최신 출제경향을 그대로 반영한

IELTS 급상승
Actual Test 1
READING & WRITING 7 Sets

IELTS급상승
Actual Test 1
[Reading & Writing]
Academic Module

저 자 James H.Lee
발행인 고본화
발 행 반석출판사

2024년 9월 15일 초판 9쇄 인쇄
2024년 9월 20일 초판 9쇄 발행

반석출판사 | www.bansok.co.kr
이메일 | bansok@bansok.co.kr
블로그 | blog.naver.com/bansokbooks

07547 서울시 강서구 양천로 583. B동 1007호
(서울시 강서구 염창동 240-21번지 우림블루나인 비즈니스센터 B동 1007호)
대표전화 02) 2093-3399 **팩 스** 02) 2093-3393
출 판 부 02) 2093-3395 **영업부** 02) 2093-3396
등록번호 제 315-2008-000033호

Copyright ⓒ James H.Lee

ISBN 978-89-7172-688-4 (13740)

- 교재 관련 문의 : bansok@bansok.co.kr을 이용해 주시기 바랍니다.
- 이 책에 게재된 내용의 일부 또는 전체를 무단으로 복제 및 발췌하는 것을 금합니다.
- 파본 및 잘못된 제품은 구입처에서 교환해 드립니다.

최신 출제경향을 그대로 반영한

IELTS 급상승
Actual Test 1
READING & WRITING 7 Sets

Bansok

머리말

지난 1989년에 첫선을 보인 IELTS(International English Language Testing System)는 영국을 비롯한 영국 문화권(호주, 뉴질랜드, 캐나다, 남아공, 미국 등)으로 이민을 가거나 유학을 갈 때 반드시 필요한 영어능력 평가시험이다. IELTS는 이민을 준비하는 사람들을 위한 제너럴 트레이닝 모듈(General Training Module)과 대학 입학을 준비하는 학생들을 위한 아카데믹 모듈(Academic Module)로 나누어진다. 점수는 0.0~9.0까지이며, 지원하는 대학(5.5~7.5)이나 이민 직종(4.5~7.0)에 따라 요구되는 점수대가 다양하다.

「IELTS 급상승」시리즈는 저자가 영국 런던에서 8년 동안 현지 유학생들을 상대로 IELTS 아카데믹 모듈(Academic Module)과 제너럴 트레이닝 모듈(General Training Module)을 전문적으로 가르쳐 오면서 체득한 강의 노하우를 상세하게 담고 있다. 또한 실전문제에 대한 면밀한 자료 분석을 통해 핵심 전략을 제공하기 때문에 IELTS를 처음 준비하는 수험생들에게 많은 도움이 된다. 이 책은 그동안 영국 현지의 많은 유학생 및 어학 연수생들에게 크게 호평을 받아 왔다.

IELTS는 듣기(Listening Comprehension: 40문항, 40분), 읽기(Reading Comprehension: 40문항, 60분), 쓰기(Writing-2 Tasks: 60분) 그리고 말하기(Speaking: 최대 14분)의 4가지 영역을 평가한다. 본 교재는 Reading과 Writing 실전문제 7세트를 싣고 있다. 본 교재는 특히 해설 부분에서 꼼꼼한 해석과 문제별 해결책을 제공하기 때문에 본인 스스로 '훈련감독(Training coach) 역할'을 할 수 있다.

저자가 직접 만든 실전 모의시험과 해설집을 통해 반복해서 공부한다면 시험장에서 정답 고르는 속도가 한결 빨라질 것이다. IELTS를 준비하는 국내 수험생들이 이 책으로 공부한다면, 불필요한 시간과 비용을 최대한 절약할 수 있을 것이라 저자는 확신한다.

끝으로 이 책으로 공부하시는 모든 수험생들께서 좋은 결과를 얻어 자신이 원하는 바를 꼭 이루시길 바랍니다. 수험생들의 건강과 행운을 빕니다.

2013년 6월

James H. Lee (이제헌)

현) 이제헌 아이엘츠 전문어학원 연구원장 (www.ielts119.com)

차례

- 머리말 • 4
- 이 책의 특징 • 9
- IELTS란? • 10

PART 1   READING & WRITING ACTUAL TEST 7 SETS

Reading Test 1 • 15   Writing Test 1 • 108
Reading Test 2 • 29   Writing Test 2 • 112
Reading Test 3 • 43   Writing Test 3 • 116
Reading Test 4 • 55   Writing Test 4 • 120
Reading Test 5 • 69   Writing Test 5 • 124
Reading Test 6 • 81   Writing Test 6 • 128
Reading Test 7 • 95   Writing Test 7 • 132

PART 2   정답 및 해설

Reading Test 1 • 139   Writing Test 1 • 252
Reading Test 2 • 157   Writing Test 2 • 261
Reading Test 3 • 173   Writing Test 3 • 269
Reading Test 4 • 189   Writing Test 4 • 277
Reading Test 5 • 205   Writing Test 5 • 285
Reading Test 6 • 219   Writing Test 6 • 293
Reading Test 7 • 237   Writing Test 7 • 301

James H. Lee

현) 이제헌 아이엘츠 전문어학원 대표 및 연구원장 (www.ielts119.com)
현) IELTS 전문 문제집 출간 및 IELTS 관련 세미나 준비 중

- M.A of Cultural Industries Management (University of Greenwich, London)
  런던 그리니치대 문화산업 경영학 석사학위과정 수료 및 (현) 박사학위 과정(ph. D) 중
- Diploma in TESOL (ASET, a national awarding body in the United Kingdom)
  영국 교육혁신부(the UK Government Department of Innovation) 산하 기관인 ASET의 TESOL 영어교사자격학위(증) 취득 (2009)
- Certificate in teaching IELTS 국제교육개발 (EDI. Education Development International)에서 후원하는 런던 Teaching Training College에서 IELTS 교사자격 수료(증) 취득 (2009)
- 대한민국 교육과학기술부 중등영어교사(2급 정교사) 자격학위(증) 취득 (2005)

■ 교육활동

- 이제헌 아이엘츠 전문어학원 연구원장
- 서울 강남 JRT어학원 IELTS 전담 수석강사 (2011~2012)
- 런던 그리니치 대학(University of Greenwich, London)에서 여름학기 교육강좌로 '대학 연구조사와 학습능력입문과정 (Introduction to Research and Study Skills)'과 '구두 대화와 발표기술법(Oral Communication and Presentation Skills)'의 학점 취득으로 본 대학의 여름학기 지원강사(Summer university teaching volunteer tutor) 자격으로 2006년~2009년 여름학기마다 정규적으로 국제학생들의 IELTS 지도 (2005)
- 런던에서 IELTS 소수개인지도와 'London IELTS Institute' 운영 및 런던소재 IELTS 어학원 강사 역임 (2002~2009)

■ 지도교수

Dr. Phyllis Vannuffel

- TESOL courses in Trinity College, London
- Teaching English as a foreign language in Teacher Training College, London since 1975
- Consultant to publishers "Longman" and "Oxford Press"
- Contributor to professional journals "English Teaching Professional", "the IATEFL newsletter" and "AGENDA, the ARELS quarterly bulletin"
- Workshops on a variety of TEFL related topics at locations "the IATEFL". Conference '99 in Edinburgh and Brighton 2001, ARELS, and The Oxford House Teacher's Club

M.A. Sebastian Power

- TESOL courses in Trinity College, London
- Tutor in TESOL & IELTS courses in Teacher Training College, London
- Methodologies of Language Teaching, The Communication Approach, The Lesson Plan

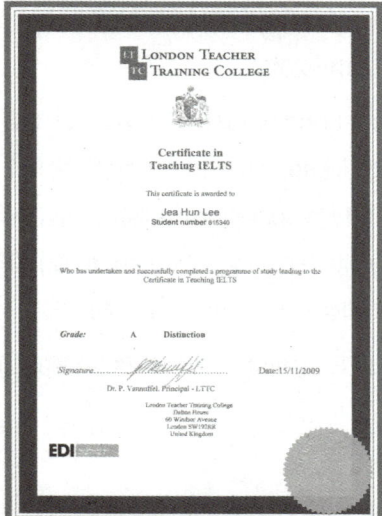
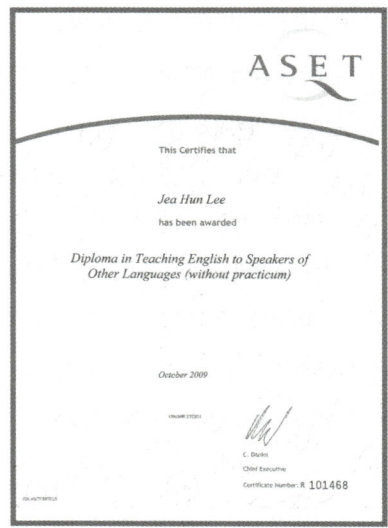

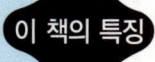 **이 책의 특징**

저자는 영국에서 8년 동안 IELTS를 전문적으로 강의해오면서 한국 유학생, 어학원생들이 가장 어려워하는 독해와 영작 그리고 기출 어휘와 문법을 체계적으로 정리했다. 이 책은 단기간에 좋은 효과를 낼 수 있는 핵심 전략집으로 독해 지문을 전반적으로 해석하지 않아도 문제를 쉽게 풀 수 있는 스킬을 제공한다.

또한 영작에 대한 부담감을 갖고 있는 학생들을 위해서 어떻게 글을 시작하고 어떤 내용으로 진술하면 고득점을 얻을 수 있는지에 대한 예문을 순서적으로 정리해서 이해하기 쉽다. IELTS의 문제방향을 정확히 분석하고 체계화시켜 놓았기 때문에 IELTS 시험을 처음 준비하는 학생들에게 나침반과 같은 역할을 할 것이다. 기대 이상의 시간과 비용을 최대한 줄여줄 수 있다.

PART 1_ Reading & Writing Actual Test 7 Sets

7회분의 리딩과 라이팅의 실전문제를 수록하였다. 시험시간은 한 테스트당 리딩 60분, 라이팅 60분을 엄수하여 실제 시험환경과 동일한 조건에서 문제를 풀어보도록 하자.

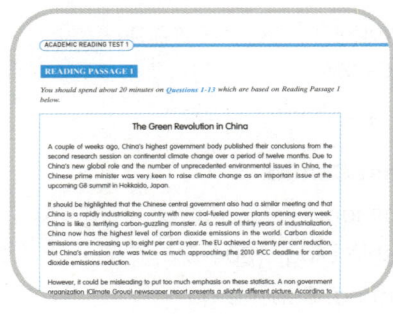

PART 2_ 정답 및 해설

정답을 채점한 후 자신이 취약한 부분의 문제 유형을 집중해서 다시 학습해본다. 문제의 키워드와 그 문제에 해당하는 지문의 문장 중 키워드를 별색으로 처리하여 키워드를 활용하여 빠른 시간 내에 문제를 해결하는 방법을 제시하고 있다.

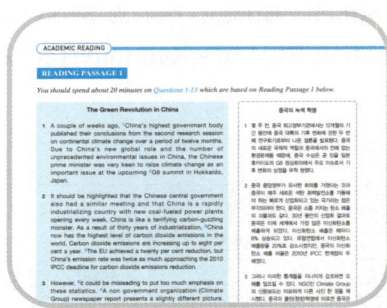

1. 시험 등록

전화·방문·인터넷 접수를 하고 있으나, 방문접수를 추천한다. 왜냐하면, 접수처에서 상담원의 도움으로 신청서를 작성하면서 혹시나 발생할 수 있는 실수를 사전에 예방할 수 있으며, 지원자들과 좋은 정보를 교환할 수 있는 기회도 얻을 수 있다.

"시험등록비는 225,000원이며, 매달 정기시험을 2회 이상 지원할 수 있다."

- **등록 시 준비물** : 주민등록증, 여권(복사본 같이) 중 택 1, 여권사진 2장, 국제신용카드(visa or master card)
- **시험점수 결과** : 시험 후 2주 안으로 성적표를 집으로 발송(점수는 24개월간 유효함)
- **전국 고사장 및 접수처 안내** : 주한 영국문화원(www.britishcouncil.org.kr/korea.htm)

IELTS Administrator
British Council Seoul, Test Centre
4F Hungkook Life Insurance Building
226 Shinmunro 1-ga, Jongro-gu
Seoul 110-786
Tel: 02-3702-0600

IELTS Test Centre
IDP Education
5F, Wooshin Bldg, 1304-5
Seocho-dong, Seocho-gu
Seoul
137-855

IDP Education Pty Ltd - Busan (Tel: 02-533-7246)
British Council - Busan (Tel: 02-3702-0600)
IDP Education Pty Ltd - Kyungin (Tel: 02-533-7246)

2. 시험 당일 시험 시간 및 준비

시간	내용
08:20	고사장 입실 및 준비
09:00 – 09:40 (제한시간: 40분)	Listening
10분간 교실 내에서 휴식 (외부출입금지)	
09:50 – 10:50 (제한시간: 60분)	Reading
10분간 교실 내에서 휴식(외부출입금지)	
11:00 – 12:00 (제한시간: 60분)	Writing
고사장 퇴실 및 말하기시험 준비	
13:00 – (제한시간: 10분)	Speaking

3. IELTS SCORE RANGE

Listening		Academic Reading		General Reading		TOEFL (CBT)	TOEIC
Number	Score	Number	Score	Number	Score	Score	Score
15~17	5.0	15~17	5.0	15~17	5.0	-	-
18~21	5.5	18~21	5.5	18~21	5.5	173	660
22~25	6.0	22~25	6.0	22~25	6.0	197	
26~28	6.5	26~28	6.5	26~28	6.5	227	810
29~31	7.0	29~31	7.0	29~31	7.0	250	
32~34	7.5	32~34	7.5	32~34	7.5	270	990
35~36	8.0	35~36	8.0	35~36	8.0	293	
37~38	8.5	37~38	8.5	37~38	8.5		
39~40	9	39~40	9.0	39~40	9.0		

IELTS 정기시험에선 Academic Module(아카데믹 모듈: 대학진학)와 General Training Module(제너널 모듈: 이민)은 듣기영역(Listening Comprehension)과 말하기(Speaking Test) 두 가지 영역은 문제가 같다. 영국 문화권 (영국, 호주, 뉴질랜드, 캐나다, 남아공, 미국) 등의 대학입학 조건은 다음과 같다.

- 일반대학 학부과정 (Bachelor of Art): 6.0~6.5
- 일반대학 대학원과정 (Master of Art): 6.5~7.5
- 일반대학 박사과정 (Philosophy of Doctor): 7.0~7.5
- 예체능대학 학부과정 (Bachelor of Art): 5.0~6.5
- 예체능대학 대학원과정 (Master of Art): 6.0~7.0
- 예체능대학 박사과정 (Philosophy of Doctor): 6.5~7.0
- 대학준비과정 (Foundation Course): 5.0~6.0
- 캐나다/미국/호주 국제간호사이민준비: 평균 7.0 (특히, speaking score: 7.0)
- 캐나다/호주기술이민(제빵, 건축, 미용, 인프라 IT 등등)준비: 평균 4.5~6.5

영국 런던 현지에서 IELTS을 지도해오면서, General Training Module 지원자들을 Academic Module로 전환시켜 지도해 왔다. 저자가 추천하는 것은 General Training Module 보단 Academic Module이다. General Training Module과 거의 비슷하며 차후에 대학 이상의 고등교육을 지원할 때 더욱 더 이득이 되는 등 선택의 폭이 넓기 때문이다. General Training Module이 쉽다고 하지만, 독해와 영작시험은 본 수험생이라면 결코 쉽지는 않다고 말한다. 두 가지 모듈을 지도한 저자 또한 거의 학습량은 큰 차이는 없다. 다만, 독해와 영작의 문제 양식이 다를 뿐이다.

PART 1
Reading & Writing Actual Test 7 Sets

IELTS
INTERNATIONAL ENGLISH LANGUAGE TESTING SYSTEM

ACADEMIC READING

TEST 1

TIME ALLOWED : 1 hour
NUMBER OF QUESTIONS : 40

Instructions

ALL ANSWERS MUST BE WRITTEN ON THE ANSWER SHEET

The test is divided as follows :

Reading Passage 1   Questions 1-13

Reading Passage 2   Questions 14-28

Reading Passage 3   Questions 29-40

Start at the beginning of the test and work through it. You should answer all the questions. If you cannot do a particular question leave it and go on to the next.

You can return to it later.

READING PASSAGE 1

You should spend about 20 minutes on **Questions 1-13** which are based on Reading Passage 1 below.

The Green Revolution in China

A couple of weeks ago, China's highest government body published their conclusions from the second research session on continental climate change over a period of twelve months. Due to China's new global role and the number of unprecedented environmental issues in China, the Chinese prime minister was very keen to raise climate change as an important issue at the upcoming G8 summit in Hokkaido, Japan.

It should be highlighted that the Chinese central government also had a similar meeting and that China is a rapidly industrializing country with new coal-fueled power plants opening every week. China is like a terrifying carbon-guzzling monster. As a result of thirty years of industrialization, China now has the highest level of carbon dioxide emissions in the world. Carbon dioxide emissions are increasing up to eight per cent a year. The EU achieved a twenty per cent reduction, but China's emission rate was twice as much approaching the 2010 IPCC deadline for carbon dioxide emissions reduction.

However, it could be misleading to put too much emphasis on these statistics. A non government organization (Climate Group) newspaper report presents a slightly different picture. According to Clean Revolution in China, China is a nation that is more than aware of its environmental issues but also has the potential to achieve a second miracle in 30 years.

The environmental price of the first, "miracle" was that Chinese people always saw their daily lives. That's why most of the policies are related to energy efficiency, energy saving and alternative other energy sources. Those policies have already been met with some concern.

Whilst the personal sectors are so strong and developing, they are able to aid the central government to introduce laws, like the National Renewable Energy Law in 2006. This has set hard targets, including increasing the amount of energy made from new renewable sources from eight per cent to fifteen per cent until 2020. Also, it has guaranteed at least three per cent of renewable energy sources, such as biomass, solar and wind.

Both wind and solar power are so successful, but their origins are very different With 6 gigawatts of energy made from wind turbines, surprisingly China is now ranked behind Germany, the US, Spain and India. Also, some believe China will reach 100 GW by 2020.

Wind and solar power successfully shows that with central government aid China is ready for new policies, subsides and advanced technology. This situation also has a role in the domestic market. The amount of electricity produced by the wind and solar farms can be a burden to fund.

Even though western countries invented an open marketplace set to dominate in China, there were few domestic incentives for solar power. In the global solar photovoltaic cell market, it is only the second to Japan and growing fast. In China, the solar market has been a small business, because the cells are so expensive. This puts pressure on the government to rapidly follow up on their policies, for example, the role of the Climate Group is important in developing domestic markets.

However, the image of new coal-fueled power stations still looms large as they are opening every week. It is hard to imagine that China has achieved a 10.5 per cent of growth rate without such stations in the last quarter. However, how many people actually know that China has been closing its small power stations over the last couple of years? Step by step China is reducing its small power stations, first the 50 megawatt ones then the 100 megawatt ones and next will be the 300 megawatt power stations.

This policy is operated by the Chinese central government and backs up the new generation of coal stations using the most advanced technologies with supercritical and ultra-supercritical improved clean coal. Capture functions and plants of carbon are researched and developed, but advanced thinking for the future is based on the technology of Integrated Gasification Combined Cycle (IGCC) that turn coal materials into synthetic gas to make power.

These days, Chinese consumers demand better homes and vehicles. Public awareness of energysaving is on the rise. The Chinese government introduced a standard fuel economy for vehicles in 2004 of 15.6 kilometers per litre. This is higher than the US, Canada and Australia but behind Europe and Japan. In the meantime, in spite of a high 20 per cent tax on SUVs (Sport Utility Vehicles) the sale of these sorts of cars continues to increase.

Up to now, China has been the kingdom of the bicycle, importing the electric bike at 1500 yuan ($ 220) per vehicle. Some of these vehicles have adopted an intelligent recovery system similar to that of hybrid cars. In 2007, the sale of electric bikes increased considerably and China is estimated to make up three quarters of the world electric vehicle market.

China, already, is doing a lot on the bottom line. So, could it do more? The answer is yes. China should learn and open its mind through the international communities. According to the Climate Group, they report the world should refine their image of China, just not fear it and, constructively, work in unison. At the same time, China's government should develop the clean revolution and maintain internal pressure for improvements.

ACADEMIC READING TEST 1

Questions 1-7

Do the following statements reflect the claims of the writer in Reading Passage 1?

In boxes 1-7 on your answer sheet write

- **YES** if the statement reflects the opinion of the writer
- **NO** if the statement contradicts the opinion of the writer
- **NOT GIVEN** if it is impossible to say what the writer thinks about this

1 The Central Government of China concluded the second research scheme of climate change in less than one year.

2 The main topic of the G8 Meeting in Japan was to discuss greenhouse gas emissions.

3 The Chinese Government must compensate the European Union for loss of climate change.

4 NGO's group reported about truth of problems of a climate change in China.

5 Solar energy has increased the amount of energy.

6 With different launching, both wind and solar power are inefficient.

7 The high cost of cells causes less activity in the solar market in China.

Questions 8-13

Complete the sentences.

Choose NO MORE THAN THREE WORDS from the passage for each answer.

8 China is emitting .... of the so outstanding rates in the world.

9 Statistics that can be misleading have been corrected by a ....

10 In 2006 .... has set a hard target, waxing the amount of renewable sources.

11 What is included in the amount of sources which are renewable is like ....

12 Wind energy is based on subsides, policies and the equitable ....

13 .... should support to develop the domestic market in China facing on financial problems.

READING PASSAGE 2

You should spend about 20 minutes on Questions 14-28 which are based on Reading Passage 2 below.

The Efficacy of Hypnotherapy

In the 1840s Scottish neurosurgeon, James Braid, coined 'Hypnotherapy'. At that time, in India, British surgeon, James Esdaile, practiced hundreds of scrotal and abdominal operations, adopting hypnosis as the only anaesthetic. It was unfortunate timing that he reported his research dissertation on hypnosis to London Royal Society just as chemical anaesthetics were discovered. The technique was not agreed on by the medical establishment.

These days, whilst an increasing number of people are asking about private practitioners, the level of studies within the hypnotherapy field is meaningful enough that it remains on the fringes of medicine. In a report on alternative and complementary medicine in 2000, the Science and Technology Committee of the UK's House of Lords has given hypnosis a bad reputation by putting it in the "poor research / regulation" category. In other word, the therapies are unlikely to enter mainstream medicine without substantial changes.

If you research the PubMed database using the term "hypnotherapy," you find 11,518 hit-words, so there are plenty of studies out there. However, most of the researchers are not satisfied with the gold standard of a Randomised Controlled Trial (RCT) instead of taking the frame of reviews or case studies. Only 91 relevant RCTs conducted in the world have worked in the past four years. The researchers propose that hypnotheraphy can be effective treatment for pain control, irritable bowel syndrome, anxiety disorders and smoking cessation.

There is clear evidence that hypnosis has psychological and physiological effects. That's why Peter Whorwell at the University of Manchester has researched the efficacy of IBS (irritable bowel syndrome) surgery for gastrointestinal modualation with hypnotherapy and possible immune function support. But even though IBS is one of the best covered areas, the action with mechanism is not clear and the Cochrane Collaboration from assessing clinical trials has criticised the size and quality of the studies.

In spite of the evidence that hypnotheraphy reduces pain, anxiety and stress, there are a couple of reasons why few trials have been done. From these stages, hypnosis's usage doesn't aid its image. Also, it has same problems as other "talking" therapies. Alternative funding should be built up, as the drug companies do not benefit from funding expensive studies

But, one of the biggest obstacles to hypnosis being considered on a more scientific basis is the therapists themselves. Its effects are a result of a unique interaction between the practitioner and the patient. The expectation is similar to that of a drug and therefore should follow the same trial testing criteria. However, this argument is not helpful.

I strongly believe that whilst meeting with a living, breathing person, it is hard to decrease the process of clinical hypnosis and to receive YES or NO responses that are able to be reliably repeated in other conditions. However, for hypnosis to be considered medical, it should be measurable, replicable and vigorous. Actually, we need to model a body of clinical evidence in order to adapt to the medical profession.

With standardising protocol used, we demand quantitative measures of the effects on the patient, so studies can be compared. Ideally, researchers would have access to state-of-the art brain scanning equipment. In a reality, we are able to get simple biochemical markets of hypnosis and after effects under suitable usage.

Coming out of such studies in England, Ursula James founded the Medical School Hypnosis Association with his colleagues. According to Complementary Therapies in Clinical Practice, he explains schemes to bring medical professors and students together with hypnotherapists to operate coordinated national trials and build up a large body of evidence from research replicated at multiple locations. Most of all, one of the first questions is whether clinical hypnosis is able to decrease stress. That is an important component potentially in an illness. We work towards using standardised questionnaires to calculate lifestyle, stress and depression and to measure various stress hormone levels in saliva samples taken from case applicants.

If we are able to present that there is a decrease in stress, we hope that hypnosis will be supplied to patients to treat their condition. With a wide range of usages, it could open up study into other areas including decreasing the thoughts of pain and improving recovery times.

ACADEMIC READING TEST 1

Questions 14-16

*Choose the appropriate letters **A-D** and write them in boxes **14-16** on your answer sheet.*

14 According to information in the text, hypnotheraphy

    A was created by British surgeon James Esdaile in 1840.
    B has already been used during an operation by James Braid.
    C originated from the work of Scottish neurosurgeon James Braid in the 1840s.
    D was created by James Esdaile and James Braid in the 1840s.

15 According to information in the text, the recent perception on hypnotheraphy among private practitioners

    A maintains plenty of research within alternative medicine.
    B is on the fringes of mainstream medicine because there hasn't been enough research.
    C means there is an neutral attitude within alternative medicine.
    D demands non-practical, but has potential.

16 According to randomised controlled trial (RCT), hypnotheraphy

    A works in a variety of cases.
    B supplied research and development in advance.
    C works in cold.
    D was found to be an antidote against irritable bowel syndrome (IBS).

Questions 17-21

Complete the summary.

Choose **ONE OR TWO WORDS** from reading passage for each answer.

Write your answers in boxes **17-21** on your answer sheet.

To show evidence of hypnosis, researchers have proved physiological and **17** -------------------------- as well. They discovered that hypnotherapy presumes to assist modulate gastrointestinal and immune function whilst operated **18** --------------------------. The mechanism of action is not justified, also, what assesses clinical trials, the **19** -------------------------- has underestimated the value and scale of studies. Despite having several effects, drug companies deny the therapies due to **20** -------------------------- it should be demanded as a substitute investment. However, an outstanding barrier is **21** --------------------------.

Questions 22 and 23

Answer the questions below.

Choose **NO MORE THAN TWO WORDS AND/OR A NUMBER** from the passage for each answer.

Write your answers in boxes **22** and **23** on your answer sheet.

22 How many relevant RCTs were there in the past four years?

23 Who reported that hypnotherapy aids gastrointestinal modulation and supports immune function?

ACADEMIC READING TEST 1

Questions 24-27

Look at the following people and the list of statements below.

Match each city with the correct statement.

Write the correct letter, **A-E**, in boxes **24-27** on your answer sheet.

24 James Braid

25 James Esdaile

26 Peter Whorwell

27 Ursula James

List of Statements

A   have founded the Medical School Hypnosis Association.
B   discovered hypnotherapy suppose to aid gastrointestinal modulation and support immune function.
C   created a new term, hypnotheraphy in the 1840s.
D   implemented over several hundred abdominal and scrotal operations.
E   criticised the quality and size of hypnotherphy.

Questions 28

Choose the appropriate letter **A-D** and write it in box **28** on your answer sheet.

Which of the following statements best describes the writer's main purpose in Reading Passage 2?

A   to inform the reader relative not to mimic during operating of hypnotheraphy
B   to encourage the reader to act against misinformation regarding hypnotheraphy
C   to make the reader spread the right perception of hypnotherapy
D   to make readers to encourage a randomised controlled trial (RCT)

READING PASSAGE 3

You should spend about 20 minutes on Questions 29-40 which are based on Reading Passage 3 on the following pages.

Questions 29-34

Reading Passage 3 has ten paragraphs, **A-J**.

Choose the correct heading for paragraph **B-G** from the list of headings below.

Write the correct number, *i-viii*, in boxes **29-34** on your answer sheet.

List of Headings

i   A lot of proof of non well-being
ii   Recent perceptional change of the environment
iii   Reviving time for private time
iv   Understanding of being valuable
v   The absurdity of our lives from the feature of economy benefit
vi   Right attitude for constant comfort and human ingenuity
vii   People and governments which continue to disagree
viii   Aspiring to the material civilisation

Example	Answer
Paragraph **A**	ii

29   Paragraph B

30   Paragraph C

31   Paragraph D

32   Paragraph E

33   Paragraph F

34   Paragraph G

The Well-being Life

A Going to back in the 1970s, few people listened to scientists' warnings of global warming. It got worse as nobody was interested in curbing economic growth to protect the environment. Nowadays, we are more cautious. We are hearing about the conflict between living on the earth and expanding the demands of the global market.

B However, Tim Jackson reports that people and governments claim the growth agenda to ensure our future and are still in denial of the conflict. A reason for this is the presumption that support for the green campaigners will ultimately make our lives worse.

C All representations of a pleasant and easy life which aspire to come from advertising do not help. Also, our happiness is dependent on consuming more and more "material." We have never listened to ways of escaping stress, noise, congestion, and the ill-health that comes from our "high" standard of living.

D Actually there is plenty of evidence to suggest that a workaholic mentality and an affluent lifestyle does not give us a pleasant life and that switching to a more sustainable community to work could make us happier. For instance, rates of depression and occupational illness have been indicated to be relative to the number of hours we are working. Once a certain income level is reached more wealth is not linked with growing happiness.

E The unreasonableness of our situation can be explained by the way in which our economy tries to sell us happiness. For example, leisure and tourism companies sell customers, "a good quality time," catering services offer us, "home cooking," dating agencies sell relationships; the sports centre sells health and as a result of modern car culture it can be unsafe to walk outside. With the economy steadily expanding, consumer culture is becoming more and more reliant on our desire to adopt this lifestyle.

F An increasing number of people are beginning to realize that there is more to life than work and money. Troubled by the effects of a stressful life, people are starting to make their lives more simple and rethinking their values and desires. If people were to switch to a less work-intensive economy, it would decrease the rate of people, products and information delivered, reducing carbon emissions and the use of resources.

G There are a number of advantages to making sacrifices to our lifestyles. We would be able to have more time for ourselves and our families. We would commute less and enjoy healthier ways of travelling such as walking, cycling, and riding a boat. Large supermarket chains would be replaced by local family businesses resulting in the creation of more communal town centres. Our local areas would become more tranquil and give us more chance to reflect on things. These changed ideas for a "good life" might also motivate less developed countries to reconsider their goals enabling them to avoid some of the less attractive aspects of the current system.

H Of course, we must sacrifice some conveniences and pleasure such as regular steaks, hot tubs, luxury cosmetics and easy foreign travel. But constant comfort can blunt as well as satisfy our desires. And human ingenuity will invent a wide range of eco-friendly excitement.

I Moving into a safe-state economy is an intimidating prospect. However, Herman Daly explains it is unrealistic to continue with current rates of development in production, work and material consumption over the next decades, let alone into the next century.

J Under the financial disorders and broad cynicism over government commitments to global warming, more honesty would win cooperation and esteem from the voter, especially if politicians emphasise the advantages of the sustainable society.

ACADEMIC READING TEST 1

Questions 35-40

Do the following statements reflect the claims of the writer in Reading Passage 3?

In boxes 35-40 on your answer sheet write

> **YES** if the statement reflects the opinion of the writer
> **NO** if the statement contradicts the opinion of the writer
> **NOT GIVEN** if it is impossible to say what the writer thinks about this

35 Most people have concentrated on global warming since 1970.

36 Tim Jackson discusses a conflict of opinions between people and government.

37 Work and material are relative to pleasant and favorable lives recently.

38 Level of income is vital for building up substantial happiness.

39 With a less work-intensive economy, it would decrease only the rate of carbon emissions.

40 Herman Daly indicates current rates of natural resources are enlarged for a sustainable society.

IELTS

INTERNATIONAL ENGLISH LANGUAGE TESTING SYSTEM

ACADEMIC READING

TEST 2

TIME ALLOWED : 1 hour
NUMBER OF QUESTIONS : 40

Instructions

ALL ANSWERS MUST BE WRITTEN ON THE ANSWER SHEET

The test is divided as follows :

Reading Passage 1   Questions 1-13

Reading Passage 2   Questions 14-26

Reading Passage 3   Questions 27-40

Start at the beginning of the test and work through it. You should answer all the questions. If you cannot do a particular question leave it and go on to the next.

You can return to it later.

ACADEMIC READING TEST 2

READING PASSAGE 1

You should spend about 20 minutes on **Questions 1-13** which are based on Reading Passage 1 on the following pages.

Questions 1-6

Reading Passage 1 has twelve paragraphs, **A-L**.

Choose the correct heading for paragraph **B-G** from the list of headings below.

Write the correct number, **i-vii**, in boxes **1-6** on your answer sheet.

List of Headings

- i   Disorders strike much later in life.
- ii Drawbacks in public health
- iii Longevity based on high education
- iv The elderly people of today got better nutrition when they were children.
- v   The elderly are becoming more well off.
- vi Most of independent people over 65 complete activities themselves.
- vii Diseases have decreased recently.

Example	Answer
Paragraph **A**	v

1   Paragraph B

2   Paragraph C

3   Paragraph D

4   Paragraph E

5   Paragraph F

6   Paragraph G

Growing of the Aging Society

A   American scientists say that the elderly are now healthier, happier and more independent. The results of a study that has take place over a 14 year period will be released at the end of the month. The research will show that common health disorders suffered by the elderly are affecting fewer people and happening later in life.

B   Over the last 14 years, The National Long-term Health Care Survey has gathered data from more than 20,000 males and females over the age of 65 about their health and lifestyles. The group has analysed the results of data gathered in 1994 on conditions such as arthritis, high blood pressure and poor circulations these were the most common medical complaints for this age group. The results show that these conditions are troubling a smaller proportion of people each year and decreasing very quickly. Other disease suffered by the elderly including dementia, emphysema and arteriosclerosis are also affecting fewer people.

C   According to Kenneth Manton, a demographer from Duke University in North Carolina, "the question of what should be considered normal ageing has really changed." he said. He also mentioned that diseases suffered by many people around the age of 65 in 1982, are now not occurring until people reach the age of 70-75.

D   It is clear that due to medical advances some diseases are not as prominent as they used to be. However, there may also be other factors influencing this change. For instance, improvements in childhood nutrition in the first quarter of the twentieth century gave many people a better start in life than was possible before.

E   The data also shows some negative changes in public health. The research suggests that the rise respiratory conditions such as lung cancer and bronchitis may reflect changing smoking habits and an increase in air pollution. Manton says that as we have been exposed to worse and worse pollution it is not surprising that some people over the age of 60 are suffering as a result.

F   Manton also found that better-educated people are likely to live longer. For instance, women of 65 with less than eight years of education are expected to live to around 82. Those who studied more could be able to live seven years longer. Whilst some of this can be attributed to better-educated people usually having a higher income, Manton believes it is mainly because they pay closer attention to their health.

G   Also, the survey estimated how independent people of 65 were, and found a striking trend. In the 1994 survey almost 80% of them were able to complete activities such as eating and dressing alone as well as handling difficult tasks, like cooking and managing their financial affairs. This situation indicates an important drop among disabled elderly people in the population. If, 14 years ago, the apparent trends in the U.S had continued, researchers believe that there would be one million disabled elderly people in today's population. Manton shows the trend saved more than $ 200 billion for the US's government's Medicare system, and it has suggested the elderly American population is less of a financial burden than expected.

H   The growing number of the independent elderly people is probably linked to the huge increase in home medical aids. For instance, the research shows the use of raising toilet seat covers and bath seats has increased by more than fifty per cent. Also, these developments about health benefits are reported by the MacArthur Foundation's research group for successful ageing. It found the elderly who are able to take care of themselves were more likely to stay healthy in their old age.

I   Retaining a certain level of daily physical activity may also help brain function, according to Carl Cotman, a neuroscientist at the University of California at Irvine. He found that rats exercising on a treadmill have higher levels of a brain-derived neurotrophic in their brains. He believes the hormone which holds neuron functions may prevent the active humans' brain function from declining.

J   Teresa Seeman, a social epidemiologist at the University of Southern California in Los Angeles, was conducting the same research. He found a link between self-esteem and stress in people over 70. The elderly who did challenging activities such as driving have more control of their mind and have a lower level of stress hormone cortisol in their brains. Chronically high levels of this hormone can cause heart disease.

K   However, an independent life may have negative points. Seeman knew that the elderly people that were living alone were able to retain higher levels of stress hormones even when sleeping. The research indicates that elderly people are happier if they can live an independent life but also acknowledge when they need help.

L   Seeman says, "With many cases of research about ageing, these results help common sense." Also, the situations show that we may be ignoring some of the simple factors. She mentions, "The sort of thing your grandmother always used to talk to you about seems to be exactly right."

Questions 7-13

Do the following statements reflect the claims of the writer in Reading Passage 1?

*In boxes **7-13** on your answer sheet write*

> **TRUE** if the statement agrees with the information
> **FALSE** if the statement contradicts the information
> **NOT GIVEN** if there is no information on this

7 Smoking habits are a crucial cause in some cancers.

8 The better-educated elderly people tend to live more longer.

9 People over 65 can independently manage a variety of tasks.

10 Elderly people have overcome dementia as a result of home medical aids.

11 Continuing physical exercise is likely to assist digestive function.

12 People over 70 who still do challenging things such as driving are able to lower their level of the hormone cortisol which is linked to heart disease.

13 Isolation may cause a higher level of stress hormones at work.

READING PASSAGE 2

You should spend about 20 minutes on **Questions 14-26** which are based on Reading Passage 2 below.

Space Flight Tourism

Falcon 1's successful launch on 28th of September was an outstanding achievement for the fledging space tourism industry. When a rocket made by Space X in Hawthorne, California, reached an orbit of 500 kilometres from the Earth, it became possible for privately developed rocket too.

Two days after the launch, Virgin Galactic started a business with the US National Oceanic and Atmospheric Administration which will be accepted by US scientists as a way of researching climate change using a spacecraft.

No doubt the civilian space flight industry is an exciting area and this was apparent at the International Aeronautical Congress in Glasgow last month. It displayed slick promotional videos, and models of the "Nearly Ready" spacecraft in orbit to the people who would be investing money in the project.

However, in spite of increasing confidence, it is also necessary to be cautious: can a civilian spacecraft be safe like holiday airlines? Gerardine Goh, a lawyer at DLR, the German Aerospace Centre in Bonn and a member of Germany's delegation to the UN's Office of Outer Space Affairs reported that as it is not global there needs to be enforceable regulations in place to guarantee the safety of a civilian spacecraft. She said "Ships should be equipped to be seaworthy, aircrafts should be equipped to be airworthy but there no legislation in place to ensure that a spacecraft is space worthy."

At the International Association for the Advancement of Space Safety, Goh is planning to press the UN to force civilian space operators to warrant which spacecrafts are designed and built to minimum safety standards. She says, "Mass commercial space flight does not currently have international safety regulations." And, "We deeply need a UN treaty which offers us this."

One way companies are planning to transport tourists into space is with a "mother ship" an aircraft which carries a rocket at an altitude of 16 kilometres before launching it, says Goh. "But with launching the aircraft, the ICAO's air safety standards only apply to the mother ship and the rocket capsule until they are separated. After that, we do not have any safety standards for the capsule itself. It is a critical problem."

From 16 kilometres to the Karman line, the point of 100 kilometres up where space is considered to start, the rocket will be travelling within a legal vacuum. Here, lawyers cannot agree on whether it is a plane or a rocket. Some insist that if you are in a well-equipped functioning rocket, more strict safety measures should try to be incorporated into the spaceship's design.

The other aspects of the UN's 1967 treaty for outer space exploration may be discussed again if civilian space flight turns out to be successful. For example, countries must consider how to rescue and repatriate astronauts crashing or landing in their land. Also, governments have to decide if the money generated by the space flight industry will be enough to cover the cost of rescuing space tourists.

Civilian space flight companies are very aware of the risks in this field as they have already had the experience of dealing with a tragedy. Unfortunately, three engineers were killed and another three were severely injured in 2007, when nitrous oxide rocket fuel suddenly exploded during fuel flow tests at a Scaled Composites facility in Mojave, California. The company is establishing WhiteKnightTwo, a carrier aircraft and SpaceShip Two, a six-seater rocket for Virgin Galactic. The facility was regulated by California's health and safety regulator, and it has now modified its technology to decrease the risks.

However, space flight's dangers are far from just fuel issues. According to Laurent Gatheir of Dassault Aviation developing the VSH of a rocket powered sub-orbital tourist space plane, other critical safety factors are with depressurization risks, passengers close to the engine and the activities of flight trajectories including cosmic ray shielding.

Civilian space companies should incorporate the safety features into their designs. For instance, the VSH will equip an ejector seat for all tourists and staff. It is a device for bailing out of the spacecraft with default of 40,000 feet (12 kilometres).

Goh's vision is essentially against the Federal Aviation Administration Office of Commercial Space Transportation (AST) and does not have any schemes to regulate civilian space flight safety until 2012. The Commercial Space Launch Amendments Act of 2004 mentions that George Nield an AST chief said, the civilian space flight regulation must not "stifle" the developing technologies with inconvenient rules.

Before launching, a hands off approach to civilian space flight could be quite risky. Goh said, "A lack of safety standards and a lot of operational burdens will leave a commercial space flight in the dangerous activity categories in terms of insurance." It means insurance costs will be very high. Critics who are developing safety standards also insist that the "at-your-own-risk" mentality that is applied to risky sports like scuba-diving should also be applied to civilian space flight.

ACADEMIC READING TEST 2

Questions 14-20

Complete the summary.

Choose **NO MORE THAN THREE WORDS** from the passage for each answer.

Write your answers in boxes **14-20** on your answer sheet.

> On 28 September the emerging space tourism industry was enormous. In Hawthorne, California, a rocket was erected by **14** --------------------. Climate change was monitored by **15** -------------------- in US National Oceanic and Atmospheric Administration using its spacecraft. In Glasgow at the international Aeronautical meeting, it is apparent that civilian space flight industry is growing, as it showed the **16** -------------------- spacecraft which promises sub-orbital flights. Although developing confirmation, non regulation is clear to guarantee **17** --------------------. A method for space business is cooperating with **18** -------------------- conveyable at 16 kilometres in the skies. From 16 kilometres to 100 kilometres' travelling may be available, but lawyers definitely cannot agree with whether it is a **19** -------------------- or a rocket. **20** -------------------- need to be revisited if civilian space flight proves successful.

Questions 21-26

Complete each sentence with the correct ending **A-I** below.

Write the correct letter **A-I** in boxes **21-26** on your answer sheet.

21   Civilian space flight companies

22   Laurent Gathier

23   VSH devised for a safety

24   AST chief George Nield

25   Insurance costs

26   Critics

A	assisted some minimum safety standards may prevent that.
B	emphasised a civilian space flight must not be under a severe regulation for technical advancement.
C	hardly need a reminder of the danger when considering past experiences.
D	will protect a commercial space flight.
E	try to develop a module of safety regulation applied to civilian space flight.
F	made up for an ejector seat for tourist and the crew in case of a craft emergency in the skies.
G	indicated main safety problems were with passengers' proximity to the power engine.
H	believed that scuba-diving should be applied to civilian space flight.
I	kept costs stratospheric.

ACADEMIC READING TEST 2

READING PASSAGE 3

You should spend about 20 minutes on Questions 27-40 which are based on Reading Passage 3 below.

Doctor's Rights and Drinks

New Yorker, John Davin started his campaign for election to Congress on 26th of September 1922. Actually, he was not a politician, but a doctor who practiced in a local city for 40 years at the top of his profession. Davin and other doctors with the same opinions were faced with the task of arguing their cases in front of the people. Also, they made a new political party, the Medical Rights League, and decided that Davin should run as a candidate for the coming election. What did they want? Beer, or more precisely, a doctor who had the right to prescribe it.

The Congress had legislated the law prohibiting the sale of alcohol in January 1920. The aim was to transform a nation of drinkers and gamblers into one of hard-working, law-abiding, teetotal citizens. It was now illegal to sell or buy a drink that included more than 0.5 per cent alcohol "for beverage purposes." Only Medical alcohol was allowed, but the conditions were so strict. Doctors could prescribe "liquor" when there was a "need to afford relief from a known ailment". Patients could not have more than a pint of liquor "within 10 days at any time". Doctors who needed to prescribe alcohol were approved for a permit. But the current law said nothing about beer, a traditional alcohol for ailments from anaemia to anthrax. So, could they prescribe beer or not?

As doctors were requesting permission to prescribe beer, someone had to make a decision. That person was Attorney General Mitchell Palmer, a staunch supporter of Prohibition. To the delight of doctors and dismay of prohibitionists, he urged "it was not the purpose of Congress to prohibit the use liquor for non-beverage usages." The Congress accepted medicinal alcohol for non beverage usages. It was for "beer and other malt liquors."

The Prohibitionists were very enraged. They had suspicions that doctors were in league with the brewers and that their intentions were more to disrupt Prohibition than for medicinal purposes. Although brandy and whisky might have some medicinal advantages, in their view, beer was not needed at pharmacies. Congressman Andrew Volstead, who drafted the

National Prohibition Act, criticized the decision saying "It is not a worthy argument that beer is medicine," "Everything in beer except the alcohol is similar to the beers that can be bought without any prescription." He immediately set up a supplementary bill that would further restrict medicinal alcohol and ban "medical beer" altogether.

Now, it was the doctors' turn out to be infuriated. How dare politicians presume to tell doctors what sort of things they could prescribe or how much. The merits of medicinal alcohol were suddenly a topic of national debate. For a couple of decades, doctors had been divided on the issue. Many insisted it was a treatment for all manners of disease. Others removed a worthless remedy left from the past. The American Medical Association (AMA), in 1971, denied the medicinal usage of alcohol, "Its value in therapeutics as a tonic, stimulant or food has no scientific basis."

However, as Prohibition hit home, doctors' enthusiasm for alcohol improved. Articles admiring beer, wine and whisky spread among medical journals. One doctor suggested champagne worked wonders in cases of scarlet fever. Beer was warranted to treat sleeplessness. One of the US's top doctors even insisted that when children with diphtheria developed secondary infections, alcohol could save them.

According to JAMA, the report said, "Impressive particularly was the sincerity of the belief of a lot of physicians in the therapeutic effect of whisky within a limited number of diseases." "But equally impressive was the expressed belief of a limited number of physicians of necessity within a lot of disease." The contents ran from anaemia to uraemia, including influenza and indigestion, cancer, colds and heart disease.

ACADEMIC READING TEST 2

Questions 27-33

Do the following statements reflect the claims of the writer in Reading Passage 3?

In boxes **27-33** on your answer sheet write

YES if the statement reflects the opinion of the writer
NO if the statement contradicts the opinion of the writer
NOT GIVEN if it is impossible to say what the writer thinks about this

27   John Davin has been ready for election to Congress.

28   The Medical Rights League was made to support the right to prescribe beer by Davin and like minded doctors.

29   It was illegal to sell or buy beverage that contained over 0.5 per cent alcohol.

30   Congress only granted beer as a medical alcohol.

31   As beer might have some benefit for medicinal use, it was in a pharmacy.

32   The American Medical Association (AMA) has funded scientific basis.

33   If children have diphtheria, alcohol may cure them.

Questions 34-35

Choose the appropriate letters **A-D** and write them in boxes **34-35** on your answer sheet.

34   In 1922 the reason John Davin begun a campaign

   A   was against beer and other malt liquors.
   B   was to assert a doctor's right to prescribe beer
   C   was for the Medical Right League's duty.
   D   was to oppose strong minded politicians.

35 In 1971, the American Medical Association (AMA)

    A   decided beer is a worthless remedy.
    B   declared beer has an effect as tonic.
    C   decided beer won't be an evidence of medical basis.
    D   assisted a patient with cancer.

Questions 36-39

*Complete the summary below. Choose **ONE** word from Reading Passage 3 for each answer.*

*Write your answers in boxes **36-39** on your answer sheet.*

Once prohibition affected homes, doctor stimulated interests in **36** --------------------. Besides, doctors affirmed the effects of alcohol, beer was guaranteered to cure **37** --------------------. When children with **38** -------------------- transferred dual-infections, alcohol could save them. According to **39** --------------------, most physicians believed the effects of therapeutic usage of whisky in the treatment of a limited number of diseases to be remarkably impressive.

Questions 40

*Choose the appropriate letter **A-D** and write it in box **40** on your answer sheet.*

This text is taken from

    A   a medical text book for a beginner.
    B   a critical research of the scientific basis of a beverage.
    C   a magazine article about alcohol issues.
    D   a document against government prohibition.

IELTS

INTERNATIONAL ENGLISH LANGUAGE TESTING SYSTEM

ACADEMIC READING

TEST 3

TIME ALLOWED : 1 hour
NUMBER OF QUESTIONS : 40

Instructions

ALL ANSWERS MUST BE WRITTEN ON THE ANSWER SHEET

The test is divided as follows :

    Reading Passage 1   Questions 1-13

    Reading Passage 2   Questions 14-27

    Reading Passage 3   Questions 28-40

Start at the beginning of the test and work through it. You should answer all the questions. If you cannot do a particular question leave it and go on to the next.

You can return to it later.

ACADEMIC READING TEST 3

READING PASSAGE 1

*You should spend about 20 minutes on **Questions 1-13** which are based on Reading Passage 1 below.*

Amazon Rainforest of Peru

A A cement maker proudly speaks about the brief history of the road: this main road was part of an incentive programme supported by the US's fund to help local people to find economic alternatives to harvesting coca, from which cocaine is produced. Four years later, the road is a global vacuum from which timber from the Peruvian rainforest is taken to China. Some wood will be polished into luxury parquet flooring for high quality homes in Shanghai and Beijing. More wood will be used in Chinese factories and made into patio furniture, decking or flooring in North America and Europe.

B Going down the street, muddy tracks show the old forest known as *Monte Alto*, where local farmers have been using the sunlight that comes through the openings in the forest canopy to grow a variety of food crops, like cassava, sweet potatoes, bananas and plantains. They are also growing a few cash crops like coffee and cacao. This also helps to fund essential services like schools and hospitals.

C As a tree ecologist and student studying about the timber trade, I am here researching a kind of Dipteryx known in the region as shihuahuaco (its international trade name is cumaru) and to research its movements from the Amazonian forest the Chinese factories. Although shihuahuaco is not particularly high profile, ecologists call it a "keystone" tree, as its large seeds are an essential food source for forest herbivores in the dry season, whilst its hollow rooms are utilized as the nesting place of parrots and macaws. It is so hard that local residents use big shihuahuco trees as a shelter when strong storms bring trees down.

D My trip began in the company of a great group of people who were logging from the sawmill town in Pucallpa. A two day trip into the forest guided us beyond the road's end to a community called Esperanza, or "Hope." In the middle of a flourishing Chacra – a farm typical of the area – there was a temporary logging camp. As well as their productive farming, the chacra had a family business called the Medinas which offered a refuge for birds, wild piglets and primates saved from logged areas. From there, I walked through the *Monte Alto* with my logging friends for 10 days, which they were soon to cut.

E The adult trees were colossal, reaching heights of up to 50 metres and a width of 1.3 metres, towering above their huge buttresses which spread up to 5 metres around the main trunk. There were one or two such trees per hectare and most of them were put forward for the long voyage across the Pacific. Whilst we found approximately 250 seedlings and saplings, there were only two young trees which had reached the canopy and therefore could be expected to harvest into adults.

F I don't want to be sentimental about trees. On one of my last nights in the rainforest when speaking to the company's chief woodsman Pedro, I felt reassured about the situation. Pedro said, "At least there are the Medias arbolitos." "What, little trees?" I asked. The next day Pedro showed me the trees he was referring to. We walked up the hill and Pedro stopped in front of a very healthy looking young shihuahuaco growing in the sun. "When do you expect to harvest them?" I had to ask. I hope he wasn't planning to profile them in a few years.

Questions 1-3

Choose **THREE** letters **A-F**.

Write your answers in boxes **1-3** on your answer sheet.

The list below gi es some features of shihuahuaco.

Which **THREE** ways are mentioned by the writer of the text?

- **A** a field to grow varied sustainable food crops
- **B** a habitat for parrots and macaws
- **C** a shelter for natives against a natural disaster
- **D** a village of palm-thatch houses
- **E** a road to help local people for finding economic alternatives
- **F** an ecologist named it a keystone tree

ACADEMIC READING TEST 3

Questions 4-6

Answer the questions below using **NO MORE THAN TWO WORDS** from the passage for each answer.

Write your answers in boxes **4-6** on your answer sheet.

4   What is the name given to the old forest of the Amazon?

5   What is called the international trade name of the cumaru?

6   What is the typical farm land area that is used as a temporary logging camp?

Questions 7-13

Reading Passage 1 has six paragraphs labeled **A-F**.

Which paragraph contains the following information?

Write the correct letter **A-F** in boxes **7-13** on your answer sheet.

NB   You may use any letter more than once.

7   the self-rescue measures there to cover essentials

8   the dimensions of timber

9   the road sponsored by the United State's fund to aid relief work scheme

10   an anecdote for the writer

11   a short camping trip of the writer

12   practical sides of shihuahuaco

13   the export of timber

READING PASSAGE 2

You should spend about 20 minutes on **Questions 14-27** *which are based on Reading Passage 2 below.*

A shot for public health

Millions of elderly people in the US, Europe and elsewhere get injections for their annual flu shots this month. It is widely seen as a largely effective public health programme which halves the risk of dying over the winter people aged 65 or over. Actually for every 200 vaccinations one life is saved. However, there is overwhelming evidence that this claim is too good to be true, and we must look for additional ways to prevent the flu.

According to the US Centres for Disease Control and Prevention (CDC), flu kills approximately 36,000 people every winter in the US. Of them about 30,000 are aged 65 or over. This is about 5% of the 650,000 winter deaths per year in this age group. Flu itself is never recorded as a cause of death: instead, it is leads to the elderly dying from other causes, like bacterial pneumonia, heart disease or a stroke.

Most rich countries are concentrated on cutting this figure by vaccinating those who are at the highest risk, but how well does this actually work? The best way to carry out research is trials that compare those who are vaccinated against those who aren't, with applicants allocated randomly from each group. But as flu shots are known to be an advantage, it would be unethical to deny some people vaccinations. Researchers compare those who choose to be vaccinated with those who don't. Then, they use the statistical methods of control to observe the differences between the two groups. One large meta-analysis of such studies concluded that those who get flu shots are half as likely to die as their unvaccinated peers over the winter. Several other studies have come to a similar conclusion.

It sounds possibly a bit too good to be true. In 2005, Lone Simonsen, a researcher at George Washington University and her colleagues, showed that the number of flu deaths among the elderly in the US has remained at about 5% of deaths in the group during winter. Vaccination coverage has skyrocketed from about 15% in 1980 to about 70% today. So how could flu vaccination be preventing half of the deaths in winter, when the flu accounted for only 5% of those deaths back in 1980, when most people were not vaccinated?

Also, in 2006 epidemiologist Lisa Jackson and her colleagues at the Centre for Health Statistics in Seattle, analysed a Seattle medical database using the same statistical methods as the previous studies. It showed that the maximum benefit of having the flu shot happened in the months before the season of flu even started.

Jackson insisted that the studies failed to give an account of ill and weak elderly people who had died but were less inclined to be vaccinated, making vaccination seem more valuable than it actually is.

But the debate was not over. Last year Kristin Nichol and her colleagues from the University of Minnesota published a dissertation using slightly different statistical methods and included records from tens of thousands of patients in three cities over 10 years. It came to the same incredible conclusion that vaccination was preventing about half of all deaths in winter. Researchers like Simonsen, Jackson and myself estimated Nichol's methods. Also, we believe this finding is subject to the sort of bias already identified by Jackson.

Last week Simonsen and Nichol discussed the issue at the Interscience Conference on Antimicrobial Agents and Chemotherapy in Washington DC. Nichol accepted that although there might still be some bias in her latest survey, flu deaths are estimated indirectly, especially counting extra deaths beyond those expected in winter. Researchers may have underestimated the number of people who have died as a result of the flu.

In conclusion, we need to improve our statistical methods for measuring the effectiveness of the flu vaccine. This issue has much wider implications as similar methods are used to analyse other areas in which randomized trials are not possible. For example, the effectiveness of cholesterol-lowering statins for pneumonia patients is also analysed in this way.

Questions 14-20

Do the following statements reflect the claims of the writer in Reading Passage 2?

*In boxes **14-20** on your answer sheet write*

> **TRUE** *if the statement agrees with the information*
> **FALSE** *if the statement contradicts the information*
> **NOT GIVEN** *if there is no information on this*

14 About 3,600 people are dying from the flu every winter in the US.

15 Although flu itself is seldom a disease that causes death, it can make the people age quicker.

16 Lots of rich countries have successfully carried out a high quality vaccination programme.

17 Flu shots should be useful for prescription but it may be immoral to hold back vaccination.

18 From meta-analysis those who get the flu shot are fifty per cent less likely to die than their unvaccinated peers.

19 Lone Simonsen indicated how many people died from flu deaths among the young.

20 The time for the highest level of efficacy of the flu shot turned out within the weeks previous to the flu season.

ACADEMIC READING TEST 3

Questions 21-25

Classify the following statements as being

- **A** US Centre for Disease Control and Prevention (CDC)
- **B** George Washington University in Washington DC
- **C** Centre for Health Statistics in Seattle
- **D** University of Minnesota in Minneapolis

Write the appropriate letters **A-D** in boxes **21-25** on your answer sheet.

NB You may use any letter more than once.

21 Vaccination extent has maximised.

22 Seattle medical database was analysed using a statistical method.

23 Around 83 per cent of flu related fatalities are in the over 65 age group.

24 Vaccination was able to prevent about fifty per cent of all winter deaths.

25 The flu death account for five per cent of annual winter deaths in the age group of 65 or over.

Questions 26-27

Complete the sentences below with taken from Reading Passage 2.

Use **ONE OR TWO WORD** for each answer.

Write your answers in boxes **26** and **27** on your answer sheet.

26 What is ONE of several diseases recorded as a cause of death if the elderly have the flu?

27 What percentage of the vaccination coverage is recently maximised by the research of Lone Simonsen?

READING PASSAGE 3

You should spend about 20 minutes on Questions 28-40 which are based on Reading Passage 3 below.

High-tech Switzerland

For a nation with a history of making sophisticated clocks, it is not surprising that Switzerland is the best place for precision and high-tech research. The country is so proud of two Federal Institutes of Technology, like the CERN of particle physics laboratory and a core of IBM research facilities. Also, there are two big pharmaceutical companies called Roche and Novartis. Also, who can forget Switzerland's world famous chocolate industry?

British citizens are able to work in Switzerland visa-free and the country offers salaries of up to £72,000 per year for highly-skilled experienced researchers with the option of skiing in the lunch break. It is easy to know why Switzerland appeals to so many. In what fields are these great opportunities available?

Computing Clout

IBM is one of the global companies that has established a research hub in Switzerland. The Ruschlikon lab located in the south of Zurich draws researchers from around the world, with 80% of them coming from abroad.

This lab is a leader in digital storage technology and semiconductor and optical electronics for on-line networks. Projects to build a top-class nanotechnology research centre in the place are on-going and will be completed by 2014.

Irene Holenweger Koeb, a manager in IBM human resources, says that the lab is looking for a wide range of disciplines including physics, chemistry and mathematics. Also, it is a thriving bioscience group working on the application of nanotechnology to life sciences and other areas. Most of the positions only accept applicants with a Ph.D. but the lab also hires approximately 100 applicants with Bachelors and Masters degrees each year.

Paul Hurley, a researcher in IBM's systems software group, is enjoying the flexible atmosphere of his work. There is a relaxed atmosphere in the office at IBM and meetings often take place over lunch or a coffee break.

As a lot of employees are not Swiss nationals, the company offers a lot of support and also has a policy of paying relocation expenses. Koeb says that it is important to gradually ease employees into their new workplace.

German lessons which are paid for by IBM, are offered to new employees working in Zurich. The standard of German is different to the German spoken in Zurich. Whilst Hurley has attended the classes, he says it a little bit more practice is needed to notice the "Swiss-isms."

Raising the Chocolate Bar

Switzerland is known for chocolate. Jose Rubio of Lindt's human resources department says "Our company has 44 nationalities and 18 languages."

Scientists are able to find jobs within quality management, research and development and in the factory working conditions. The work of R&D is to help improve new recipes and products as well as designing and building new machines for making them. You are able to hone your skills in a well managed company and have the pleasant task of testing the products to make sure they meet the company's high standards.

Rubio says that a foreign staff must speak at least one of the official Swiss languages. Most of the positions need a good level of German, as it is vital when working with Swiss coworkers in the production lines.

The ETH in German-speaking Zurich has a sister institution, which is the Federal Institute of Technology in French-speaking Lausanne (EPFL). With over 250 research groups and 10,000 students and faculties, it is focused on interdisciplinary scientific research. The institute's technology transfer programmes ensure that practical tools and methods make it out of the lab and into industry.

Questions 28-30

*Choose the appropriate letters **A-D** and write them in boxes **28-30** on your answer sheet.*

28 Ruschlikon lab located in Zurich attracts

    A almost 80 per cent of research staff from overseas.
    B 80 per cent of research staff domestically.
    C at least 80 per cent of engineers from abroad.
    D 80 per cent of staff with a PhD staff from overseas.

29 The lab has a plan to complete in 2014

    A founding a top-class Ruschlikon lab.
    B making a world-famous chocolate industry.
    C founding the best nanotechnology research centre.
    D researching digital storage marketing.

30 According to information in the text, the main purpose of the writer is

    A to survey various high-tech research in Switzerland.
    B to introduce attractive research centres in Switzerland.
    C to recruit a variety of human resources in Switzerland.
    D to understand the world-famous chocolate in Switzerland.

Questions 31-35

*Complete the summary below. Choose **NO MORE THAN TWO WORDS** from Reading Passage 3 for each answer.*

*Write your answers in boxes **31- 35** on your answer sheet.*

Raising the chocolate bar

Switzerland famous for **31** --------------------, attracted scientists in quality management, research and development. Those working in R&D aid to improve new version of recipes, products and design and build on **32** --------------------. Foreign staff should fluently speak one of **33** -------------------- official tongues in the least. Especially, a number of workplaces need to have an advanced level of **34** --------------------. With over 250 research groups and 10,000 students and faculty, it emphasises **35** -------------------- scientific research.

ACADEMIC READING TEST 3

Questions 36-40

Do the following statements reflect the claims of the writer in Reading Passage 3?

In boxes 36-40 on your answer sheet write

    TRUE   *if the statement agrees with the information*
    FALSE   *if the statement contradicts the information*
    NOT GIVEN *if there is no information on this*

36   Switzerland has a reputation for history of making precise clockwork.

37   Coffee in Switzerland is world-famous.

38   Four-fifths of the staff at the Ruschlikon in Zurich are from overseas.

39   The Ruschlikon lab is a traiblazer in only the field of semiconductors in digital storage technology.

40   Most study fields need a high level of English.

IELTS

INTERNATIONAL ENGLISH LANGUAGE TESTING SYSTEM

ACADEMIC READING

TEST 4

TIME ALLOWED : 1 hour

NUMBER OF QUESTIONS : 40

Instructions

ALL ANSWERS MUST BE WRITTEN ON THE ANSWER SHEET

The test is divided as follows :

    Reading Passage 1   Questions 1-13

    Reading Passage 2   Questions 14-28

    Reading Passage 3   Questions 29-40

Start at the beginning of the test and work through it. You should answer all the questions. If you cannot do a particular question leave it and go on to the next.

You can return to it later.

READING PASSAGE 1

You should spend about 20 minutes on **Questions 1-13** which are based on Reading Passage 1 below.

THE SWINE FLU PANDEMIC

The swine flu pandemic has become more problematic. The White House will meet with state representatives on the 9th of July to talk about the preparation for the autumn flu season in the US, whilst the UK has focused their response on the H_1N_1 virus to cope with widespread infection.

Meantime, the southern hemisphere is going into the middle of the winter flu season, and the swine H_1N_1 virus seems to be replacing the seasonal flu viruses that have been circulating until now. This is related to the seasonal flu vaccine which several companies are still producing. It could cause some problems when the northern hemisphere flu season comes at the end of this year.

The flu pandemics of 1918, 1957 and 1968 showed a high level of seasonal change and also released mild form of the H_1N_1 virus which circulates through the existing flu virus, H_3N_2. So, nobody knows how the H_1N_1 virus is going to behave. If it is not exchanged with the seasonal virus the milder H_1N_1 and H_3N_2 - the world is facing the prospect of catching all three viruses at once. It would be a complicated scenario, such as both seasonal and pandemic vaccines would be wanted and patients from different age groups would be affected. Although, based on what is happening in the southern hemisphere, it does not seem that this will be the case.

In the northern hemisphere, swine flu has spread to the extent that over 98% of flu cases genotyped in the US towards the end of June were caused by the pandemic virus. This is to be expected. Whilst the seasonal flu viruses generally die out during the summer season, the pandemic virus can be more powerful as fewer people have built up immunity to it.

The state of Victoria in Australia reported this week that the H_1N_1 virus is now considered for 99% of all flu cases. There are reports of a similar situation in South America. In Chile, the H_1N_1 virus is also much stronger than other seasonal viruses. "98% of the flu cases we now take are caused by H1N1," Jeanette Vega, Chile's under-secretary of public health, said last week about a pandemic peak in Cancun, Mexico. "The seasonal vaccine is not used."

In the Argentine capital Buenos Aires, Juan Manzur, the health minister, reported last week about the emergency situation in that 90% of the flu in a result of the H_1N_1 virus.

During this winter in the northern hemisphere, it is an important matter. "If the pandemic virus greatly attacks the seasonal viruses in a regular flu season, the seasonal viruses are likely to be exchanged by the new virus, like in the 1968 pandemic," says Ab Osterhaus in the University of Rotterdam in the Netherlands.

In previous pandemics, the virus has changed, producing negative side effects. So far for H_1N_1, there have only been a few ominous signs.

The mutation of the virus's polymerase enzyme has been replicated efficiently from a sample taken in Shanghai. Ron Fouchier at the University of Rotterdam says that this could spread if it makes the virus more contagious, but the virus may also improve pathogenicity.

Also last week, two cases of the H_1N_1 virus with resistance to the main antiviral drug, Tamiflu, were found in people using the drug. Another was found in a girl who had never take the drug, suggesting Tamiflu - resistant to the H_1N_1 virus might already be in circulation.

Questions 1-9

Complete the summary below.

Choose **NO MORE THAN THREE WORDS** from the passage for each answer.

Write your answers in boxes *1-9* on your answer sheet.

There is currently severe problem of **1** -------------------- in the world, especially both the US and the UK are making strenuous efforts to solve the problem.

In the meantime, during the middle of winter flu season, **2** -------------------- is likely to substitute the seasonal flu viruses in the southern hemisphere. Also, over 98 per cent out of flu cases genotyped in the US were generated by **3** --------------------. Whilst seasonal flu viruses usually fade out in **4** --------------------, the pandemic virus has the advantage that few people have immunity to it.

There are reports that the H_1N_1 virus accounts for more than 90 per cent of all flu cases in countries, such as **5** -----------------, **6** ----------------- and **7** -----------------.

According to Ab Osterhaus, **8** -------------------- in a regular flu season can be replaced by the pandemic virus. New viruses were found to be resistant to the antiviral drug, **9** -----------------.

ACADEMIC READING TEST 4

Questions 10-13

Do the following statements reflect the claims of the writer in Reading Passage1?

*In boxes **10-13** on your answer sheet write*

> **YES**   *if the statement reflects the opinion of the writer*
> **NO**   *if the statement contradicts the opinion of the writer*
> **NOT GIVEN**   *if it is impossible to say what the writer thinks about this*

10   The UK and the US had discussed and worked together on the swine flu pandemic in the past.

11   Over 98 per cent of flu cases in the US were motivated by the pandemic virus.

12   In Argentina, 60 per cent of the flu virus in circulation is the H_1N_1 virus.

13   Tamiflu is the crucial antiviral medicine which is resistant to the H_1N_1 virus.

READING PASSAGE 2

*You should spend about 20 minutes on **Questions 14-28** which are based on Reading Passage 2 on the following pages.*

Questions 14-20

Reading Passage 2 has nine paragraphs, **A-I**.

Choose the correct heading for paragraph **B-I** from the list of headings below.

Write the correct number, ***i-ix***, in boxes **14-20** on your answer sheet.

	List of Headings
i	The scientific value of the rocks
ii	The craters of the moon
iii	The mission to collect material on the moon
iv	The impact of the rocks discovered
v	The surprise evidence about the lunar
vi	The history of the early solar system
vii	The unknown questions left for future
viii	NASA's lunar rock collection
ix	Study of lunar history

Example	Answer
Paragraph **A**	iii

14   Paragraph **B**

15   Paragraph **C**

16   Paragraph **E**

17   Paragraph **F**

18   Paragraph **G**

19   Paragraph **H**

20   Paragraph **I**

ACADEMIC READING TEST 4

Mission to Collect Materials on the Moon

A Whilst the world watched in excitement as Neil Armstrong and Buzz Aldrin landed on the moon, planetary scientists were focused on something else. For them, the value of the mission was in the cargo they brought back to earth. By the time Armstrong and Aldrin climbed into the lunar for the last time, they had gathered 22 kilograms of moon rocks, completely filling a small suitcase. Over five Apollo crews brought back a total collection of 382 kilograms of material containing 2,200 samples.

B The rocks were known at the time as a scientific treasure and they did not disappoint. Paul Spudis, a geologist of the Lunar and Planetary Institute in Houston, Texas, said "Our ideas about planetary formation and evolution must be rewritten after the discoveries made by the Apollo crews." Harold Urey, a Nobel prizewinner, and one of the advocates of lunar exploration, had predicted that the moon was composed of primitive meteoritic material. But his conclusion was wrong. Some of the rocks looked just like the rocks on earth.

C Many clues that the lunar rocks contained have taken a couple of years to effectively analyse. Also, some of the conclusions are still debated. A big surprise was the evidence that the early moon was covered by a lot of molten rock. The moon's mountainous regions are made of anorthosite, a rare rock on Earth that forms when light, aluminum-rich minerals floats to the top of lava.

D Nowadays, the smart money is on the idea that the moon was created as a result of something that occurred around 50 million years after the solar system was created, when the Earth was in its infancy. From this hypothesis, earliest Earth ran into a planet that was a similar size to Mars and debris from the collision went into orbit around Earth which rapidly came together to form the moon.

E The "giant impact" scenario led to a radical re-evaluation of the history of the early solar system. Before Apollo, planetary scientists watched the collection of objects orbiting the sun like a clockwork mechanism in which collisions were rare and trivial. Now, it is accepted as being a far more active environment, shuffling, colliding or ejecting. This history of all the inner planets has been shaped by collisions and nowhere is that history more visible than the moon.

F Another surprise was the rocks from the moon's largest impact craters indicate that all craters are roughly the same age, between 3.8 and 4 billion years old. It never coincided. The moon – and by extension, Earth must have been caused by a devastating barrage half a billion years after the solar system formed. To causing this process, something big must have been going back to the outer solar system, but what? Surprisingly, this episode in the history of the solar system has come to be known as the last heavy bombardment, and ended at roughly the same time as the first signs of life on Earth.

G These key discoveries about our planet's history may never have been made without the samples taken from the moon for chemical analysis and isotopic dating. So do the Apollo rocks hide any more secrets? All 2,200 samples have been researched, and Randy Korotev, a lunar geochemist at Washington University in St Louis, Missouri, says that it is unlikely that there will be anything groundbreaking left to find from them. However, they may yet keep some more delicate secrets. Korotev says "We are steadily developing better tools and asking better questions." Especially, the instruments for dating mineral samples have been more delicate, enabling researchers to study the age of ever smaller samples, like tiny mineral grains within a rock.

H These techniques have stimulated a rethink of some key dates in lunar history in the past two years. A team at the Swiss Federal Institute of Technology dated the formation of the moon's magma oceans. Also, by inference, the creation of the moon itself is estimated to have happened between 20 and 30 million years later than we originally thought, at approximately 4.5 billion years ago. Alexander Nemchin with five colleagues in Cutin University of Technology in Perth, Western Australia also estimated that a lunar zircon was around 4.417 billion years old when the last of the magma oceans solidified.

I The Apollo rock samples are not finished answering some of the bigger picture questions. What will we discover on the opposite side of the moon's surface that we are unable to see from Earth? Can we put together a detailed history of the lava flows that formed the basalts of the lunar seas? Can we discover any samples from deep inside the moon? These are all seen as very good reasons for coming back to the moon. The big picture needs more samples, more data and more contexts. According to Gary Lofgren, a curator of NASA's lunar rock collection at Johnson Space Centre in Huston, "There's no lack of target and scientific questions. It's not just about the moon but about the solar system's history. This is the lesson that we have learned from Apollo."

ACADEMIC READING TEST 4

Questions 21-23

Choose the correct letter, A, B, C and D.

*Write the correct letter in boxes **21-23** on your answer sheet.*

21 The scenario "giant impact" is mainly concerned with

    A ways of finding the history of the early solar system.
    B the history of the early solar craters.
    C the origin of the earth.
    D ways of learning about orbiting the sun.

22 The samples taken from the moon help

    A planetary scientists have made for dating mineral.
    B geochemists to study some craters.
    C planetary scientists to make key discoveries about the earth's history
    D geologists to predict the moon's primitive material.

23 Gary Lofgren's quote says that, when we try to remember things,

    A the remaining big picture questions will never come true.
    B the history of the lava flows will be returned.
    C plenty of targets and scientific questions will be collected.
    D the earth's development will be the milestone in the solar system's history.

Questions 24-28

Do the following statements reflect the claims of the writer in Reading Passage1?

In boxes 24-28 on your answer sheet write

> **TRUE**   *if the statement agrees with the information*
> **FALSE**   *if the statement contradicts the information*
> **NOT GIVEN** *if there is no information on this*

24 The rocks which Neil Armstrong and Buzz Aldrin collected were more valuable than those of Russian astronauts.

25 The lunar rocks taken are critical to beginning to understand the history.

26 All craters on the moon are of a similar age, up to 5 billion years old.

27 The main clues for discovering the earthquake are given by the samples taken from the moon.

28 The half of the moon's surface that we can never see is related to the solar system's history.

READING PASSAGE 3

You should spend about 20 minutes on *Questions 29-40* which are based on Reading Passage 3 on the following pages.

Organism's Appearance

As Darwin discovered his evolution theory, the earliest known fossils were left in rocks which he called the Silurian age. Older rocks seemed to contain no fossils. The apparently sudden appearance of subtle animals like trilobites was not inconsistent with Darwin's thoughts of gradual evolution. "If my theory will be true, it is unquestionable that before the lowest Silurian stratum was deposited ... the world swarmed with living creatures. To the question why we do not find records of these vast primordial periods, I can give no satisfactory answer," Darwin wrote in the first edition of *On the Origin of Species*. His puzzle is known as Darwin's dilemma.

Of course, we have discovered a lot of fossils from the earliest periods. Rocks of 3.8 billion years old have signs of life, and the first recognizable bacteria to come out in rocks of 3.5 billion years old. During the Ediacaran, approximately one billion years ago, Multi-cellular plants with red and green algae appeared and approximately 575 million years ago was found in the first multi-cellular animals.

Even so, there are many perplexing questions. Why did animals evolve so late in the day? And why did the ancestors of modern animals apparently evolve in a geological blink of an eye during the early Cambrian period between 542 and 520 million years ago? Recently, a series of discoveries could help to explain these long-lasting mysteries. These discoveries suggest that the earliest animals evolved much earlier than we thought, perhaps over 850 million years ago. However, the really extraordinary part is that these early animals may have completely changed the planet, paving the way for the larger and more complex animals to follow them.

Several aspects of the biggest discoveries have come from an ancient seabed in China, called the Doushantuo Formation, where unusual conditions conserved some extraordinary fossils. During the last part of the Ediacaran period, layers between 550 and 580 million years old include tiny spheres made of from one to dozens of different cells – just like animals' first embryos. A couple of things have suggested that they are the property of giant bacteria, but a series of studies over the past decade have left little doubt that they are really animal embryos.

Leiming Yin, a researcher at the Nanjing Institute of Geology and Paleontology in China, reported discovering embryos encased inside hard, spiky shells unlike anything produced by bacteria in 2007. Furthermore evidence of shells that apart from the deficiency of conserved embryos on the inside are identical, can be seen in rocks as old as 632 million years – the appearance of the Ediacaran period – suggesting that the animal embryos themselves go back this far.

Other more tentative discoveries push the appearance of animals back even further. Roger Summons, a researcher in the Massachusetts Institute of Technology and his colleague Gordon Love studied brownish, oily sandstone cores drilled from 4 kilometres below the desert of Oman. The oily remains of dead organisms drifted down to the depths of ancient oceans, where they decomposed slowly because of the lack of oxygen. No visible fossils are present but within that oil are molecular fossils – chemicals taken from the ancient organisms. In layers that are 635 to 713 million years old, Summons and Love discovered 24-isopropylcholestane (24-IPC), a stable form of a kind of cholesterol that these days are only discovered in the cell membranes of certain sponges. "The sponges biomass must have been so substantial," says Love, now at the University of California, Riverside. "They were ecologically outstanding."

Fuel of Life

With the oceans changed, the stage was finally set for the evolution of more complicated body forms. The idea that increasing oxygen levels played a major role in the explosion of life during the Cambrian period is far from new, but most of the researchers attribute the increase in oceanic oxygen to the increase in the atmosphere. If Butterfield is right, it was basically because of animals taking over from bacteria. "These geochemical signatures [of oxygenation] are not causing the evolution of animals," he insists. "They're consequences of the dawn of animals."

"He is right," says Brasier. In fact, he thinks the link between complex life and the transformation of the planet runs even deeper. In Darwin's Lost World, a book published earlier this year, Brasier suggests that the improved burial of carbon resulting from the rising of large cells and groups of cells – perhaps with plants, like seaweed – sucked carbon dioxide out of the atmosphere, setting off the series of ice ages that aided the first animals to wrestle for control of the oceans with bacteria. "Rather than being the cause of animal evolution, the ice ages may well have been the response to it," he says.

ACADEMIC READING TEST 4

Questions 29-33

Look at the following statements Questions 29-33 and the list of researchers below.

Match each statement with the correct researcher(s), **A-E**.

Write the correct letter, **A-E**, in boxes **29-33** on your answer sheet.

NB You may use any letter more than once.

29   studied brownish, oily sandstone cores.

30   announced embryos on the inside surrounded by hard, spiky shells.

31   claimed that the expanded burial of carbon resulted in the series of ice ages.

32   wrote in the first edition of On the Origin of Species.

33   discovered 24-isopropylcholestane.

List of Researchers

A	Darwin
B	Leiming Yin
C	Summons and Love
D	Elizabeth Turner
E	Brasier

Questions 34-36

Complete the sentences below.

Choose **NO MORE THAN THREE WORDS** from the passage for each answer.

Write your answers in boxes **34-36** on your answer sheet.

34 What is an ancient seabed in China, conserving some weird fossils?

35 What made organisms decompose in the depths of ancient oceans?

36 What was written by Brasier to swell burial of carbon resulting from the rise of large cells and groups of cells?

Questions 37-40

Complete the summary below.

Choose **NO MORE THAN TWO WORDS** from the passage for each answer.

Write your answers in boxes **37-40** on your answer sheet.

Fuel of Life

From the oceans fluctuated, **37** ––––––––––––––––––– of increasing levels which played a vital part in the increase of oceanic oxygen in the atmosphere. Actually, Brasier considers the connection of **38** ––––––––––––––––––– and **39** ––––––––––––––––––– goes deeper. According to *Darwin's Lost World*, he claims that carbon burial was getting more inhaled **40** ––––––––––––––––––– outside of the atmosphere, caused the series of ice ages that was supported with the first organism generated from bacteria.

IELTS
INTERNATIONAL ENGLISH LANGUAGE TESTING SYSTEM

ACADEMIC READING

TEST 5

TIME ALLOWED : 1 hour
NUMBER OF QUESTIONS : 40

Instructions

ALL ANSWERS MUST BE WRITTEN ON THE ANSWER SHEET

The test is divided as follows :

   Reading Passage 1   Questions 1-13

   Reading Passage 2   Questions 14-28

   Reading Passage 3   Questions 29-40

Start at the beginning of the test and work through it. You should answer all the questions. If you cannot do a particular question leave it and go on to the next.

You can return to it later.

READING PASSAGE 1

You should spend about 20 minutes on **Questions 1-13** which are based on Reading Passage 1 below.

Parasitic Worms' Efficacy

A   Parasitic worms, like hookworms, whipworms, pinworms and flukes that plague humans are enough to make most of us shudder. Except John Turton, in the middle of 1970s, whilst working at the UK's Medical Research Council Laboratories in Surrey, he intentionally infected himself with hookworms in an attempt to alleviate his chronic hay fever. It worked. During two summer seasons whilst he held the parasites, his allergy diminished.

B   In regions where parasitic worm infections are rife, when the remedy was emerged, Turton's vital experiment came. In 1913 W. Herrick, a doctor from Columbia University in New York, found a very different link between parasitic worms, or helminthes, and allergies. Lab workers analysed the gut-dwelling roundworm Ascaris that often caused tenderness and swelling around the fingers, and more severely asthma after longer exposure.

C   Researchers have been trying to make sense of these contradicting findings since the 1970s in the hope of being able to use the power of parasites to help free people of their allergies, without making things worse. They know they are playing with fire. After all, helminthes are responsible for some truly horrible diseases and cause great suffering around the world. However, as the effects of helminthes on the human body become clearer, it looks like their healing powers may have potential benefits.

D   Not surprisingly, no researchers have been willing to take the risk of deliberately infecting themselves as Turton had done. Instead, most studies are dependent on populations in countries where people are already infected. This research tends to emphasis on three commonly diagnosed allergic conditions: asthma, eczema and hay fever. The results have been confusing, but now researchers are beginning to have a better understanding.

E   For instance, a study conducted in Taiwan showed that people infected with Enterobius vermicularis, a pinworm that is one of the most common gut parasites in the world, were less likely to have hay fever than the rest of the general population. But the results from Ecuador show a different story. Hay fever was not more common in children living in urban areas than it was in children living in rural areas. The parasite was equally common in both groups, so the researchers concluded that something else must be responsible for the prevalence of hay fever.

F   Knowing about eczema has proved as difficult to interpret. For instance, a study in Uganda discovered that eczema was less common among babies whose mothers had been infected with helminthes whilst being pregnant. But, another study this time in Ethiopia, discovered that children with Trichuris worms, and whipworms that infest the large intestine, were more likely to have eczema than uninfected children.

G   Regarding asthma, Herrick's discovery that it can be started by contact with the Ascaris was confirmed in the 1970s. But, hookworms decreased the extremity of asthma in a group of Ethiopians and similar benefits have been seen in Brazilian asthma sufferers infected with the Schistosoma mansoni, the flatworm responsible for schistosomiasis, which damages internal organs. What are we to make of all this? The outstanding link between allergies and parasites is the human immune system. Allergies are caused by an overactive immune response, and helminthes have strategies to dampen down our immune response to stimulate their survival. After all, they have evolved alongside humans for several thousands of years.

H   In people with no allergies, foreign material entering the body stimulates the release of cytokines, molecules that sound the alarm to get the attention of other immune cells. As immune cells set to attack the intruder, another set of molecules is released to prohibit the immune response from overreacting. One of the main molecules responsible for keeping reactions in check is interleukin-10, which inhibits the release of certain cytokines. People with allergies tend to have lower than normal levels of interleukin-10, so their immune responses frequently get out of hand. In contrast, people infected with helminthes have above average levels of the molecule, and research on schistosomiasis patients indicates that this is at least partially because of the worms that set free chemicals that trigger the production of interleukin-10 in their host.

Questions 1-8

*Reading Passage 1 has eight paragraphs, **A-H**.*

Which paragraph contains the following information?

*Write the correct letter, **A-E**, in boxes **1-8** on your answer sheet.*

NB   *You may use any letter more than once.*

1   Lab workers' duties

2   Contrary results between surveys

3   A voluntary attempt against allergy

4   The same results between surveys

5   A powerful remedy for allergies

6   Understanding of immune responses

7   Critical connection between allergies and parasites

8   Three most commonly allergies

Questions 9-13

Do the following statements reflect the claims of the writer in Reading Passage1?

In boxes **9-13** on your answer sheet write

TRUE   if the statement agrees with the information
FALSE   if the statement contradicts the information
NOT GIVEN   if there is no information on this

9   John Turton infected himself with hookworms by mistake.

10 Dr Herrick has found a different feature between worms and allergies.

11 Researchers have not known the healing potential of parasites since the 1970s.

12 Allergies have the same appearance as parasites.

13 People with allergies may have higher than ordinary levels of interleukin-10.

READING PASSAGE 2

You should spend about 20 minutes on **Questions 14-28** which are based on Reading Passage 2 below.

The Nagymaros Dam

When Janos Vargha, a biologist from the Hungarian Academy of Sciences, began a new career as a writer with a small monthly nature magazine called Buvar, it was 9 years after the story behind the fall of the Berlin Wall had started to unfold. During his early research, he went to a beauty spot on the river Danube outside Budapest known as the Danube Bend to interview local officials about plans to build a small park on the site of an ancient Hungarian capital.

One official mentioned in passing that this tree-lined curve in the river, a popular tourism spot for Hungarians, was monotonous. Also, it was to be submerged by a giant hydroelectric dam in secret by a much-feared state agency known simply as the Water Management.

Vargha investigated and learned that the Nagymaros dam (pronounced "nosh-marosh") would cause pollution, destroy underground water reserves, dry out wetlands and wreck the unique ecosystem of central Europe's longest river. Unfortunately, nobody objected. "Of course, I wrote an article. But there was a director of the Water Management on the magazine's editorial board. The last time, he went to the printers and stopped the presses, the article was never published. I was frustrated and angry, but I was ultimately interested in why they cared to ban my article," he remembers today.

He found that the Nagymaros dam was part of a joint project with neighbouring Czechoslovakia to produce hydroelectricity, irrigate farms and enhance navigation. They would build two dams and re-engineer the Danube for 200 kilometres where it created the border between them. "The Russians were working together, too. They wanted to take their big ships from the Black Sea right up the Danube to the border with Austria."

Vargha was soon under vigorous investigation, and some of his articles got past the censors. He gathered supporters for some years, but he was one of only a few people who believed the dam should be stopped. He was hardly surprised when the Water Management refused to debate the project in public. After a public meeting, the bureaucrats had pulled out at the last minute. Vargha knew he had to take the next step. "We decided it wasn't enough to talk and write, so we set up an organization, the Danube Circle. We announced that we didn't agree with censorship. We would act as if we were living in a democracy." he says.

The Danube Circle was illegal and the secret publications it produced turned out to be samizdat leaflets. In an extraordinary act of defiance, it gathered 10,000 signatures for a petition objecting to the dam and made links with environmentalists in the west, inviting them to Budapest for a press conference.

The Hungarian government enforced a news blackout on the dam, but articles about the Danube Circle began to be published and appear in the western media. In 1985, the Circle and Vargha, a public spokesman, won the Right Livelihood award known as the alternative Nobel prize. Officials told Vargha he should not take the prize but he ignored them. The following year when Austrian environmentalists joined a protest in Budapest, they were met with tear gas and batons. Then the Politburo had Vargha taken from his new job as editor of the Hungarian version of Scientific American.

The dam became a focus for opposition to the hated regime. Communists tried to hold back the waters in the Danube and resist the will of the people. Vargha says, "Opposing the state directly was still hard." "Objecting to the dam was less of a hazard, but it was still considered a resistance to the state."

Under increasing pressure from the anti-dam movement, the Hungarian Communist party was divided. Vargha says, "Reformists found that the dam was not very popular and economical. It would be cheaper to generate electricity by burning coal or nuclear power." "But hardliners were standing for Stalinist ideas of large dams which mean symbols of progress." Environmental issues seemed to be a weak point of east European communism in its final years. During the 1970s under the support of the Young Communist Leagues, a host of environmental groups had been founded. Party officials saw them as a harmless product of youthful idealism created by Boy Scouts and natural history societies.

Green idealism steadily became a focal point for political opposition. In Czechoslovakia, the human rights of Charter 77 took up environmentalism. The green-minded people of both Poland and Estonia participated in the Friends of the Earth International to protest against air pollution. Bulgarian environmentalists built a resistance group, called Ecoglasnost, which held huge rallies in 1989. Big water engineering projects were potent symbols of the old Stalinism.

Questions 14-21

Complete the summary using the list of words and phrases, **A-L**, below.

Write the correct letter, **A-L**, in boxes **14-21** on your answer sheet.

The story of the fall of the Berlin Wall had started to unfold 9 years earlier. Janos Vargha visited the river Danube out of Budapest to discuss a matter of **14** -------------------- with executives. However, unfortunately, the tree-lined curve in the river was **15** -------------------- by a colossal dam which caused a lot of fear. He noticed the negative impact of the Nagymaros dam would be **16** -------------------- on the ecosystem around the main river. Besides, the dam was engineering public works, generating hydroelectricity, irrigating farmlands and developing sailing trade which was **17** -------------------- with border of Czechoslovakia.

After one public meeting, Vargha **18** --------------------, the Danube Circle for showing the autonomy of the people in a democracy. Despite of every effort, he who would eventually become the editor of the Hungarian edition was **19** -------------------- by the Politburo. Fortunately, with plenty of pressure from the anti-dam movement, east European communism's final symbol was opposed by the **20** --------------------. Overall, between political processing and environmentalists have been on a **21** -------------------- of views.

A severe	**B** discharged	**C** constructing a park of small-scale
D passed	**E** reformist	**F** swallowed up
G separated	**H** favourable	**I** established
J collision	**K** combined	**L** environmentalist

Questions 22-26

Do the following statements reflect the claims of the writer in Reading Passage 2?

In boxes 22-26 on your answer sheet write

> **TRUE** if the statement agrees with the information
> **FALSE** if the statement contradicts the information
> **NOT GIVEN** if there is no information on this

22 Janos Vargha predicted that the Nagymaros dam would be wreck the natural atmosphere before it was built.

23 The Nagymaros dam's project was managed by the Russians only.

24 The Danube Circle was an unauthorised group for opposing the dam.

25 The Politburo accepted Vargha as editor of the Hungarian edition.

26 The human rights Charter 77 in Czechoslovakia accepted green thoughts.

Questions 27-28

Choose the correct letter, A, B, C or D.

Write the correct letter in boxes 27-28 on your answer sheet.

27 In this passage, the Nagymaros dam's main purpose was

   A related to the Russian Water Management.
   B to develop a source of electronic power, farming and sail.
   C to connect the Black Sea and the Danube.
   D to develop a beauty spot on the river Danube.

28 Vargha claims that opposing the dam was

   A to preserve precious ecosystem around the river Danube.
   B to protest against air pollution.
   C to supply plenty of water for fishing and aquaculture in the river Danube.
   D to preserve the site of an ancient Hungarian capital.

READING PASSAGE 3

You should spend about 20 minutes on Questions 29-40 which are based on Reading Passage 3 on the following pages.

Human Guinea Pig

There are 50 million people in the world being used as guinea pigs in clinical trials testing experimental drugs. Apart from potentially risking part of their lives, applicants must pass a severe series of tests just to be able to participate in some trials. However, acceptance means more tests, negative side effects and a considerable disturbance to their daily lives. So what's in it for them? As journalist Alex O'Meara explains in *Chasing Medical Miracles*, some participate out of genuine altruism, whilst some are looking for cures for their own disorders. O'Meara having diabetes himself volunteered for a risky transplant of insulin-producing cells from the liver, and his story spread through the book.

O'Meara knows people choose to participate for life's great motivator: money. Clinical trials are a huge business, making up to $ 24 billion annually, and the cash they offer as compensation has become a sought-after way to make extra money. This exchange of money often involves people who are sick and vulnerable, and emphasises the dark ethical waters in which current clinical trials are mired.

At intervals, the ill feel compelled to join a trial to get medical care. Some unethical researchers, desperate to recruit the large numbers needed to make their researches statistically valid, take advantage of this. It can be difficult for ill people to take that, at best, they are taking experimental medicine and at worst they are taking nothing at all.

Desperation for money or medicine is never a basis for unbiased decision-making. How can a researcher be sure a person is giving their true consent? And if a person gets better as a result of taking an experimental drug, what happens when their drug supply finishes after the trial?

These ethical quandaries have influenced healthcare in developing countries where clinical trials are a prospering industry. According to Adriana Petryna in *When Experiments Travel*, in spite of the fact that drug companies are moving their trials to developing countries, only 10% of drug research addresses disorders that influence the world's poor. Such diseases make up to 90% of the global disease burden. Establishing ethical and legal responsibilities is also becoming harder, she reports. With an increased number of subcontractors included in trials, it is clear that no one is overly concerned about patient welfare.

ACADEMIC READING TEST 5

> From this theory, international human rights frameworks, such as the Nuremberg Code should ensure that participants are not taking any positive effect. In reality, largely poor and illiterate populations are being exploited. Besides, ethical regulations in poor countries are rarely strict, therefore researchers can get away with recruiting people into HIV trials knowing that they will die without the experimental drug.
>
> O'Meara also reports about drug company's greed and the inability of regulators to control the rapidly increasing number of trials. The US Food and Drug Administration inspects less than 1% of the 350,000 registered trial sites. Drug firms are managing non-profit organizations that are undertaking just 30% of trials. However, in spite of their faults, clinical trials are still an essential tool of modern medicine.

Questions 29-36

Complete the summary below.

Choose **NO MORE THAN THREE WORDS** from the passage for each answer.

Write your answers in boxes **29-36** on your answer sheet.

For testing experimental **29** --------------------, there are 50 million people being used as guinea pigs looking for remedies to **30** -------------------- in clinical trial in spite of the risks through the world. Actually, that means people are both eager for life's considerable milestone of **31** -------------------- to make up insufficient labour pay in their lives and **32** -------------------- to participate in a trial. These ethical dilemmas have influenced health problems in **33** -------------------- which drug companies encouraged their trials.

From these situations between **34** -------------- and --------------, international human rights frameworks like **35** -------------------- should inform people of poverty of the poor countries which have a lack of **36** -------------------- ethical regulations.

Questions 37-39

Complete the summary below.

Choose **NO MORE THAN TWO WORDS** from the passage for each answer.

Write your answers in boxes **37-39** on your answer sheet.

37 Whilst some choose to cure for themselves, some participated due to -------------------.

38 Hopeless for either ------------------- or ------------------- does not work for fair decision-making.

39 Drug companies invest a lot of money in developing countries, causing ----------------.

Questions 40

Complete the correct letter, *A*, *B*, *C* or *D*.

Write the correct letter in box **40** on your answer sheet.

Which of the following phrases best describes the main aim of Reading Passage 3?

    A   to warn that guinea pigs are likely to have financial problems
    B   to describe how clinical trial were rapidly increasing and how serious it was
    C   to suggest that the Nuremberg Code is needed in other countries
    D   to examine how drug companies promoted the use of guinea pigs

IELTS
INTERNATIONAL ENGLISH LANGUAGE TESTING SYSTEM

ACADEMIC READING

TEST 6

TIME ALLOWED : 1 hour

NUMBER OF QUESTIONS : 40

Instructions

ALL ANSWERS MUST BE WRITTEN ON THE ANSWER SHEET

The test is divided as follows :

    Reading Passage 1   Questions 1-13

    Reading Passage 2   Questions 14-28

    Reading Passage 3   Questions 29-40

Start at the beginning of the test and work through it. You should answer all the questions. If you cannot do a particular question leave it and go on to the next.

You can return to it later.

READING PASSAGE 1

You should spend about 20 minutes on **Questions 1-13** which are based on Reading Passage 1 below.

Extraterrestrial National Park

The message to visitors at many beauty spots is "TAKE only pictures, leave only footprints." Although you won't see the actual place, Apollo11 astronauts Neil Armstrong and Buzz Aldrin took their giant leap for mankind on the moon. It will be the first extraterrestrial national park.

It may still be some years off, but the imminent reality of space tourism is already stimulating some archaeologists to begin to plan how to protect historic sites in space. With further moon missions planned, the fear is that the principle sites like Apollo11's landing place may be in danger. According to Beth O'Leary, a researcher in New Mexico State University in Las Cruces, "Technologically, probably the most important event in human history was to land on another celestial body," "It's like the discovery of fire, or the first stone tools. They should be protected and conserved."

In September 1959 since the Soviet Union's Luna2 crashed into the moon, a total of 40 expeditions have touched down on the moon's surface. 22 of them were launched by the US with the six, crewed Apollo missions launching between 1969 and 1972. The Apollo missions alone left behind 23 large artefacts including the descent and ascent stages of the lunar module landing equipment, the stage three Saturn rockets used to fly them there, and the lunar rovers or "moon buggies" the astronauts used to explore when they arrived.

As well as these, there are also smaller artefacts and personal items scattered around, such as Neil Armstrong's boots and portable life-support system, scientific instruments and their power generators. Of course, the iconic US flag planted in the moon's surface is there too. There are also the footprints and rover tread paths. In spite of the passing of the years, these remains are carved into the dust, since the moon has no wind or rain to wash them away.

P.J. Capelotti, an anthropologist at Penn State University in Abington, has mapped out five "lunar parks." These are the areas where the majority of the artefacts are concentrated and will be used as a basis for future preservation efforts. "Although nobody's saying that the whole moon has to be off-limits, people are starting to make plans for tourism and mineral extraction, or for putting a base there, needing to be aware of them and work around them."

More technological developments are also on their way. NASA's LCROSS mission plans to crash an SUV-sized rocket into one of the moon's poles later this year with the hope of finding water there. At the same time, teams competing for the Google Lunar X Prize for the first privately funded robot to reach the moon have been offered a $ 5 million bonus if they take a picture of artefacts like the Apollo11 landing equipment. Already, a question to be reported is how national governments and private companies should cooperate to ensure that artefacts are protected. There is some evidence that the US government is interested in working alongside other governments.

A space-flight company called TransOrbital, based in Palo Alto, California, presented its plans for sending a commercial mission to the moon by the end of the 1990s. These plans include making detailed maps of the moon and landing a capsule containing personal items, like business cards and cremated ashes. The US National Oceanic and Atmospheric Administration stipulated that TransOrbital's rockets must crash well away from any historic US artefacts when its flight was over. Although ultimately TransOrbital were unable to fund the mission, it might try again in the near future.

According to Phil Stooke, a planetary cartographer of the University of Western Ontario in London, he agrees Luna 2 also has great significance. "It crashed, but that impact site is every bit as historic as Apollo11." Another one is Luna9, the first spacecraft to land sending back pictures. "They must be preserved."

On the remaining Apollo sites, Stooke is searching how electronics, metal and paints have degraded after years of exposure to solar radiation and extremes of temperature. Also, he suggests that another Apollo site could be turned into a biological research centre, analysing the DNA and bacteria left behind from astronauts' life-support packs.

Once a consensus has been reached as to which sites are worthy of conservation, and guidelines have been built up to protect them from being damaged by future missions, the next question will be how future space tourists should be allowed to interact with them. Capelotti says, "Looking at grey dust is going to hold its attraction for only so long," "People are going to make pilgrimages to these sites."

There is a suggestion to build domes over historic sites, or perhaps even hotels, with the artefacts displayed in the "lobby." Another idea is to build up a raised railway track over the sites, so visitors could look at them without touching them. Capelotti says, "If Walt Disney was developing it, he would put a monorail around all five 'lunar parks,' so you could do the entire Apollo tour."

ACADEMIC READING TEST 6

Questions 1-7

Do the following statements reflect the claims of the writer in Reading Passage 1?

In boxes 1-7 on your answer sheet write

> **TRUE**   *if the statement agrees with the information*
> **FALSE**   *if the statement contradicts the information*
> **NOT GIVEN**   *if there is no information on this*

1   Archaeologists have established links between space tourism and Apollo11.

2   Of the 40 expeditions that landed on the lunar, the US embarked on more than half of them.

3   Between 1969 and 1972, there were not remarkable issues in the Apollo missions.

4   Neil Armstrong made up his mind to exploit the natural resources of the moon.

5   Astronauts' traces marked on the surface of the moon remain unchanged due to the lack of wind and rain.

6   Commercial space-flight companies planned to place both business cards and ashes on the moon.

7   In spite of financial problems, TransOrbital plan to launch their mission again in the foreseeable future.

Questions 8-13

Complete each sentence with the correct ending, *A-H*, below.

Write the correct letter, *A-H*, in boxes *8-13* on your answer sheet.

8 Archaeologists

9 The Apollo missions

10 Anthropologist P.J. Capelotti

11 SUV-sized rocket into the moon's pole

12 TransOrbital

13 The impact site of Luna2

A	left various artefacts on the moon's surface.
B	discovered water supported by NASA's LCROSS mission scheme.
C	aimed to launch a project to preserve relic sites in space.
D	funded a robot to reach the moon.
E	promoted commercial business on the moon.
F	designed the lunar parks for cultural industries resources.
G	had a similar historic impact to Apollo11.
H	made detailed maps of the moon and personal items.

READING PASSAGE 2

You should spend about 20 minutes on **Questions 14-28** which are based on Reading Passage 2 below.

Asiatic black bear

Known as a moon bear, Jasper is an Asiatic black bear with a yellow crescent on his chest. The bear came to the Animals Asia Moon Bear Rescue Centre in Chengdu, China, from a bear farm in 2000.

When Jasper arrived, rescuers had to cut Jasper out of a tiny "crush cage." Bear bile has been used in traditional Chinese medicine and fetches a high price. The wholesale price is approximately 4000 yuan (approximately $ 580) per kilogram with each bear producing up to 5 kilograms every year in China. But it comes at a high price.

Jasper normally spent 15 years in a cage. Other bears spend up to 25 years without moving in cages no bigger than their bodies. Bears are milked for bile twice a day. In China, farmers use a catheter inserted into the gall bladder or permanently open wound. In Vietnam, Farmers use long hypodermic needles.

The Animals Asia has rescued 260 bears from Chinese bear farms over the past 10 years. These bears are lucky. The official number of reared bears in China is 7,000, but the Animals Asia fears the real figure is close to 10,000.

In spite of the obvious cruelty, bear farming is legal in China. Whilst the Convention on International Trade in Endangered Species lists Asiatic black bears as being at the highest level of endangerment, China grants them only second-level protection allowing them to be farmed. Although some have reported there are 15,000 bears, its figure is not a true estimate of the remaining wild population in China.

Bear farming is also practiced in Vietnam where it is illegal but remains common due to a lack of enforcement. There are approximately 4,000 bears on Vietnamese farms but even more in Laos, Cambodia and Korea.

Bear farming is justified on the grounds that it satisfies the local demand for bile in China, therefore decreasing the number of bears are taken from the wild. Since 1989 farmers have been allowed to breed bears in captivity and hunting wild bears has been illegal. In spite of this, a lot of wild bears are still poached for their gall bladders or to restock the farms. Sometimes bears arrive at the rescue centre with missing ribs after being caught in the wild.

Those bears that arrived at the centre have suffered from severe physical and psychological trauma. Rescued bears can't be set free into the wild due to the long-term damage caused by their incarceration. They all need surgery to get rid of damaged gall bladders and many need additional surgery and long-term medical care because of missing claws or paws, infected necrotic wounds along with broken and missing teeth caused by biting at bars or because farmers break them to make the bears less of a hazard. Also, many have liver cancer as a result of being continually milked for bile and suffer from litany of other ailments including blindness, arthritis, peritonitis, weeping ulcers and ingrown claws.

On the other hand, with the horrors of bear farming, the rehabilitation process is amazing and inspiring to witness. It takes around a year to rehabilitate a bear. Although some have to be kept alone for the rest of their lives, most can eventually be housed with other bears. The transition in personality from animals who are violent and fearful to ones who are trusting, inquisitive and completely at ease with people is truly remarkable, Robinson says, "I have visited the rescue centre and it changed my life." That is how powerful the bears' stories are.

In spite of the rescue programme, bear bile extraction remains a cause of wanton and remorseless abuse. It is difficult to change attitudes when bear bile has been used in Chinese medicine for over 3,000 years to cope with "heat related" ailments, such as eye conditions, liver disease. These days, it is used to treat conditions from hangovers to haemorrhoids. There is some evidence from western medicine that a synthetic version of the active ingredient in bear bile, ursodeoxycholic acid, is able to treat a range of disorders including hepatitis C. But traditional Chinese medicine still insists on using natural bear bile which is often contaminated with pus, blood, urine and faeces. Although healthy bear bile is free flowing and orangey-green, veterinarians describe bile leaking from the diseased gall bladders of rescued bears as "black sludge."

The half-moon bear rescue project raises a number of critical questions. For instance, why do bears show large individual differences in response to persecution, and

ACADEMIC READING TEST 6

variations in recovery? Rescued bears are powerful ambassadors, but should so much time and money be invested in saving the lives of individuals who will not make any direct contributions to saving their species? How can people from outside China work to free bears whilst respecting their Chinese colleagues and remaining sensitive to cultural traditions?

Efforts to quit bear farming will continue. Soon after Robinson established the Animals Asia in 1998, she negotiated an agreement with the Chinese government to work towards the eradication of bear farming. All farmers are cruel, but the very worst are identified for closure by the government and the farmers have their licences revoked. It is bears from these farms that come to the rescue centre. The Animals Asia compensates the farmers so that they can begin another business or retire. More than 40 farms have so far been closed, and China has not issued any new licences since 1994.

Questions 14-20

Complete the summary below.

Choose **NO MORE THAN THREE WORDS** from the passage for each answer.

Write your answer in boxes *14-20* on your answer sheet.

In 2000 Jasper, an Asiatic black bear, in China, was called a moon bear due to embedding **14** -------------------- on the chest. Whilst bear farming is illegal, it is prevalent because of weak **15** -------------------- in Vietnam. Since 1989 hunting wild bears has been illegal in China, breeding bears in the farmland is not prohibited, at intervals, bears are delivered to the rescue centre without **16** -------------------- by poachers.

Most bears arrived at the centre have experienced **17** -------------------- of both physical and psychological problems to be continued. Besides, **18** -------------------- is caused by extracting the bile from bear's gall. Over 3,000 years Chinese has made use of the bile for healing illness like both **19** --------------- and ---------------. In 1998 Animals Asia was established by Robinson. She made an agreement against bear farming. Actually, she negotiated with Chinese government to eliminate **20** --------------------.

Questions 21-25

Do the following statements reflect the claims of the writer in Reading Passage 2?

In boxes 21-25 on your answer sheet write

> **YES** if the statement reflects the opinion of the writer
> **NO** if the statement contradicts the opinion of the writer
> **NOT GIVEN** if it is impossible to say what the writer thinks about this

21 Jasper is an Asiatic black bear and it had grown in the wild.

22 China is accustomed to use the bear bile as traditional medicine from the old times.

23 The bile from bear's gall is extracted every day.

24 Even though bear bile use has spread among Chinese, it had no effect on them.

25 In 1998 Robinson has reported the Animals Asia to the United Nations.

Questions 26-27

Choose the correct letter, A, B, C and D.

Write the correct letter in boxes 26-27 on your answer sheet.

26 The writer reports that bear bile have been prevalent in China due to

    A working a sense of beauty for women.
    B using traditional medicine and a little expense.
    C delaying the ageing and relieving mental fatigue.
    D using traditional medicine and its price being skyrocketing.

27 Jill Robinson founded the Animals Asia in 1998 in order to

    A protect animals in Asian zoo.
    B promote the bear rescue project to the United Nations.
    C protect the bear and prohibit brutal farming in Asia.
    D support bear farms.

ACADEMIC READING TEST 6

Questions 28

From the list below choose the most suitable title for Reading Passage 2.

Write the appropriate letter A-E in boxes 28 on your answer sheet.

- A   Cruel bear bile business
- B   Increasing the bear bile supply
- C   Traditional Chinese medicine
- D   Rescue project forward
- E   Bear farming enforcement

READING PASSAGE 3

You should spend about 20 minutes on *Questions 29-40* which are based on Reading Passage 3 on the following pages.

Questions 29-35

Reading Passage 3 has eight sections, **A-H**.

Choose the correct heading for sections **B-H** from the list of headings below.

Write the correct number, *i-viii*, in boxes **29-35** on your answer sheet.

List of Headings

i   The opposite of Adolph's view
ii Adolph's studies to guarantee in the book
iii The utmost limits for survival
iv Positive evidence of Adolph's research
v   A barren landscape for marching
vi Noakes' stance on humans of drinking
vii A simple solution for developing performance
viii Misjudgment of Salazar's thought

Example	Answer
Paragraph **A**	v

29   Section **B**

30   Section **C**

31   Section **D**

32   Section **E**

33   Section **F**

34   Section **G**

35   Section **H**

Colorado Desert

A Particularly in the summer, California's lower Colorado desert is a harsh place. It's a barren landscape of rocks and rattlesnakes that little grows in but creosote bushes and cactus. Midday temperatures can reach 43℃ and searing winds and afternoon sun combine to suck moisture from the body. This is not the place for a midday march, but that is precisely what Edward Adolph had in mind when, in the summer of 1942, he took a group of soldiers and researchers there. Adolph, a physiologist at the University of Rochester in New York state, wanted to investigate how people could live and work efficiently in the desert and how to get the best out of them.

B He wasn't the first to consider the effects of hot, dry conditions on the human body. The image of the traveler lost in the desert, crawling towards a shimmering mirage, is probably as old as desert travel itself. But earlier researchers mainly focused on survival. According to Timothy Noakes, an exercise physiologist at the University of Cape Town and master of some of the world's toughest ultra-marathons, "They never looked at performance." Adolph was the first to test the presumptions most of the people still have about what to do if forced to make any sort of effort in unbearable heat. He discovered most were myths. For example, Stripping to T-shirt and shorts is not the best way to treat dehydration. Although long sleeves and long trousers may feel hotter, they'll slow the loss of water. Nor is there any point in rationing water when supplies are low. Postponing drinking it only makes you unhappier sooner. Adolph wrote "It is better to drink the water and have it inside you than to carry it."

C The most critical of Adolph's discoveries was the simplest: drinking during exercise enhances performance. Nowadays, we take this for granted, but generations of coaches and distance runners were taught that drinking during exercise was for wimps. Some claimed it would only make you thirstier. Others said it could even trigger a heart attack. The author of Marathon Running in 1909 advised, "Don't buy into the habit of drinking and eating in a marathon race," "Some outstanding runners do, but it is not helpful." Adolph tested these old assumptions by splitting his soldiers into two groups. When the average afternoon high was up to 42℃, both marched through the desert for 8 hours. The soldiers in one group were allowed to drink as much water as they needed and the others weren't allowed any water. The results were obvious, the drinkers outperformed the non-drinkers, but the men in both groups back out once they had sweated off 7 to 10% of their body weight.

D To Adolph, this made perfect sense. On days when the temperature is hotter than the average person's skin temperature – approximately 33℃ the only way for the body to cool itself is by the evaporation of sweat, and he could estimate how much moisture that required. A brisk walk could easily need three quarters of a litre or more, of evaporative cooling each hour. Adolph's research was launched by the North Africa campaign, and he finished in 1943. But he came back to the desert every summer and supplemented his experiments with tests in his heated lab. His discoveries stayed secret until 1947, when published *Physiology of Man* in the Desert. It went almost entirely unnoticed. In the late 1960s, marathon runners were still advised not to drink water during races. Until 1977, runners in international competitions were prohibited from drinking water in the first 11 kilometres and after that were allowed water only every 5 kilometres.

E However, there was a complete reversal of opinion. A study began to warn of the dangers of running a marathon without enough water and suddenly runners were told they must drink during the race – and if they didn't feel like it they should force themselves or risk heatstroke. In 1978, Alberto Salazar, one of America's great distance runners, ran a 7.1-mile race in temperatures of 29℃. At mile six, he was in second place. He said later, "The last thing I remember, and I was watching Bill Rodgers pull away from me. It was dreamlike. Bill was floating away, and I wasn't able to follow the energy to go after him. In the next mile, I faded from second to tenth, but I do not have any memory of being passed by anyone."

F Salazar almost died. At the finish, his body temperature was 42℃ and he was saved only as a result of a quick-thinking member of the medical crew promptly dumping him into a tub of iced water. Everyone "found" what Salazar had done wrong: Salazar hadn't drunk enough before or during the race. He therefore became dehydrated and nearly killed himself. Even Salazar accepted this. "Dehydration is insidious," he would later say. At first glance, Adolph's discoveries seem to support this. His notes about his dehydrated soldiers are a litany of sorrow. "Their only desire is to stop and to rest," he wrote of one man, after 13.4 waterless kilometres in 40℃ heat. "He had an unsocial attitude, began to lag and finally stopped," he wrote of another, who managed 29.8 kilometres at 34℃.

Both 1970s and 1980s runners and coaches assumed that collapsing athletes like Salazar were simply extreme cases of the same thing. Dehydration and heat collapse were virtually synonymous in many minds. "Drink early and often," athletes were told it and not just when thirsty. However, as Noakes points out, none of Adolph's dehydrated soldiers suffered heatstroke. "They just got very angry and stopped walking." What's more, they recovered quickly when allowed to rest and drink. "They were able to walk almost immediately after drinking water," Adolph wrote in one case. In another: "exhaustion relieved by water." Salazar's brush with death wasn't the result of drinking too little: on a very hot day he had simply tried to run a world-class race. Under these kinds of conditions, heat is the enemy, not dehydration.

G Adolph had accepted this but thought it too clear to guarantee more than a few lines in his book. He had conducted most of his tests on marches, not because he wasn't interested in the effects of running in the heat, but because when he made his soldiers run, even at a slow jog their body temperature soared by 2.5℃ in 30 minutes. "There is no doubt that men are limited in the physical work they can do in the desert," he wrote. The advocates of drinking-early-and-often had also overlooked Adolph's discovery that even soldiers who were able to drink what they wanted still tended to dehydrate, and only made up their deficiencies at mealtimes. Adolph disregarded this as a "peculiarity of dehydration," but Noakes believes he had stumbled upon a quirk of human evolution.

H Humans, Noakes observed are "delayed drinkers." He supposes that this is a consequence of early humans hunting and chasing game for long distances under the African sun. There are good reasons for not stopping to drink during a hunt, not least the expectation of the prey escaping. There's also the fact that we are not built like camels and other animals that are able to drink deeply and quickly. That makes us better runners — and running hunters — but means we cannot drink as much as we can sweat, so we delay our thirst until it's comfortable to drink, says Noakes. Adolph never used the word evolution in his book but he would have understood Noakes's point.

Questions 36-40

Complete the sentences below.

Choose **NO MORE THAN TWO WORDS** from the passage for each answer.

Write your answers in boxes *36-40* on your answer sheet.

36 Adolph found out that a critical way for improving a marathon race is -------------------- during performance.

37 During walking, the body needs approximately -------------------- of a litre moisture per hour.

38 International competitions didn't allow water within racing -------------------- kilometres.

39 Salazar nearly died at the end of the race as a result of --------------------.

40 In this final section, Noakes indicates humans are part of the concept of --------------------.

IELTS
INTERNATIONAL ENGLISH LANGUAGE TESTING SYSTEM

ACADEMIC READING

TEST 7

TIME ALLOWED : 1 hour

NUMBER OF QUESTIONS : 40

Instructions

ALL ANSWERS MUST BE WRITTEN ON THE ANSWER SHEET

The test is divided as follows :

    Reading Passage 1   Questions 1-13

    Reading Passage 2   Questions 14-28

    Reading Passage 3   Questions 29-40

Start at the beginning of the test and work through it. You should answer all the questions. If you cannot do a particular question leave it and go on to the next.

You can return to it later.

READING PASSAGE 1

You should spend about 20 minutes on **Questions 1-13** which are based on Reading Passage 1 on the following pages.

Questions 1-5

Reading Passage 1 has six sections, **A-F**.

Choose the correct heading for sections **B-F** from the list of headings below.

Write the correct number, *i-viii*, in boxes **1-5** on your answer sheet.

List of Headings
i   a significant role to creatures
ii   spectrum's previous models
iii   a distinction of hydrogen bonds
iv   nature's mysteries in the small place
v   the effect of spectrum on liquid water
vi   molecular composition of water
vii   water based on infrared light
viii   one-body structure of water

Example	Answer
Paragraph **A**	iv

1   Section **B**

2   Section **C**

3   Section **D**

4   Section **E**

5   Section **F**

The Mysteries of Water

Section A
From the nature of dark matter and the origin of the universe to the research for a theory of everything, we come across many mysteries. Whilst these are all puzzles on a grand scale, there is another not quite so grand but equally confusing mystery of the physical world that you can observe from the comfort of your own kitchen. Simply fill a tall glass with chilled water, throw in an ice cube and leave it to stand. The fact that the ice cube floats is the first oddity. And the mystery deepens if you take a thermometer and measure the temperature of the water at various depths. At the top, near the ice cube, you'll find it to be around 0℃, but at the bottom it should be about 4℃. That's why water is denser at 4℃ than it is at any other temperature which is another strange feature that sets it apart from other liquids.

Section B
Water's odd but essential qualities don't stop there, for ice is less dense than water, and water is less dense at its freezing point than it is when it is slightly warmer. It freezes from the top down rather than the bottom up. So even during the ice ages, life kept going on to flourish on lake floors and in the deep ocean. Also, water has an extraordinary capacity to absorb up heat, and this helps smooth out climatic changes that could otherwise lay waste to ecosystems. However, in spite of water's enormous importance to life, no single theory had been able to satisfactorily explain its mysterious qualities — until now. If we can believe physicists Anders Nilsson at Stanford University, California, and Lars Pettersson of Stockholm University, Sweden, we could at last be getting to the bottom of many of these anomalies.

Section C
Their disputed ideas expand on a theory proposed more than a century ago. According to Wilhelm Roentgen, the man who discovered the X-ray, claimed that the molecule in liquid water packs together not in just one way, as today's textbooks would have us believe, but in two different ways. The way its molecules are composed of two hydrogen atoms and one oxygen atom and how they interact with one another is essential to the understanding of water's mysteries. The oxygen atom has a slight negative charge whilst the hydrogen atoms share a compensating positive charge. Through this process, the hydrogen and oxygen atoms of neighbouring molecules are drawn to one another, forming a link called a hydrogen bond.

Section D
Hydrogen bonds are even weaker than the bonds that link the atoms within molecules together, so keep going to break and reform, but they are at their strongest when molecules are organized so that each hydrogen bond lines up with a molecular bond. The shaping of a water molecule is such that each H_2O molecule is surrounded by four neighbours organized in the shaping of a triangular

pyramid better known as a tetrahedron. At least, that's the way the molecules organize themselves in ice. From the conventional view, liquid water has a similar, although less hard, structure, in which extra molecules are able to pack into some of the open gaps in the tetrahedral arrangement. It explains why liquid water is denser than ice – and it seems to comply with the results of various experiments that beams of X-rays, infrared light and neutrons are bounced off samples of water.

Section E
Some physicists had suggested that water placed under certain extreme conditions may separate into two different structures, but most had assumed it resumes a single structure under normal conditions. And then, 10 years ago, a change found by Pettersson and Nilsson called this idea into question. They were using X-ray absorption spectroscopy to research the amino acid glycine. The peaks in the X-ray absorption spectrum can shed light on the accurate nature of the target substance's chemical bonds on its structure. Critically, the researchers had got hold of a new, high-power X-ray source with which they could make more sensitive and precise measurements than had ever been possible. They soon knew that the water containing their glycine sample was producing a far more interesting spectrum than the amino acids did. Nilsson recalls, "What we saw there was sensational, so we had to get to the bottom of it."

Section F
The characteristic that sparked their interest was a peak point in the absorption spectrum that is not anticipated by the traditional model of liquid water. Actually, in a paper published in 2004 concludes that at any given moment 85% of the hydrogen bonds in water must be weakened or broken. This is far more than the 10% anticipated by the textbook model. The hints of this finding are dramatic: it claims that a total rethink of the structure of water is needed. So, both Nilsson and Pettersson turned to other X-ray experiments to confirm these claims. Their first move was to enlist the aid of Shik Shin of the University of Tokyo who specialises in a technique called X-ray emission spectroscopy. The main thing about these spectra is that the shorter the wavelength of the X-ray in a substance's emission spectrum is, the looser the hydrogen bonding must be.

The team struck gold: the two peak spectrum of discharged X-ray might correspond to two separate structures. The researchers insisted that the spike of the longer-wavelength X-ray, indicated the proportion of tetrahedrally organized molecules, whilst the shorter-wavelength peak reflects the proportion of disordered molecules. Critically, the shorter-wavelength peak in the X-ray emissions was the more intense of the two, suggesting that the loosely bound molecules must be more outstanding within the sample, an assertion that fitted the team's previous models. What's more, they also recognised that this peak shifts to an even shorter wave length, as if the water was heated, the other peak remains more or less fixed.

Questions 6-13

Do the following statements reflect the claims of the writer in Reading Passage 1?

In boxes 6-13 on your answer sheet write

YES	*if the statement reflects the opinion of the writer*
NO	*if the statement contradicts the opinion of the writer*
NOT GIVEN	*if it is impossible to say what the writer thinks about this*

6 Water's temperature of top and bottom is generally the same.

7 During the ice ages, there was life in the deep ocean because of warmth.

8 Wilhelm Roentgen discovered X-rays for water molecules.

9 Both hydrogen and oxygen's atoms are similar to a positive charge.

10 A single H_2O molecule is composed entirely of five-angled shape.

11 Pettersson and Nilsson were scrutinising the amino acid glycine by using X-ray absorption spectroscopy.

12 The water which including glycine was making superior spectrum to the amino acid.

13 The shorter-wavelength is subjected to the longer-wavelength.

READING PASSAGE 2

You should spend about 20 minutes on **Questions 14-28** which are based on Reading Passage 2 below.

Vehicle Safety Systems

Although drivers and their passengers are encased in the event of a crash, people hit by a car have no protection. Now that could change thanks to a new system that built into a vehicle will enhance a pedestrian's safety. Every month about 3,400 pedestrians are killed in traffic accidents on the roads in the US, and a similar number die in Europe. Some 30% of the injuries included in this group are caused by an impact with a windscreen or its frame.

A European-wide collaboration led by Roger Hardy of the Cranfield Impact Centre at Cranfield University close to Bedford in the UK has devised an experimental system for cars that aims to cut this death toll and decrease the risk of injuries. When the system registers that the car is about to hit a pedestrian, it automatically raises the rear of the bonnet (hood), releasing a giant airbag in front of the windscreen.

"The raised bonnet absorbs some of the energy of the impact, decreasing the risk of severe injury to the pedestrian," says Hardy, whose project forms part of the European Union-funded Integrated Project on Advanced Protection Systems (APROSYS). "If it's a large pedestrian or on a small town car, the airbag also offers a cushioning effect around the stiff peripheral regions of the windscreen," he says. The airbag system used by Hardy was enhanced by the German company Takata Petri. To test its efficacy when combined with the raised bonnet, they cooperated into developing a prototype Fiat Stilo by engineers at the Fiat Research Centre in Turin, Italy. Then the team estimated the danger of head injuries in test collisions with a dummy pedestrian.

A standard Stilo test hitting a pedestrian at 40 kilometres per hour would have a score of around 1,000 on the Head Impact Criterion (HIC) scale. That is the equivalent of an 18% chance of a life-threatening injury. For pedestrians hitting Hardy's bonnet, the scores were reduced to between 234 and 682, whilst the normal windscreen airbag scores ranged between 692 and 945. Hardy's team has also introduced a design in which a windscreen mounting system cushions the impact with the edge of the windscreen. This consists of a flexible Z-shaped section of metal, that is a maximum of 15 millimetres wide, separating the windscreen from its frame so that it is able to flex inwards to absorb energy in a collision. The team says it could decrease HIC scores by over 50%.

Another APROSYS collaboration led by Jurgen Gugler at Graz University of Technology in Austria researched how changing the shaping of the front of a truck could reduce the risk to pedestrians. Computer stimulations of 20 accident scenarios indicated that a smooth sloping surface with a central bulge decreases the likelihood of a pedestrian involved in a front-end accident being run over by 80 to 90%. Gugler says, "The pedestrian is knocked to the side, rotated and pushed towards the ground. You are out of the path of the oncoming truck."

Fiat researchers managed by Roberto Puppini have also had some success in early tests of an adaptive bumper system. Four gas springs kick in at high speeds to move the bumper forward so that it will absorb energy of an impact. So will manufacturers actually incorporate any of these safety innovations into their cars? Over the next two years, the European car safety commission (Euro NCAP), will be phasing the results of pedestrian safety tests into its essential rating system. Poor Euro NCAP test results could result in less safe car models being withdrawn from the market. This suggests that buyers and manufacturers can be persuaded to take the safety of drivers and their passengers seriously, but it remains to be seen whether the welfare of pedestrians is as persuasive a selling point.

For now at least, there is little else to convince car-manufacturers to install these safety devices. Hardy says, "Recently, from the legislative point of view, there is not a colossal incentive for manufacturers to utilise these technologies." Perhaps ultimately the law will have to step in so that external airbags and energy-absorbing bodywork enhance pedestrian safety as dramatically as seat belts and internal airbags have enhanced driver and passenger safety.

ACADEMIC READING TEST 7

Questions 14-20

Complete the summary below.

Choose **NO MORE THAN THREE WORDS** from the passage for each answer.

Write your answers in boxes **14-20** on your answer sheet.

Every month there are about 3,400 people hit by a car in the US and a similar number of casualties in **14** --------------------. Actually, around 30% of them are a result of **15** -------------------- or its frame. To decrease road traffic accidents, a European-wide collaboration devised automatic lifting rear of **16** --------------------, and a **17** -------------------- ahead of the windscreen working at the same time.

Hardy's team has researched a system to cushion impacts with the outline of **18** --------------------. It includes an easily bent and **19** -------------------- metal frame with the windscreen and frame seperated. But he said: According to law, although having safety devices for protection against a crash, now any manufacture companies to harness these devises could not have **20** --------------------.

Questions 21-25

Complete the each sentence with the correct ending, *A-G*, below.

Write the correct letter, *A-G*, in boxes *21-25* on your answer sheet.

21   A European-wide collaboration

22   European Union-funded Integrated Project

23   APROSYS collaboration

24   Euro NCAP

25   Poor Euro NCAP

A	be part of schemes to decrease hazardous situations for pedestrians.
B	help judge less safe vehicle models between buyers and companies.
C	improve testing under the condition that a crash decreased.
D	make a solution within the frequency of tests for safe pedestrians.
E	study how replacing a lorry's front side protects pedestrians.
F	be persuasive as a selling point.
G	improve a pedestrian's chances.

Questions 26-28

*Choose the correct letter in boxes, **A**, **B**, **C** or **D**.*

*Write the correct letter in boxes **26-28** on your answer sheet.*

26 Which one of the following is found in the passage?

    A the number of traffic accidents and rubbish on the road
    B the amount of petrol gas misused and recycled
    C the number of casualties in traffic accidents on the road
    D the cases of car insurance in a court

27 What are the main technical devices made by Roger Hardy?

    A brake system
    B automatic both bonnet and airbag system
    C instant front door and trunk open
    D anti-slip tires whilst heavy rain and snow

28 The writer believed that the "Hardy's team" on the system could

    A decrease the Head Impact Criterion (HIC) score until over half per cent.
    B be almost as safe as computer simulation tests.
    C be causing significant damage to half a per cent of the Head Impact Criterion (HIC).
    D reduce converting the windscreen airbag.

READING PASSAGE 3

You should spend about 20 minutes on *Questions 29-40* which are based on Reading Passage 3 on the following pages.

The Harmony of Food and Drink

A

Food is not only a necessity for life, but also our greatest sources of pleasure. The taste of things such as champagne, chocolate and chips offer your brain a big "pleasure hit" that keeps us coming back for more. And the preparation of food is as important as the ingredients. Recently, food, science and technology have become more closely linked than ever. Scientifically-minded chefs like Harold McGee, Heston Blumenthal and Ferran Adria sometimes utilise science to enhance startling new dishes.

B

Before the Agricultural Age, humans were hunter-gatherers. Sheep were probably the first animals to be farmed, followed by cattle and pigs. We are still unsure what our earliest ancestors actually ate and how much of their diet was meat. We know that Otzi the iceman had consumed ibex, deer, vegetables and possibly grains.

C

Controversially, it has been suggested that the invention of cooking was a main factor in human evolution (as well as our alveolar bone) – a question that partly depends on when humans discovered fire. Like us, apes also prefer cooked food to raw – possibly because cooked food offers more energy than raw food does. Recently, almost all our food comes from farming for the huge increase in human population over the last 200 years. Farming has become much more intensive and dependant on technology and the so-called Green Revolution in the 20th century was a vital boost. At the same time, technologies for conserving food have come along in leaps and bounds.

D

But, the grains have not been without cost. Soil quality has been damaged, and crops like bananas have become less genetically diverse, rare breeds of animals have been pushed close to extinction, and habitats have been destroyed. Also, the increasing demand for meat puts pressure on agriculture. One possible solution to food shortages is genetic modification of crops plants to enhance yield and to make them resistant to disorder. But GM has proved unpopular with the public, in spite of efforts to grow environmentally friendly solutions. Concern for environmental damage from farming led to the development of "sustainable" techniques, like organic farming which rejects the use of artificial fertilisers, pesticides and other agricultural technologies. Organic farming produces lower yields, but there is evidence that it produces suitable amounts of food with less environmental damage.

E

The overfishing of the world's oceans has also led to serious damage, causing population crashes in many species. Recently, fish farming has become more widespread. It decreases the burden on wild fish, but has other problems such as escaping fish, excessive food consumption, infectious viruses and louse infestation. Unless the population recessions are stopped, we will have to turn to less appetizing species for our seafood like jellyfish.

F

Nowadays, many people suffer from food allergies, and must avoid common foods like peanuts and wheat. A condition called food intolerance looks the same on the surface, but its effects are slower to appear and longer lasting. Charles Darwin may have been a sufferer of this condition. The allergy epidemic has been related to modern clean living.

G

Today, one of the biggest health problems is obesity. Through a diet rich in fats and sugars, many people in developed countries are overweight increasing the risk of cancer, diabetes and an early death. Unfortunately, mild obesity takes two to four years off the average lifespan. The risks are particularly concerning for children and being overweight as a child makes you more obese as an adult. The causes of obesity have been a source of debate. Surprisingly, a lack of exercise may not be a critical factor. It is possible that it could be a genetic condition and may also be caused by eating lots of fructose. Some cases have been linked to a virus that causes fat cells to increase. Also, obesity is socially contagious. A huge range of possible treatments for obesity have been developed.

ACADEMIC READING TEST 7

Questions 29-34

Reading Passage 3 has seven paragraphs, **A-G**.

Which paragraph contains the following information?

Write the correct letter, **A-G**, in boxes **29-34** on your answer sheet.

29 cooked food relative to human evolution and structure of teeth

30 a change of food taste and importance of preparation

31 problems of population crash caused by overfishing

32 the earlier hunting of humans

33 overweight influenced with gene and overeating

34 indifference of genetic modification crops

Questions 35-40

Complete the sentences below.

Choose **NO MORE THAN TWO WORDS** from the passage for each answer.

Write your answers in boxes **35-40** on your answer sheet.

35 Food is one of human's sustainable materials of --------------------.

36 -------------------- might be the first creature to be tamed for farming.

37 The population has increased over the last 200 years, accelerating with technology triggered --------------------.

38 -------------------- is yielded with less environmental damage and non-fertilisers.

39 From overeating fats and sugars, modern people are suffering from -----------------.

40 Health problems have been linked to -------------------- which makes fat cells.

IELTS
INTERNATIONAL ENGLISH LANGUAGE TESTING SYSTEM

ACADEMIC WRITING

PRACTICE TEST

ACADEMIC WRITING TEST 1

WRITING TASK 1

You should spend about 20 minutes on this task.

> *The bar chart below shows the number of employees from the European Union in the United States (1999).*
>
> *Write a report for a university lecturer describing the information shown below.*

You should write at least 150 words.

EU-Born Science & Technology Employees Working in the US in 1999

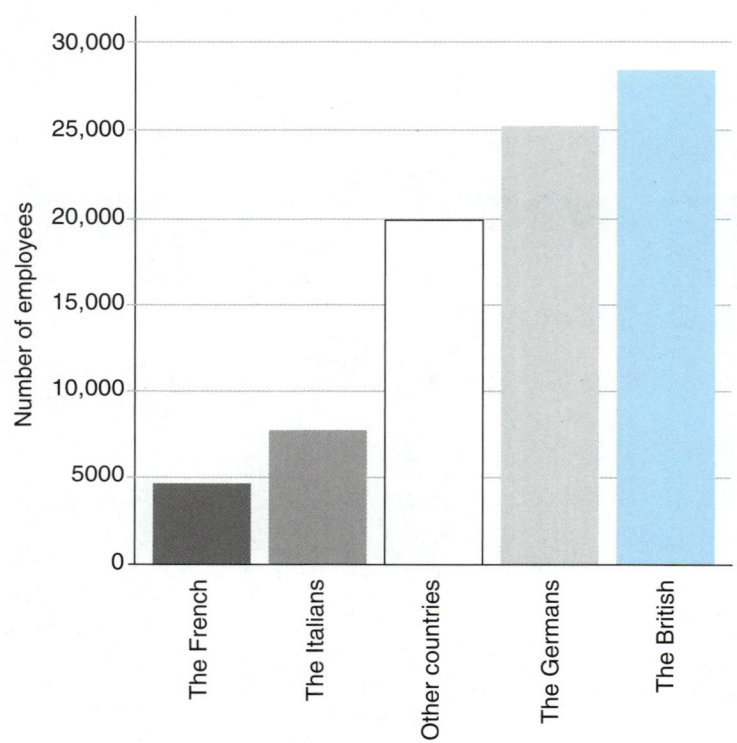

WRITING ANSWER SHEET

Candidate Name: _____ Candidate Number: _____

Centre Name: _____ Date: _____

Module: ACADEMIC ☐   GENERAL TRAINING ☐   (Tick as appropriate)

TASK 1

_____
_____
_____
_____
_____
_____
_____
_____
_____
_____
_____
_____
_____
_____
_____
_____
_____
_____
_____
_____

EXAMINER'S USE ONLY

EXAMINER TASK1	TA	CC	LR	GRA

UNDERLENGTH	NO OF WORDS	PENALTY
OFF-TOPIC	MEMORISED	ILLEGIBLE

WRITING TASK 2

You should spend about 40 minutes on this task.

> *Central and local governments make a frantic attempt to promote festivals to create a lot of revenue. Some people think this money should be invested in social programmes for the poor.*
>
> *To what extent do you agree or disagree with this statement?*
>
> *Give reasons for your answer.*

You should write at least 250 words.

You should use your own idea, knowledge and experience and support your arguments with examples and relevant evidence.

TASK 2

WRITING TASK 1

You should spend about 20 minutes on this task.

The chart below shows the number of hidden costs of the UK's annual food bill.

Write a report for a university lecturer describing the information shown below.

You should write at least 150 words.

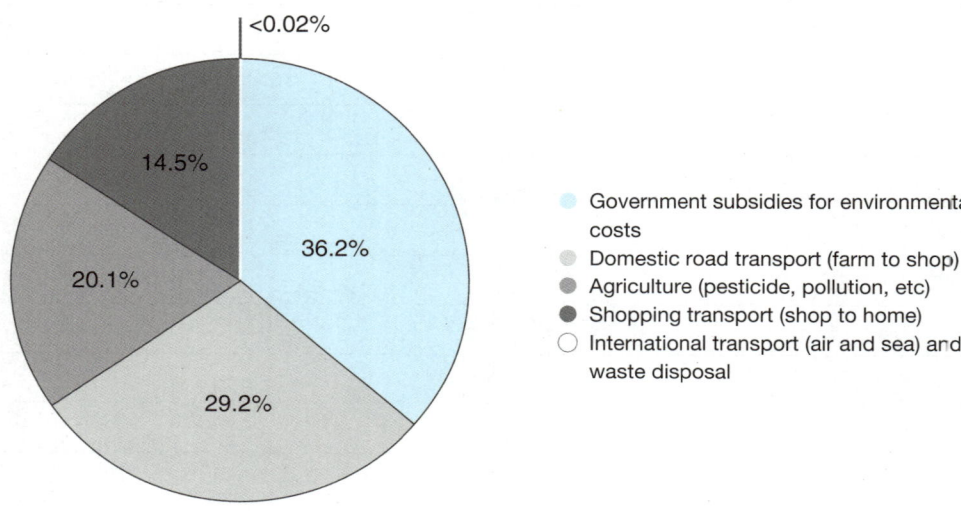

The hidden costs of the UK's annual food bill

- Government subsidies for environmental costs
- Domestic road transport (farm to shop)
- Agriculture (pesticide, pollution, etc)
- Shopping transport (shop to home)
- International transport (air and sea) and waste disposal

WRITING ANSWER SHEET

Candidate Name: _____   Candidate Number: _____

Centre Name: _____   Date: _____

Module: ACADEMIC ☐   GENERAL TRAINING ☐   (Tick as appropriate)

TASK 1

EXAMINER'S USE ONLY

EXAMINER TASK1	TA	CC	LR	GRA

UNDERLENGTH		NO OF WORDS		PENALTY	
OFF-TOPIC		MEMORISED		ILLEGIBLE	

ACADEMIC WRITING TEST 2

WRITING TASK 2

You should spend about 40 minutes on this task.

> *Studying abroad can be highly motivational for students and also inspire their dreams. However, whilst studying abroad can have a number of positive effects on students, there are also many difficulties that they may meet along the way. With this in mind, it is more advantageous to study at home.*
>
> *To what extent do you agree or disagree with this statement?*
>
> *Give reasons for your answer.*

You should write at least 250 words.

You should use your own idea, knowledge and experience and support your arguments with examples and relevant evidence.

TASK 2

WRITING TASK 1

You should spend about 20 minutes on this task.

> *The graph below shows the average levels of Methane (CH₄) globally. Line A shows the trend together with seasonal variations. Line B indicates the trend that emerges when the seasonal cycle has been removed.*
>
> *Write a report for a university lecturer describing the information shown below.*

You should write at least 150 words.

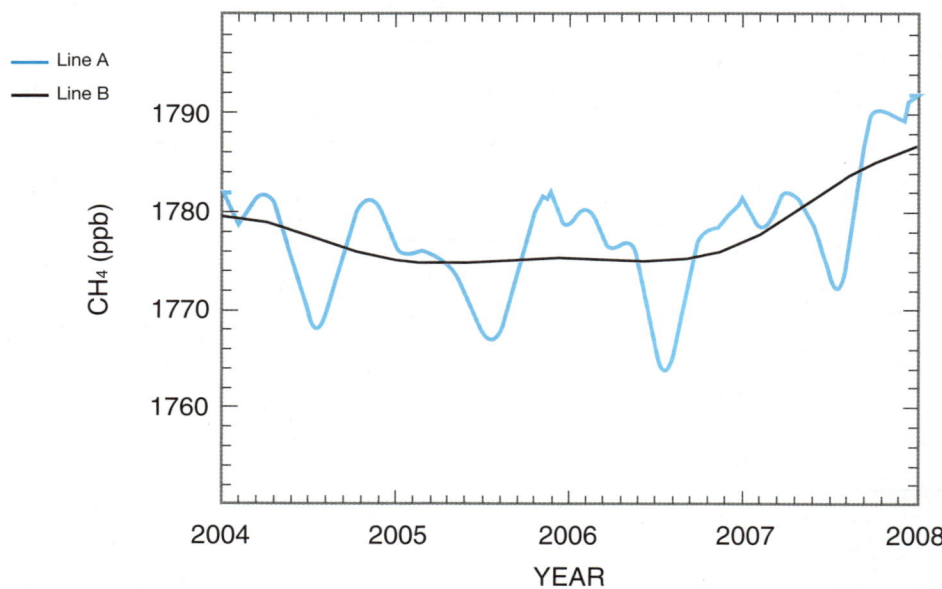

WRITING ANSWER SHEET

Candidate Name: _____ Candidate Number: _____

Centre Name: _____ Date: _____

Module: ACADEMIC ☐   GENERAL TRAINING ☐   (Tick as appropriate)

TASK 1

EXAMINER'S USE ONLY

EXAMINER TASK1	TA	CC	LR	GRA

UNDERLENGTH		NO OF WORDS		PENALTY	
OFF-TOPIC		MEMORISED		ILLEGIBLE	

WRITING TASK 2

You should spend about 40 minutes on this task.

> *Due to the increasing density of living areas in a city, most residents are suffering from physical and social dangers so that they are against it.*
>
> *To what extent to you agree or disagree with this statement?*
>
> *Give reasons for your answer.*

You should write at least 250 words.

You should use your own idea, knowledge and experience and support your arguments with examples and relevant evidence.

TASK 2

WRITING TASK 1

You should spend about 20 minutes on this task.

> *The table below shows the percentage of electronic products used in UK homes in 2005 and 2008.*
>
> *Summarise the information by selecting and reporting the main features, and make comparisons where relevant.*

You should write at least 150 words.

Percentage of electronic categories in UK Homes both in 2005 and 2008

	2005	2008
TV	93	94
computer	50	72
microwave oven	80	85
washing machine	95	95
video recorder	82	65
digital camera	15	90
Humidifier	20	62

WRITING ANSWER SHEET

Candidate Name: _____ Candidate Number: _____

Centre Name: _____ Date: _____

Module: ACADEMIC ☐   GENERAL TRAINING ☐   (Tick as appropriate)

TASK 1

EXAMINER'S USE ONLY

EXAMINER TASK1	TA		CC		LR		GRA	

UNDERLENGTH	NO OF WORDS	PENALTY
OFF-TOPIC	MEMORISED	ILLEGIBLE

ACADEMIC WRITING TEST 4

WRITING TASK 2

You should spend about 40 minutes on this task.

> *Modern society is becoming more concerned with the increase in juvenile crime.*
>
> *What do you think is the cause of the increase in juvenile crime?*
>
> *What solutions can you suggest?*

You should write at least 250 words.

You should use your own idea, knowledge and experience and support your arguments with examples and relevant evidence.

TASK 2

ACADEMIC WRITING TEST 5

WRITING TASK 1

You should spend about 20 minutes on this task.

The table below shows the reasons why people in Australia use on-line services according to the ages.

Summarise the information by selecting and reporting the main features, and make comparisons where relevant.

You should write at least 150 words.

Percentage of using on-line services in Australia according to the ages and the purpose of use

	11~19	20~29	30~39	40 and over
Academic study	36	31	27	18
E-Banking	2	5	11	20
E-mail	40	41	41	38
Online shopping	5	8	15	20
Online Chatting	15	12	5	3
Others	2	3	1	1

WRITING ANSWER SHEET

Candidate Name: _____ Candidate Number: _____

Centre Name: _____ Date: _____

Module: ACADEMIC ☐   GENERAL TRAINING ☐   (Tick as appropriate)

TASK 1

_____
_____
_____
_____
_____
_____
_____
_____
_____
_____
_____
_____
_____
_____
_____
_____
_____
_____
_____
_____

EXAMINER'S USE ONLY

EXAMINER TASK1	TA	CC	LR	GRA

UNDERLENGTH	NO OF WORDS	PENALTY
OFF-TOPIC	MEMORISED	ILLEGIBLE

WRITING TASK 2

You should spend about 40 minutes on this task.

> *Whilst informational systems are now being utilised to aid the old, some people are worrying about the possible negative outcomes.*
>
> *To what extent do you agree with this statement?*
>
> *Give reasons for your answer.*

You should write at least 250 words.

You should use your own idea, knowledge and experience and support your arguments with examples and relevant evidence.

TASK 2

WRITING TASK 1

You should spend about 20 minutes on this task.

> *The pie chart below shows the causes of worldwide global warming and the table shows the percentage of CO_2 by causes in three continents.*
>
> *Write a report for a university lecturer describing the information shown below.*

You should write at least 150 words.

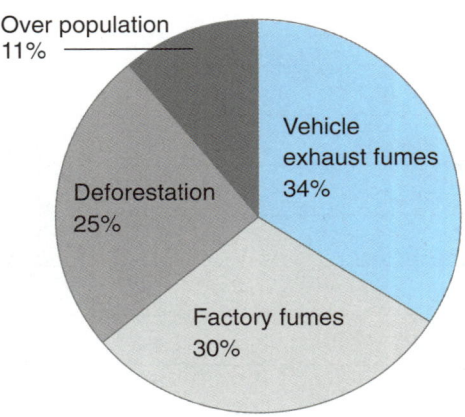

Causes of worldwide global warming

Percentage of CO_2 by Causes in three continents

	Percentage of CO_2				Total percentage of CO_2
	Vehicle	**Factory**	**Deforestation**	**Population**	
Europe	35	33	15	17	100
America	33	19	31	17	100
Asia	33	27	9	31	100

WRITING ANSWER SHEET

Candidate Name: _____ Candidate Number: _____

Centre Name: _____ Date: _____

Module: ACADEMIC ☐   GENERAL TRAINING ☐   (Tick as appropriate)

TASK 1

_____
_____
_____
_____
_____
_____
_____
_____
_____
_____
_____
_____
_____
_____
_____
_____
_____
_____
_____
_____
_____

EXAMINER'S USE ONLY

EXAMINER TASK1

TA	CC	LR	GRA

UNDERLENGTH	NO OF WORDS	PENALTY
OFF-TOPIC	MEMORISED	ILLEGIBLE

WRITING TASK 2

You should spend about 40 minutes on this task.

> *With the increase in global tourism, it has become obvious that there are many advantages and disadvantages that can be found from the effects of tourism.*
>
> *Do you believe that the advantages outweigh the disadvantages?*
>
> *Give reasons for your answer.*

You should write at least 250 words.

You should use your own idea, knowledge and experience and support your arguments with examples and relevant evidence.

TASK 2

ACADEMIC WRITING TEST 7

WRITING TASK 1

You should spend about 20 minutes on this task.

> *The diagram below shows the visual apparent motion.*
>
> *Write a report for a university lecturer describing the information shown below.*

You should write at least 150 words.

Visual apparent motion

When displayed on a screen, this creates an impression of motion that doesn't exist.

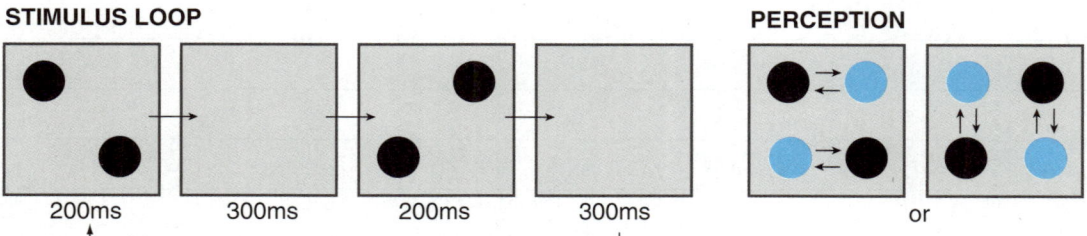

WRITING ANSWER SHEET

Candidate Name: _____   Candidate Number: _____

Centre Name: _____   Date: _____

Module: ACADEMIC ☐   GENERAL TRAINING ☐   (Tick as appropriate)

TASK 1

EXAMINER'S USE ONLY

EXAMINER TASK1	TA	CC	LR	GRA

UNDERLENGTH		NO OF WORDS		PENALTY	
OFF-TOPIC		MEMORISED		ILLEGIBLE	

WRITING TASK 2

You should spend about 40 minutes on this task.

> *Due to the increase of technology, people today have greater amounts of free time.*
>
> *What are the advantages and disadvantages of the conveniences created by modern technology?*

You should write at least 250 words.

You should use your own idea, knowledge and experience and support your arguments with examples and relevant evidence.

TASK 2

PART 2
정답 및 해설

Academic Reading

Actual Test 1

Answer Sheet

1	YES	11	solar, wind, biomass	21	therapists temselves	31	i
2	NO	12	technology	22	91	32	v
3	NOT GIVEN	13	The Climate Group	23	Peter Whorwell	33	iv
4	YES	14	C	24	C	34	iii
5	NOT GIVEN	15	B	25	D	35	NO
6	YES	16	A	26	B	36	YES
7	YES	17	psychological effects	27	A	37	NO
8	carbon dioxide	18	IBS	28	C	38	NO
9	NGO	19	cochrance collaboration	29	vii	39	NO
10	Renewable Energy Law	20	expensive studies	30	viii	40	NOT GIVEN

ACADEMIC READING

READING PASSAGE 1

You should spend about 20 minutes on Questions 1-13 which are based on Reading Passage 1 below.

The Green Revolution in China

1   A couple of weeks ago, [1]China's highest government body published their conclusions from the second research session on continental climate change over a period of twelve months. Due to China's new global role and the number of unprecedented environmental issues in China, the Chinese prime minister was very keen to raise climate change as an important issue at the upcoming [2]G8 summit in Hokkaido, Japan.

2   It should be highlighted that the Chinese central government also had a similar meeting and that China is a rapidly industrializing country with new coal-fueled power plants opening every week. China is like a terrifying carbon-guzzling monster. As a result of thirty years of industrialization, [8]China now has the highest level of carbon dioxide emissions in the world. Carbon dioxide emissions are increasing up to eight per cent a year. [3]The EU achieved a twenty per cent reduction, but China's emission rate was twice as much approaching the 2010 IPCC deadline for carbon dioxide emissions reduction.

3   However, [9]it could be misleading to put too much emphasis on these statistics. [4]A non government organization (Climate Group) newspaper report presents a slightly different picture. According to *Clean Revolution* in China, China is a nation that is more than aware of its environmental issues but also has the potential to achieve a second miracle in 30 years.

4   The environmental price of the first, "miracle" was that Chinese people always saw their daily lives. That's why most of the policies are related to energy efficiency, energy saving and alternative other energy sources. Those policies have already been met with some concern.

5   Whilst the personal sectors are so strong and developing, they are able to aid the central government to introduce laws, like the National Renewable Energy Law [10]in 2006. This has set [10]hard targets, including increasing the amount of energy made from new renewable sources from eight per cent to fifteen per cent until 2020. Also, it has guaranteed at least three per cent of renewable energy sources, [11]such as biomass, [5]solar and wind.

6   Both wind and solar power are so successful, but their origins are very different With 6 gigawatts of energy made from wind turbines, surprisingly China is now ranked behind Germany, the

중국의 녹색 혁명

1   몇 주 전, 중국 최고정부기관에서는 12개월의 기간 동안에 중국 대륙의 기후 변화에 관한 두 번째 연구회기로부터 나온 결론을 발표했다. 중국의 새로운 국제적 역할과 중국에서의 전례 없는 환경문제들 때문에, 중국 수상은 곧 있을 일본 홋카이도의 G8 정상회의에서 주요 이슈로서 기후 변화의 상정을 무척 원했다.

2   중국 중앙정부가 유사한 회의를 가졌다는 것과 중국이 매주 새로운 석탄 화력발전소를 가동해야 하는 빠르게 산업화되고 있는 국가라는 점은 부각되어야 한다. 중국은 소름 끼치는 탄소 배출의 괴물과도 같다. 30년 동안의 산업화 결과로 중국은 이제 세계에서 가장 많은 이산화탄소를 배출하게 되었다. 이산화탄소 배출은 해마다 8% 상승되고 있다. 유럽연합에서 이산화탄소 배출량을 20%로 감소시켰지만, 중국의 이산화탄소 배출 비율은 2010년 IPCC 한계점의 두 배였다.

3   그러나 이러한 통계들을 지나치게 강조하면 오해를 일으킬 수 있다. NGC인 Climate Group의 신문보도는 미묘하게 다른 사진 한 장을 제시했다. 중국의 클린(청정)혁명에 따르면 중국은 자신들의 환경문제를 인식하고 있으며 30년 이내에 두 번째 기적을 이루어 낼 잠재력 역시 가지고 있다.

4   그 첫 번째 '기적'의 환경적 대가는 중국인들은 항상 그들의 일상생활을 본다는 것이다. 이것이 오늘날 수많은 정책이 에너지 효율성, 에너지 절약, 그리고 대체 에너지 자원과 관련이 있는 이유다. 이 정책은 이미 몇몇 우려와 맞닥뜨렸다.

5   사적인 영역이 강하게 성장을 하면서, 그들은 2006년 국제재생에너지 법안과 같은 법이 중앙정부의 법안으로 도입이 될 수 있게 도움을 주고 있다. 그것은 어려운 목표를 설정하였는데 재생에너지의 양을 2020년까지 8%에서 15%까지 늘리고 또한 생물량, 태양, 바람 같은 자원을 최소 3%까지 보장한다는 것 다.

6   바람과 태양에너지는 이미 성공적이었지만, 이것들의 시작점은 매우 달랐다. 풍력발전용 터빈으로부터 얻은 6기가와트 에너지를 가진 중국은 현재 독일, 미국, 스페인 그리고 인도 다음을 차

US, Spain and India. Also, some believe China will reach 100 GW by 2020.

7 [6,12]Wind and solar power successfully shows that with central government aid China is ready for new policies, [12]subsides and advanced technology. This situation also has a role in the domestic market. [6]The amount of electricity produced by the wind and solar farms can be a burden to fund.

8 Even though western countries invented an open marketplace set to dominate in China, there were few domestic incentives for solar power. In the global solar photovoltaic cell market, it is only the second to Japan and growing fast. In China, the solar market has been a small business, because [7]the cells are so expensive. This puts pressure on the government to rapidly follow up on their policies, for example, [13]the role of the Climate Group is important in developing domestic markets.

9 However, the image of new coal-fueled power stations still looms large as they are opening every week. It is hard to imagine that China has achieved a 10.5 per cent of growth rate without such stations in the last quarter. However, how many people actually know that China has been closing its small power stations over the last couple of years? Step by step China is reducing its small power stations, first the 50 megawatt ones then the 100 megawatt ones and next will be the 300 megawatt power stations.

10 This policy is operated by the Chinese central government and backs up the new generation of coal stations using the most advanced technologies with supercritical and ultra-supercritical improved clean coal. Capture functions and plants of carbon are researched and developed, but advanced thinking for the future is based on the technology of Integrated Gasification Combined Cycle (IGCC) that turn coal materials into synthetic gas to make power.

11 These days, Chinese consumers demand better homes and vehicles. Public awareness of energysaving is on the rise. The Chinese government introduced a standard fuel economy for vehicles in 2004 of 15.6 kilometers per litre. This is higher than the US, Canada and Australia but behind Europe and Japan. In the meantime, in spite of a high 20 per cent tax on SUVs (Sport Utility Vehicles) the sale of these sorts of cars continues to increase.

12 Up to now, China has been the kingdom of the bicycle, importing the electric bike at 1500 yuan ($ 220) per vehicle. Some of these vehicles have adopted an intelligent recovery system similar to that of hybrid cars. In 2007, the sale of electric bikes increased considerably and China is estimated to make up three quarters of the world electric vehicle market.

지하고 있다. 역시 사람들은 중국이 2020년경에 100기가와트에 도달할 걸로 기대하고 있다.

7 풍력과 태양에너지는 중앙정부의 도움을 받은 중국이 새로운 정책, 보조금, 첨단기술 등을 준비하고 있다는 것을 성공적으로 보여준다. 이런 상황은 또한 국내 시장에서도 역할을 가지고 있다. 다시 말해서, 풍력과 태양에너지로 농사짓는 것은 많은 비용이 든다.

8 비록 서양 국가들이 중국에서 우위를 점하기 위해 자유시장을 만들었지만 태양에너지에 대한 국내 혜택은 거의 없었다. 세계 태양광전지 셀시장에서 중국은 일본 다음으로 빠르게 성장하고 있다. 중국의 태양에너지시장은 여전히 작다. 셀의 가격이 무척 비싸기 때문이다. 그래서 그들의 정책을 빠르게 따를 수 있게 하기 위해 정부에 압력을 가한다. 예를 들어 Climate Group의 역할이 국내시장을 개발시키는 데 있어 중요하다.

9 그러나, 심지어 매주 가동하는 새로운 석탄 화력 발전소의 이미지는 무척 무시무시하게 보이기도 한다. 이런 발전소가 없었다면 중국이 지난 1/4분기에 10.5% 성장을 달성한다는 것을 상상하기란 힘든 일이다. 그러나 중국이 지난 2년간 규모가 작은 발전소를 폐쇄해 왔던 사실을 정확하게 몇 명이나 알고 있을까? 중국은 단계적으로 소규모 발전소들을 줄이고 있다. 먼저, 50메가와트와 더 낮은 에너지로 시작해 100메가와트와 더 낮은 에너지, 그 다음에는 300메가와트의 발전소들이 줄어들 것이다.

10 이런 정책은 중국 중앙정부에 의해서 운영되어 왔으며, (물리) 초임계와 울트라초임계의 개선된 깨끗한 석탄을 갖춘 새로운 차세대 석탄공장을 지원하고 있다. 탄소를 채취하여 저장하는 공장은 연구개발 중이지만, 미래에 대한 진보적인 사고가 통합가스화 결합순환(IGCC)기술에 기반을 두고 있으며, 이는 에너지를 얻기 위해 석탄을 합성가스로 변화시키는 방식이다.

11 요즘에는 중국 소비자들이 더 좋은 주택과 자동차를 요구한다. 그들은 에너지 절약에 대한 인식이 높다. 2004년에 중국 정부는 리터당 15.6km의 자동차 연료경제지표를 보고했다. 이것은 호주, 캐나다 그리고 미국보다 효율이 높지만, 일본과 유럽보다는 낮다. 그 동안에 SUVs에 붙는 부가세 20%라는 높은 세금에도 불구하고 이런 종류의 자동차 판매는 계속 증가하고 있다.

12 지금까지 중국은 여전히 자전거의 왕국이었지만, 전기자전거는 대당 1500위엔(약 220달러)로

ACADEMIC READING

13 China, already, is doing a lot on the bottom line. So, could it do more? The answer is yes. China should learn and open its mind through the international communities. According to the Climate Group, they report the world should refine their image of China, just not fear it and, constructively, work in unison. At the same time, China's government should develop the clean revolution and maintain internal pressure for improvements.

unprecedented a. 전례(선례)가 없는   carbon-guzzling n. 탄소과용
carbon dioxide n. 이산화탄소   reduction n. 감소   efficiency n. 능률
biomass n. 생물량   photovoltaic a. 광전지의   supercritical a. 극단적으로 엄격한
synthetic a. 종합적인

수입되고 있다. 몇몇 종류는 하이브리드 자동차와 비슷한 지능에너지 복구시스템을 장착하고 있다. 2007년 전기자전거의 판매는 상당히 증가하였고, 전 세계 전기자동차시장의 3/4을 차지하는 것으로 추정되었다.

13 중국은 이미 출발점에서 많은 것들을 진행하고 있다. 그래서 앞으로 그것들을 더할 수 있을까? 대답은 '그렇다'이다. 중국은 국제사회로부터 배우고 개방을 유지해야만 한다. Climate Group에 따르면, 세계는 중국의 이미지를 다시 재고해야 하고, 불안감 없이 그러나 건설적으로 작업을 진행하고 있다고 보고한다. 동시에, 중국 정부는 청정혁명을 개발하고 개선하기 위해 내부 압력을 유지해야만 한다.

Questions 1-7

Do the following statements reflect the claims of the writer in Reading Passage 1?

In boxes **1-7** on your answer sheet write

YES	if the statement reflects the opinion of the writer
NO	if the statement contradicts the opinion of the writer
NOT GIVEN	if it is impossible to say what the writer thinks about this

1 The Central Government of China concluded the second research scheme of climate change in less than one year.

○ 키워드 The Central Government of China와 the second research scheme을 본문 첫째 단락에서 찾는다.
concluded = published
the second research scheme = the second research session
in less than one year = over a period of twelve months

중국 중앙정부에서는 1년 이내에 기후변화의 두 번째 연구 계획을 종결했다.

정답 YES

2 The main topic of the G8 Meeting in Japan was to discuss greenhouse gas emissions.

○ 키워드 G8 Meeting을 본문 첫째 단락에서 찾는다.
to discuss greenhouse gas emission ≠ Due to ~ unprecedented environmental issues in China,

일본에서의 G8회의의 주제는 온실가스 방출에 대해서 토의하는 것이었다.

정답 NO

3 The Chinese government must compensate the European Union for loss of climate change.

○ 문제에서 먼저 키워드인 the European Union을 두 번째 단락의 다섯 번째 문장에서 찾는다. 그러나 '중국 정부에서 기온변화의 손실에 대해서 유럽연합에 보상해주어야 한다(must compensate).'라는 의미를 위 문장에서 찾을 수 없다.

중국 정부는 기후변화의 손실에 대해서 유럽연합에 보상해줘야 한다.

정답 NOT GIVEN

4 NGO's group reported about truth of problems of a climate change in China.

◎ 키워드 NGO's group을 셋째 단락의 두 번째 문장과 세 번째 문장에서 찾는다. NGO's group reported about truth of problems of a climate change in China. = A non government organization (Climate Group) newspaper report presents a slightly different picture. ~

NGO(비정부기구)는 중국의 기후변화에 대한 문제의 진실성을 보도했다.

정답 YES

5 Solar energy has increased the amount of energy.

◎ 문제에서 먼저 키워드인 Solar energy를 다섯 번째 단락의 마지막 문장에서 찾는다. 그러나 태양에너지가 예전부터(has + p.p.: 현재완료-계속) 에너지양을 증가시켰는지는 알 수 없다. 본문에선 지금 8%에서 2020년에 15%까지 재생 가능한 에너지의 양을 증가시키되, solar, wind and biomass의 양을 적어도 3%를 이용하는 것이 보장되어야 한다고만 나와 있다.

태양에너지는 에너지의 양을 증가시켰다.

정답 NOT GIVEN

6 With different launching, both wind and solar power are inefficient.

◎ 키워드 both wind and solar power를 일곱 번째 단락 첫 문장에서 찾을 수 있고, 마지막 부분에 '풍력과 태양으로 농사짓는 것은 많은 비용이 든다'고 했으므로 효율성이 떨어진다.

시작점은 다르지만, 풍력과 태양에너지는 비효율적이다.

정답 YES

7 The high cost of cells causes less activity in the solar market in China. *cell (전기)전지

◎ 키워드 The high cost of cell를 여덟 번째 단락의 세 번째 문장에서 찾을 수 있다.
high cost = expensive
less activity = small business

셀의 높은 비용이 중국의 태양에너지 시장의 활동성을 줄여 놓은 원인이 되었다.

정답 YES

Questions 8-13

Complete the sentences.

Choose **NO MORE THAN THREE WORDS** *from the passage for each answer.*

8 China is emitting _____ of the so outstanding rates in the world.

◎ 본문 두 번째 지문 세 번째 문장을 보면 중국은 세계에서 가장 많은 이산화탄소를 배출하게 되었다(~, China now has the highest level of carbon dioxide emissions in the world.)고 나와 있으므로 정답은 이산화탄소라는 것을 알 수 있다.

전 세계적으로 중국이 이산화탄소 방출 비율이 가장 높다.

정답 carbon dioxide (CO_2)

143

ACADEMIC READING

9 Statistics that can be misleading have been corrected by a _____.

○ 키워드는 statistics와 misleading이다. 이 두 단어는 본문 세 번째 단락, 첫째 문장에서 찾을 수 있다. 즉, 이러한 통계를 지나치게 강조하면 오해를 일으킬 수 있다고 하면서 다음 문장에서 NGO가 신문보도를 제시했다고 했다. 즉, NGO가 오해를 낳을 수 있는 통계를 수정했다는 것과 같은 의미이다.

오해를 낳을 수 있는 통계가 NGO에 의해서 수정되었다.

정답 NGO

10 In 2006 _____ has set a hard target, waxing the amount of renewable sources.

○ 키워드는 In 2006과 a hard target이다. 이 두 단어는 본문 다섯 번째 단락의 첫 번째, 두 번째 문장에서 찾을 수 있다.

2006년 재생가능한 에너지법안은 어려운 목표를 설정하였는데, 재생 가능한 에너지원의 양을 증가시키는 것이다.

정답 Rerewable Energy Law

11 What is included in the amount of sources which are renewable is like _____.

○ 키워드는 sources which are renewable와 like이다. 이 두 단어는 본문 다섯 번째 단락의 마지막 문장에서 찾을 수 있다.
sources which are renewable~ = renewable energy sources
like = such as

재생가능한 자원의 양에 포함되는 것은 이를테면 태양과 바람 그리고 바이오매스가 있다.

정답 solar, wind, biomass

12 Wind energy is based on subsides, policies and the equitable _____.

○ 키워드는 Wind energy와 subsides, policies and equitable이다. 이 두 단어는 본문 일곱 번째 단락의 첫째 문장에서 찾을 수 있다.
Wind energy = Wind power

바람(풍력)에너지는 보조금과 정책 그리고 적절한 기술이 기본이다.

정답 technology

13 _____ should support to develop the domestic market in China facing on financial problems.

○ 키워드는 to develop the domestic market이다. 이 단어는 본문 여덟 번째 단락의 마지막 문장에서 찾을 수 있다.
support to develop the domestic market = the role of the Climate Group is important in developing domestic markets.

The Climate Group에서는 재정적인 문제에 직면한 중국의 국내 시장 발달을 후원해야만 한다.

정답 The Climate Group

READING PASSAGE 2

You should spend about 20 minutes on Questions 14-28 which are based on Reading Passage 2 below.

The Efficacy of Hypnotherapy

1   [14, 24]In the 1840s Scottish neurosurgeon, James Braid, coined 'Hypnotherapy'. At that time, in India, British surgeon, [25]James Esdaile, practiced hundreds of scrotal and abdominal operations, adopting hypnosis as the only anaesthetic. It was unfortunate timing that he reported his research dissertation on hypnosis to London Royal Society just as chemical anaesthetics were discovered The technique was not agreed on by the medical establishment.

2   These days, whilst an increasing number of people are asking about private practitioners, [15]the level of studies within the hypnotherapy field is meaningful enough that it remains on the fringes of medicine. In a report on alternative and complementary medicine in 2000, the Science and Technology Committee of the UK's House of Lords has given hypnosis a bad reputation by putting it in the "poor research / regulation" category. In other word, the therapies unlikely to enter mainstream medicine without substantial changes.

3   If you research the PubMed database using the term "hypnotherapy," you find 11,518 hit-words, so there are plenty of studies out there. However, most of the researchers are not satisfied with the gold standard of [16]a Randomised Controlled Trial (RCT) instead of taking the frame of reviews or case studies. [22]Only 91 relevant RCTs conducted in the world have worked in the past four years. The researchers propose that [16]hypnotheraphy can be effective treatment for pain control, irritable bowel syndrome, anxiety disorders and smoking cessation.

4   [17]There is clear evidence that hypnosis has psychological and physiological effects. That's why [23, 26]Peter Whorwell at the University of Manchester [18]has researched the efficacy of IBS (irritable bowel syndrome) surgery for gastrointestinal modualation with hypnotherapy and possible immune function support. But even though IBS is one of the best covered areas, the action with mechanism [19]is not clear and the Cochrane Collaboration from assessing clinical trials has criticised the size and quality of the studies.

5   In spite of the evidence that hypnotheraphy reduces pain, anxiety and stress, there are a couple of reasons why few trials have been done. From these stages, hypnosis's usage doesn't aid its image. Also, it has same problems as other "talking"

therapies. [20]Alternative funding should be built up, as the drug companies do not benefit from funding expensive studies

6 But, [21]one of the biggest obstacles to hypnosis being considered on a more scientific basis is the therapists themselves. Its effects are a result of a unique interaction between the practitioner and the patient. The expectation is similar to that of a drug and therefore should follow the same trial testing criteria. However, this argument is not helpful.

7 I strongly believe that whilst meeting with a living, breathing person, it is hard to decrease the process of clinical hypnosis and to receive YES or NO responses that are able to be reliably repeated in other conditions. However, for hypnosis to be considered medical, it should be measurable, replicable and vigorous. Actually, we need to model a body of clinical evidence in order to adapt to the medical profession.

8 With standardising protocol used, we demand quantitative measures of the effects on the patient, so studies can be compared. Ideally, researchers would have access to state-of-the art brain scanning equipment. In a reality, we are able to get simple biochemical markets of hypnosis and after effects under suitable usage.

9 Coming out of such studies in England, [27]Ursula James founded the Medical School Hypnosis Association with his colleagues. According to *Complementary Therapies in Clinical Practice*, he explains schemes to bring medical professors and students together with hypnotherapists to operate coordinated national trials and build up a large body of evidence from research replicated at multiple locations. Most of all, one of the first questions is whether clinical hypnosis is able to decrease stress. That is an important component potentially in an illness. We work towards using standardised questionnaires to calculate lifestyle, stress and depression and to measure various stress hormone levels in saliva samples taken from case applicants.

10 If we are able to present that there is a decrease in stress, we hope that hypnosis will be supplied to patients to treat their condition. With a wide range of usages, it could open up study into other areas including decreasing the thoughts of pain and improving recovery times.

---

neurosurgeon n. 신경외과의   coined a. 신조어로 만들어진   hypnotherapy n. 최면요법   abdominal a. 복부질환자의   hypnosis n. 최면상태   dissertation n. 학술논문   fringe n. 변두리   complementary a. 보충이 되는   reputation n. 명성   gastrointestinal a. (해부)위장에 관한   coordinated a. 복수의 근육계를 사용할 수 있는   saliva n. 침(타액)

---

6 그러나 최면술이 좀 더 과학적 기반에 위치하는 데 가장 큰 장애물들 가운데 하나는 치료사들 자신이다. 최면술의 효과들은 의사와 환자 사이에 독특한 상호작용의 결과이다. 기대치는 약물의 임상실험과 비슷하며 따라서 동일한 임상실험 기준을 따라야 한다. 그러나 이런 논쟁은 도움이 되지 않는다.

7 나는 살아 숨쉬는 사람과 만날 때, 다른 상황에서 쉽게 반복될 수 있는 YES / NO를 얻기 위해 그리고 임상최면술 과정을 줄이기가 어렵다는 것을 굳게 믿고 있다. 그러나 최면술이 의학의 일부분이 되기 위해서, 측정할 수 있고 반복 가능하며 활발해야 한다. 실제로 우리는 의학분야에서 받아들일 수 있는 임상증거의 실체를 만들 필요가 있다.

8 표준화된 계획서를 사용하여 우리는 환자에게 나타나는 효과의 양적인 측정을 요구하고 그럼으로써 연구가 비교되어야 한다. 이상적으로 연구원들은 최신의 뇌 스캔장비를 이용하는 것이다. 현실적으로 우리는 적절한 용례 하에서 차후 효과와 단순한 최면술의 성화학시장을 얻을 수 있다.

9 영국에서 이러한 연구의 시작으로, Ursula James와 그의 동료들은 최면의학회기구를 설립했다. '임상실험의 상호보완적인 요법'에 따라서 그는 의학전문가와 학생들을 최면요법 전문가들과 함께 초빙해 여러 지역에서 같은 연구를 통해 국가적인 실험을 실행해 증거의 실체를 형성하겠다는 계획을 설명했다. 일단, 첫 번째 문제들 중 하나는 임상최면술이 스트레스를 완화시킬 수 있느냐는 것이다. 즉, 이것은 병에 있어 잠재적으로 중요한 요소이다. 우리는 라이프 스타일, 스트레스 그리고 우울증을 측정하기 위한 표준화된 질문지법을 이용하고 연구 참여자들로부터 얻는 침(타액)을 채취하여 다양한 스트레스 호르몬 단계를 측정하는 데 목적이 있다.

10 만약 우리가 스트레스가 감소한다는 것을 보여준다면, 최면술이 환자들 질환을 치료하는데 쓰이기를 바란다. 이것이 더욱 널리 사용된다면, 회복시간을 단축시키고 통증의 인식을 감소시키는 것 등을 포함하여 다른 영역까지 연구가 확장될 수 있을 것이다.

Questions 14-16

*Choose the appropriate letters **A-D** and write them in boxes **14-16** on your answer sheet.*

14 According to information in the text, hypnotheraphy
   A was created by British surgeon James Esdaile in 1840.
   B has already been used during an operation by James Braid.
   C originated from the work of Scottish neurosurgeon James Braid in the 1840s.
   D was created by James Esdaile and James Braid in the 1840s.

글의 정보에 따르면, 최면요법은
A 1840년 영국 의사 James Esdaile에 의해서 창안 되었다.
B 이미 James Braid에 의해서 시술되어 만들어졌다.
C 1840년대 스코틀랜드 신경외과의사인 James Braid에 의해서 만들어졌다.
D 1840년대 James Esdaile과 James Braid에 의해 창안되었다.

◐ 키워드 hypnotheraphy(최면요법)를 첫째 단락의 첫 문장에서 찾을 수 있다.
originated = coined: ~ 신조어를 만들다 ~ 창조하다

정답 C

15 According to information in the text, the recent perception on hypnotheraphy among private practitioners
   A maintains plenty of research within alternative medicine.
   B is on the fringes of mainstream medicine because there hasn't been enough research.
   C means there is an neutral attitude within alternative medicine.
   D demands non-practical, but has potential.

글의 정보에 따르면, 개인병원 의사들 사이에서 최면 요법에 대한 최근에 인식은
A 대체의학 내에서 풍부한 연구를 유지하고 있다.
B 부족한 연구로 의학의 변두리 취급을 받고 있다.
C 대체의학 내에서 중립적 태도를 갖고 있다.
D 비실용적이지만, 잠재성을 요구한다.

◐ 키워드 the recent와 private practitioners를 둘째 단락의 첫 문장에서 찾을 수 있다.
outer edges of medicine = on the fringe of medicine (의학의 변두리 취급)

정답 B

16 According to randomised controlled trial (RCT), hypnotheraphy
   A works in a variety of cases.
   B supplied research and development in advance.
   C works in cold.
   D was found to be an antidote against irritable bowel syndrome (IBS).

무작위 대조비교실험에 의하면, 최면요법은
A 다양한 사례에 효과가 있다.
B 사전에 연구와 개발을 제공했다.
C 감기에 효과가 있다.
D IBS에 저항할 수 있는 해독제를 만들었다.

◐ 키워드 randomised controlled trial(RCT)와 hypnotheraphy를 셋째 단락의 두 번째와 네 번째 문장에서 찾을 수 있다.

정답 A

ACADEMIC READING

Questions 17-21

Complete the summary.

Choose **ONE OR TWO WORDS** from reading passage for each answer.

Write your answers in boxes **17-21** on your answer sheet.

To show evidence of hypnosis, researchers have proved physiological and **17** psychological effects as well. They discovered that hypnotherapy presumes to assist modulate gastrointestinal and immune function whilst operated **18** IBS. The mechanism of action is not justified, also, what assesses clinical trials, the **19** Cochrance Collaboration has underestimated the value and scale of studies. Despite having several effects, drug companies deny the therapies due to **20** expensive studies it should be demanded as a substitute investment. However, an outstanding barrier is **21** therapists themselves.

최면의 증거를 보여 주기 위해서 연구원들은 생리학과 17. 심리학적인 효과를 입증해 왔다. 그들은 최면 요법이 위장을 조절하고 심지어 면역 기능이 있다는 것을 18. IBS를 처리하면서 밝혔냈다. 작용 메커니즘은 밝혀지지 않았지만 임상실험을 평가하는 19. Cochrane Collaboration은 연구의 크기와 가치를 평가절하하였다. 여러 가지 효고-가 있음에도 불구하고 제약회사들은 20. 고비용의 연구들 때문에 치료법을 거부하였기 때문에 상당한 대체 투자가 필요하다. 그러나 주된 걸림돌은 21. 치료사들 자신이었다.

17 ○ 키워드 evidence of hypnosis와 physiological은 네 번째 단락에서 찾을 수 있다.
show evidence of hypnosis = is clear evidence

정답 psychological effects

18 ○ 키워드 modulate gastrointestinal과 immune-function은 네 번째 단락에서 찾을 수 있다.
hypnotherapy presume to assist modulate gastrointestinal and besides, immune function = has researched the efficacy of IBS (irritable bowel syndrome) surgery for gastrointestinal modulation with hypnotherapy and possible immune function support.

정답 IBS

19 ○ 키워드 is not justified와 assesses clinical trials는 네 번째 단락에서 찾을 수 있다.
is not justified = is not clear

정답 Cochrance Collaboration

20 ○ 키워드 drug companies와 substitute investment는 다섯 번째 단락에서 찾을 수 있다.
substitute investment = alternative funding

정답 expensive studies

21 ○ 키워드 an outstanding barrier은 여섯 번째 단락에서 찾을 수 있다.
outstanding barrier = one of the biggest obstacles

정답 therapists themselves

Questions 22-23

Answer the questions below.

Choose **NO MORE THAN TWO WORDS AND/OR A NUMBER** from the passage for each answer.

Write your answers in boxes **22** and **23** on your answer sheet.

22 How many relevant RCTs were there in the past four years?

○ 키워드 relevant RCTs와 in the past four years는 세 번째 단락의 세 번째 문장에서 찾을 수 있다. "지난 4년간 단지 91건의 관련 RCT만이 실행되었다."고 명시하고 있다.

지난 4년 동안에 관련 무작위 대조비교실험은 몇 번이나 이뤄졌는가?

정답 91

23 Who reported that hypnotherapy aids gastrointestinal modulation and supports immune function?

○ 키워드 gastrointestinal modulation과 immune function은 네 번째 단락에서 찾을 수 있다. 네 번째 단락의 두 번째 문장에서 최면요법이 위장완화와 면역기능에 도움이 된다는 연구는 Peter Whorwell이 했다고 말한다.

최면요법이 위장조절과 면역기능을 도와준다는 사실을 누가 발표했는가?

정답 Peter Whorwell

Questions 24-27

Look at the following people and the list of statements below.

Match each city with the correct statement.

Write the correct letter, **A-E**, in boxes **24-27** on your answer sheet.

List of Statements

A have founded the Medical School Hypnosis Association.
B discovered hypnotherapy suppose to aid gastrointestinal modulation and support immune function.
C created a new term, hypnotheraphy in the 1840s.
D implemented over several hundred abdominal and scrotal operations.
E criticised the quality and size of hypnotherphy.

A 의학최면요법협회 학술기관을 설립하였다.
B 최면요법이 위장완화와 면역기능을 돕는다는 것을 발견하였다.
C 1840년대 최면요법이라는 신조어를 만들었다.
D 복부와 음낭시술을 수백 번 이상 시행했다.
E 최면요법의 질과 정도를 비난하였다.

24 James Braid [키워드]

○ 첫 번째 단락의 첫째 문장에서 키워드를 찾는다.
created = coined

정답 C

ACADEMIC READING

25 James Esdaile [키워드]

○ 첫 번째 단락의 둘째 문장에서 키워드를 찾는다.
implemented = practiced

정답 **D**

26 Peter Whorwell [키워드]

○ 네 번째 단락의 둘째 문장에서 Peter Whorwell이 '최면요법이 위장완화와 면역 기능을 돕는다.' 라고 언급하고 있다.

정답 **B**

27 Ursula James [키워드]

○ 아홉 번째 단락의 첫째 문장에서 Ursula James가 '최면의학학회 기관을 설립하였다' 라고 언급하고 있다.

정답 **A**

Questions 28

*Choose the appropriate letter **A-D** and write it in box **28** on your answer sheet.*

28 Which of the following statements best describes the writer's main purpose in Reading Passage 2?
  A to inform the reader relative not to mimic during operating of hypnotheraphy
  B to encourage the reader to act against misinformation regarding hypnotheraphy
  C to explain make the reader spread the right perception of hypnotherapy
  D to make readers to encourage a randomised controlled trial (RCT)

지문 2에서 저자의 주요 목적을 가장 잘 설명한 것은 어떤 것인가?
A 최면요법 시행 중 관련 요법을 독자들이 흉내내지 말 것을 알리기 위해서
B 최면요법에 대한 오용에 대처할 수 있는 독자들을 격려하기 위해서
C 최면요법의 올바른 확산을 독자에게 설명하기 위해서
D 독자들에게 RCT를 장려하기 위해서

○ 문제의 요지는 저자의 주요 목적(writer's main purpose)이므로, 이것은 첫 번째 단락과 두 번째 단락에서 찾을 수 있다. 저자는 hypnotheraphy(최면요법)에 대한 올바른 인식과 보급에 대해서 관련 독자에게 알리는 글이다. 이런 주제와 관련된 글은 서론에 위치하는 두괄식 문형으로 글의 앞부분에서 찾는다.

정답 **C**

READING PASSAGE 3

You should spend about 20 minutes on *Questions 29-40* which are based on Reading Passage 3 on the following pages.

Questions 29-34

Reading Passage 3 has ten paragraphs, **A-J**.

Choose the correct heading for paragraph **B-G** from the list of headings below.

Write the correct number, *i-viii*, in boxes **29-34** on your answer sheet.

List of Headings
i   A lot of proof of non well-being
ii   Recent perceptional change of the environment
iii   Reviving time for private time
iv   Understanding of being valuable
v   The absurdity of our lives from the feature of economy benefit
vi   Right attitude for constant comfort and human ingenuity
vii   People and governments which continue to disagree
viii Aspiring to the material civilization

i	행복하지 못한 많은 증거들
ii	최근 환경의 변화인식
iii	개인 시간에 대한 회생 시간
iv	삶을 더 가치있게 하는 것에 대한 이해
v	경제 혜택의 모습으로 인한 우리 삶의 불합리
vi	계속적인 안락과 인간의 창의력에 대한 올바른 자세
vii	반대를 유지하는 시민과 정부
viii	물질 문명에 대한 열망

Example	Answer
Paragraph **A**	**ii**

29   Paragraph **B**

> B단락의 첫 번째 문장에서 '국민과 정부가 성장 의제를 계속적으로 주장하지만 갈등에 대해 부정하고 있다.'라고 서술하고 있다.

정답 vii

30   Paragraph **C**

> C단락에서 '광고에 나오는 모든 즐겁고 편한 삶의 모습은 도움이 되지 않으며, 우리의 행복은 보다 더 많은 물질을 소비하는 데 의존한다'고 말하고 있다.

정답 viii

31   Paragraph **D**

> D단락의 첫 번째 문장에서 '일에 치어 사는 수많은 증거가 있으며, ~'에서 행복하지 못한 증거들을 서술하고 있다.

정답 i

ACADEMIC READING

32 Paragraph **E**

➤ E단락에서 '우리의 현실 상황의 불합리는 과로한 업무를 통해서 우리가 잃었던 기쁨을 우리에게 되파는 경제적 이점으로 설명된다.' 라고 서술하고 있다.

정답 v

33 Paragraph **F**

➤ F단락의 첫 번째 문장에서 '많은 사람들이 일과 돈보다는 삶에 더 많은 것이 있을 수 있다는 사실을 깨닫기 시작했다.' 라고 서술하고 있다.

정답 iv

34 Paragraph **G**

➤ G단락의 첫 번째 문장에서 '우리의 생활 방식을 희생한다면 장점이 많아질 것이다.' 라고 서술하고 있다.

정답 iii

The Well-being Life

A [35]Going to back in the 1970s, few people listened to scientists' warnings of global warming. It got worse as nobody was interested in curbing economic growth to protect the environment. Nowadays, we are more cautious. We are hearing about the conflict between living on the earth and expanding the demands of the global market.

B However, [36]Tim Jackson reports that [29]people and governments claim the growth agenda to ensure our future and are still in denial of the conflict. A reason for this is the presumption that support for the green campaigners will ultimately make our lives worse.

C [30]All representations of a pleasant and easy life which aspire to come from advertising do not help. Also, our happiness is dependent on consuming more and more "material." We have never listened to ways of escaping stress, noise, congestion, and the ill-health that comes from our "high" standard of living.

D [31]Actually there is plenty of evidence to suggest that a [37]workaholic mentality and an affluent lifestyle does not give us a pleasant life and that switching to a more sustainable community to work could make us happier. For instance, rates of depression and occupational illness have been indicated to be relative to the number of hours we are working. [38]Once a certain income level is reached more wealth is not linked with growing happiness.

행복한 삶

A 1970년대로 거슬러 올라가면, 과학자들의 지구 온난화의 경고에 귀를 기울이는 사람들은 거의 없었다. 심지어 환경을 보호하기 위해 경제성장을 억제하는 데 관심을 갖는 이들은 더더욱 없었다. 오늘날, 우리는 좀 더 신중해야 한다. 우리는 지구에 생활하는 것과 확장된 국제시장의 요구 사이에서의 갈등에 대해 듣고 있다.

B 그러나 Tim Jackson은 국민과 정부가 우리의 미래를 보장하기 위해 성장 의제를 주장하고 있지만, 여전히 이런 갈등에 대해 부인을 하고 있다는 사실을 보고했다. 여기에는 환경운동가들이 궁극적으로 우리의 삶이 나빠지게 될 거라는 가정에 그 이유가 있다.

C 광고에 나오는 모든 즐겁고 편한 삶의 모습은 도움이 되지 않는다. 또한 우리의 행복은 보다 더 많은 '물질'을 소비하는 데 의존하고 있다. 우리는 '높은' 수준의 삶에서 오는 스트레스, 소음, 억압, 질병을 탈출하는 방법에 대해 결코 들어본 적이 없다.

D 실제로 일중독적인 사고방식과 부유한 생활방식은 우리에게 즐거운 삶을 제공하지 못하며 좀 더 지속가능한 사회로의 변환은 우리에게 더 큰 행복을 줄 수 있다고 제안하는 수많은 증거가 있다. 예를 들어, 경기침체와 직업병의 비율은 우리가 일하는 시간 수와 관련이 있음을 보여주고 있었다. 일단 소득 수준이 어느 정도에 이르면, 더 많은 부는 행복의 증가와 관련이 없다.

E [32]The unreasonableness of our situation can be explained by the way in which our economy tries to sell us happiness. For example, leisure and tourism companies sell customers, "a good quality time," catering services offer us, "home cooking," dating agencies sell relationships; the sports centre sells health and as a result of modern car culture it can be unsafe to walk outside. With the economy steadily expanding, consumer culture is becoming more and more reliant on our desire to adopt this lifestyle.

F [33]An increasing number of people are beginning to realize that there is more to life than work and money. Troubled by the effects of a stressful life, people are starting to make their lives more simple and rethinking their values and desires. If people were to switch to a less work-intensive economy, [39]it would decrease the rate of people, products and information delivered, reducing carbon emissions and the use of resources.

G [34]There are a number of advantages to making sacrifices to our lifestyles. We would be able to have more time for ourselves and our families. We would commute less and enjoy healthier ways of travelling such as walking, cycling, and riding a boat. Large supermarket chains would be replaced by local family businesses resulting in the creation of more communal town centres. Our local areas would become more tranquil and give us more chance to reflect on things. These changed ideas for a "good life" might also motivate less developed countries to reconsider their goals enabling them to avoid some of the less attractive aspects of the current system.

H Of course, we must sacrifice some conveniences and pleasure such as regular steaks, hot tubs, luxury cosmetics and easy foreign travel. But constant comfort can blunt as well as satisfy our desires. And human ingenuity will invent a wide range of eco-friendly excitement.

I Moving into a safe-state economy is an intimidating prospect. However, [40]Herman Daly explains it is unrealistic to continue with current rates of development in production, work and material consumption over the next decades, let alone into the next century.

J Under the financial disorders and broad cynicism over government commitments to global warming, more honesty would win cooperation and esteem from the voter, especially if

ACADEMIC READING

> politicians emphasise the advantages of the sustainable society.
>
> presumption n. 추정(가정)　aspire v. 열망하다　workaholic n. 지나치게 일하는 사람
> commute v. 대체하다　tranquil a. 평온한　ingenuity n. 정교(교묘)
> intimidating a. 위협하는　cynicism n. 비꼬는 말　commitments n. 위임(위탁)

Questions 35-40

Do the following statements reflect the claims of the writer in Reading Passage 3?

In boxes **35-40** on your answer sheet write

　　YES　　　　if the statement reflects the opinion of the writer
　　NO　　　　if the statement contradicts the opinion of the writer
　　NOT GIVEN　if it is impossible to say what the writer thinks about this

35　Most people have concentrated on global warming since 1970.

　◯ 문제에서 먼저 키워드인 global warming since 1970은 A단락의 첫 문장에서 찾을 수 있다. 본문에서는 소수의 사람들만이 온난화에 관심을 가졌다고 언급하고 있다.

1970년 이래로 지구온난화에 대해 대부분의 사람들은 집중해 왔다.

정답 NO

36　Tim Jackson discusses a conflict of opinions between people and government.

　◯ 키워드 Time Jackson과 people and government는 B단락의 첫 문장에서 찾을 수 있다

국민과 정부 사이의 갈등에 대해서 Tim Jackson은 의견을 제기한다.

정답 YES

37　Work and material are relative to pleasant and favorable lives recently.

　◯ 키워드인 Work and material은 D단락의 첫 문장에서 찾을 수 있다. 그러나 서로간의 의미가 다르기 때문에 답은 NO이다.

최근에 일과 물질은 기쁨과 호의적인 삶과 관계가 있다.

정답 NO

38　Level of income is vital for building up substantial happiness.

　◯ 키워드인 Level of income과 substantial happiness는 D단락의 마지막 문장에서 찾을 수 있다. 그러나 서로간의 의미가 다르기 때문에 답은 NO이다.

소득 수준은 실질적인 행복을 증진시키는 데 중요한 요소이다.

정답 NO

39 With a less work-intensive economy, it would decrease only the rate of carbon emissions.

○ 키워드인 less work-intensive economy와 carbon emissions는 F단락의 마지막 문장에서 찾을 수 있다. 서로간의 의미가 다르기 때문에 답은 NO이다. 본문에선 자원 활용과 이산화탄소 두 가지를 줄일 수 있다고 진술하기 때문이다.

일에 덜 집중하는 경제는, 오직 이산화탄소 방출비율만을 감소시킬 수 있다.

정답 NO

40 Herman Daly indicates current rates of natural resources are enlarged for a sustainable society.

○ 키워드인 Herman Daly는 I단락의 두 번째 문장에서 찾을 수 있다. 문제에선 Herman Daly가 '천연자원 증가가 사회를 확장시킨다.'고 했지만, 본문에선 찾을 수 없다.

천연자원의 현재 비율이 지속가능한 사회를 확장시킬 수 있다고 Herman Daly가 지적한다.

정답 NOT GIVEN

Academic Reading

Actual Test 2

Answer Sheet

#		#		#		#	
1	vii	11	FALSE	21	C	31	NO
2	i	12	TRUE	22	G	32	NOT GIVEN
3	iv	13	NOT GIVEN	23	F	33	YES
4	ii	14	Space X	24	B	34	B
5	iii	15	US scientists	25	I	35	C
6	vi	16	Nearly Ready	26	E	36	alcohol
7	FALSE	17	safety	27	NOT GIVEN	37	sleeplessness
8	TRUE	18	mother ship	28	YES	38	diphtheria
9	TRUE	19	plane	29	YES	39	JAMA
10	NOT GIVEN	20	UN's 1967 treaty	30	NO	40	C

ACADEMIC READING

READING PASSAGE 1

You should spend about 20 minutes on *Questions 1-13* which are based on Reading Passage 1 on the following pages.

Questions 1-6

Reading Passage 1 has twelve paragraphs, **A-L**.

Choose the correct heading for paragraph **B-G** from the list of headings below.

Write the correct number, *i-vii*, in boxes **1-6** on your answer sheet.

List of Headings

i	Disorders strike much later in life.
ii	Drawbacks in public health
iii	Longevity based on high education
iv	The elderly people of today got better nutrition when they were children.
v	The elderly are becoming more well off.
vi	Most of independent people over 65 complete activities themselves.
vii	Diseases have decreased recently.

i	질병이 인생의 아주 후반기에 발생한다.
ii	공중보건의 실패
iii	장수는 고등교육에 기초한다.
iv	오늘날 노인들은 유년기에 더 나은 영양을 섭취했다.
v	노인들은 더 유복한 상태에 있다.
vi	65세 이상의 자립 고령자들 대부분은 그들 스스로 행동을 한다.
vii	최근에 질병이 감소했다.

Example	*Answer*
Paragraph **A**	v

1 Paragraph B

▶ B단락 세 번째 문장, '이런 건강질환들로 인해 소수만이 고통 받고 있으며, 해마다 무척 빠르게 그 비율이 감소하고 있다는 것을 조사결과가 보여준다.(The results show that these conditions are troubling~)' 참고.

정답 vii

2 Paragraph C

▶ C단락 두 번째 문장, '그는 역시 1982년에 65세 정도의 많은 사람들이 시달리던 그런 질환들이 지금은 70세 혹은 75세까지도 나타나지 않는다고 언급했다.(He also mentioned that diseases suffered by~)' 참고.

정답 i

3 Paragraph D

▶ D단락 세 번째 문장, '예를 들어, 20세기 1/4분기에 유년기의 영양 향상이 오늘날 노인층에게 그 전 세대보다 인생의 출발을 순조롭게 하였다.(For instance, improvements in childhood nutrition~)' 참고.

정답 iv

4 Paragraph E

● E단락 첫 번째 문장, '이 자료들은 또한 공중보건에서 몇 가지 부정적인 변화들을 보여준다.(The data also shows some negative changes in public health.)' 참고.

정답 ii

5 Paragraph F

● F단락 첫 번째 문장, 'Manton이 발견한 사실은 고등교육을 받은 사람들은 좀 더 오래 살 가능성이 있다는 것이다.(Manton also found that better-educated people are likely to live longer.)' 참고

정답 iii

6 Paragraph G

● G단락 두 번째 문장, '1994년의 통계조사에서 그들의 거의 80%는 매일 식사를 준비하고 옷을 갈아입는 것부터 복잡한 일, 이를 테면 요리와 재산 관리까지 남의 도움을 받지 않고 혼자서 해 나간다는 것이다.(In the 1994 survey almost 80% of them~)' 참고.

정답 vi

Growing of the Aging Society

A American scientists say that the elderly are now healthier, happier and more independent. The results of a study that has taken place over a 14 year period will be released at the end of the month. The research will show that common health disorders suffered by the elderly are affecting fewer people and happening later in life.

B Over the last 14 years, The National Long-term Health Care Survey has gathered data from more than 20,000 males and females over the age of 65 about their health and lifestyles. The group has analysed the results of data gathered in 1994 on conditions such as arthritis, high blood pressure and poor circulations these were the most common medical complaints for this age group. [1]The results show that these conditions are troubling a smaller proportion of people each year and decreasing very quickly. Other diseases suffered by the elderly including dementia, emphysema and arteriosclerosis are also affecting fewer people.

C According to Kenneth Manton, a demographer from Duke University in North Carolina, "the question of what should be considered normal ageing has really changed." he said. [2]He also mentioned that diseases suffered by many people around the age of 65 in 1982, are now not occurring until people reach the age of 70-75.

D It is clear that due to medical advances some diseases are not

노령화 사회의 증가

A 미국 과학자들은 노인들이 현재 더 건강하고, 더 행복하고 더 독립적이라고 말한다. 14년간에 걸쳐 행해진 연구 결과가 이번 달 말에 발표될 것이다. 그 보고서는 일반 건강장애로 고통 받는 노인들은 별로 없으며 인생의 후반기에 일반 건강장애가 발생한다는 것을 보여주고 있다.

B 지난 14년 동안, '국제장기건강보호 통계조사'는 65세 이상의 남성과 여성 20,000명 이상으로부터 그들의 생활방식과 건강에 대한 자료를 수집해왔다. 그 집단은 1994년에 이 연령대에서 가장 일반적인 의학적 불평들인 관절염, 고혈압 그리고 순환장애 같은 건강상태들이 수집된 자료를 분석했다. 이런 건강질환들로 인해 소수만이 고통 받고 있으며, 해마다 무척 빠르게 그 비율이 감소하고 있다는 것을 조사결과가 보여준다. 치매, 폐기종, 동맥경화 등을 가진 노인들에게 고통을 주는 다른 질환들 역시 소수 사람들에게 영향을 미치고 있다.

C North Carolina Duke대학의 인구통계학자인 Kenneth Manton에 따르면, '무엇을 일반 노화과정으로 고려해야 할지에 대한 문제가 정말로 변화되었다.'고 말했다. 그는 역시 1982년에 65세 정도의 많은 사람들이 시달리던 그런 질환들이 지금은 70세 혹은 75세까지의 노인들에게 나타나지 않는다고 언급했다.

D 분명하게도, 의학의 발전으로 몇몇 질환들은 예

as prominent as they used to be. However, there may also be other factors influencing this change. [3]For instance, improvements in childhood nutrition in the first quarter of the twentieth century gave many people a better start in life than was possible before.

E [4]The data also shows some negative changes in public health. The research suggests that the rise respiratory conditions such as lung cancer and bronchitis may reflect changing [7]smoking habits and an increase in air pollution. Manton says that as we have been exposed to worse and worse pollution it is not surprising that some people over the age of 60 are suffering as a result.

F Manton also found that [5, 8]better-educated people are likely to live longer. For instance, women of 65 with less than eight years of education are expected to live to around 82. Those who studied more could be able to live seven years longer. Whilst some of this can be attributed to better-educated people usually having a higher income, Manton believes it is mainly because they pay closer attention to their health.

G Also, the survey estimated how independent people of 65 were, and found a striking trend. [6, 9]In the 1994 survey almost 80% of them were able to complete activities such as eating and dressing alone as well as handling difficult tasks, like cooking and managing their financial affairs. This situation indicates an important drop among disabled elderly people in the population. If, 14 years ago, the apparent trends in the U.S had continued, researchers believe that there would be one million disabled elderly people in today's population. Manton shows the trend saved more than $ 200 billion for the US's government's Medicare system, and it has suggested the elderly American population is less of a financial burden than expected.

H [10]The growing number of the independent elderly people is probably linked to the huge increase in home medical aids. For instance, the research shows the use of raising toilet seat covers and bath seats has increased by more than fifty per cent. Also, these developments about health benefits are reported by the MacArthur Foundation's research group for successful ageing. It found the elderly who are able to take care of themselves were more likely to stay healthy in their old age.

I [11]Retaining a certain level of daily physical activity may also help brain function, according to Carl Cotman, a neuroscientist at the University of California at Irvine. He found that rats exercising on a treadmill have higher levels of a brain-derived neurotrophic in their brains. He believes the hormone which holds neuron functions may prevent the active humans' brain function from declining.

J Teresa Seeman, a social epidemiologist at the University of Southern California in Los Angeles, was conducting the same research. He found a link between self-esteem and stress in people over 70. [12]The elderly who did challenging activities such as driving have more control of their mind and have a lower level of stress hormone cortisol in their brains. Chronically high levels of this hormone can cause heart disease.

K However, an independent life may have negative points. Seeman knew that [13]the elderly people that were living alone were able to retain higher levels of stress hormones even when sleeping. The research indicates that elderly people are happier if they can live an independent life but also acknowledge when they need help.

L Seeman says, "With many cases of research about ageing, these results help common sense." Also, the situations show that we may be ignoring some of the simple factors. She mentions, "The sort of thing your grandmother always used to talk to you about seems to be exactly right."

---

arthritis n. (병리)관절염   dementia n. (정신의학)치매   arteriosclerosis n. (병리)동맥경화   emphysema n. (병리)기종   demographer n. 인구통계학자   bronchitis n. (병리)기관지염   neuroscientist n. 신경정신의   treadmill n. 단조롭고 피곤한 일   chronically ad. 만성적으로   retain v. ~을 보유하다

Questions 7-13

Do the following statements reflect the claims of the writer in Reading Passage 1?

In boxes **7-13** on your answer sheet write

> **TRUE**   if the statement agrees with the information
> **FALSE**   if the statement contradicts the information
> **NOT GIVEN**   if there is no information on this

7 Smoking habits are a crucial cause in some cancers.

  ○ 키워드 Smoking habits는 E단락의 두 번째 문장에서 찾을 수 있다. 본문에서 암의 원인은 smoking habits과 air pollution이라고만 나와 있지 결정적인 원인이라고는 언급되지 않았으므로 FALSE이다.

정답 FALSE

ACADEMIC READING

8 The better-educated elderly people tend to live longer.

○ 키워드 better-educated는 F단락의 첫 번째 문장에서 찾을 수 있다. 본문에서 '더 나은 교육을 받은 사람은 더 오래 사는 경향이 있다.' 라는 의미가 문제와 본문이 같으므로 TRUE이다.

더 좋은 교육을 받은 노인들은 좀 더 오래 사는 경향이 있다.

정답 TRUE

9 People over 65 can independently manage a variety of tasks.

○ 키워드 People over 65 can independently manage는 G단락의 두 번째 문장에서 찾을 수 있다. '65세 이상의 노인층은 여러 다양한 업무를 혼자 힘으로 해나간다.' 라는 의미가 문제와 본문이 같으므로 TRUE이다.

65세 이상의 노인들은 여러 가지 다양한 업무를 혼자서 수행할 수 있다.

정답 TRUE

10 Elderly people have overcome dementia as a result of home medical aids.

○ 키워드인 home medical aids은 H단락의 첫 번째 문장에서 찾을 수 있다. 그러나 치매를 극복해 왔다는 의미는 본문에서 찾을 수는 없다. 문제의 관련된 정보가 본문에 없으므로 답은 NOT GIVEN이다.

노인들은 가정의료지원으로 치매를 극복해왔다.

정답 NOT GIVEN

11 Continuing physical exercise is likely to assist digestive function.

○ 키워드인 Continuing physical exercise는 I단락의 첫 번째 문장에서 찾을 수 있다. 그러나 본문에선 '매일 육체적인 활동을 하는 것은 정신기능(mental functioning)에 도움을 줄 수 있다'고 했기 때문에 답은 FALSE이다.

꾸준한 물리적 운동은 소화기능을 도와주는 경향이 있다.

정답 FALSE

12 People over 70 who still do challenging things such as driving are able to lower their level of the hormone cortisol which is linked to heart disease.

○ 키워드인 over 70 / challenging / driving은 J단락의 세 번째, 네 번째 문장에서 찾을 수 있다. '운전과 같은 도전적인 활동들을 하는 노인들은 그들의 마음을 훨씬 더 통제하며 그들의 뇌에는 스트레스 호르몬 코티졸(부신 피질에서 생기는 스테로이드 호르몬의 일종)이 낮았다. 만성적으로 이러한 호르몬이 높으면 심장 질환을 유발한다.' 라는 의미가 질문과 일치한다.

운전에 도전하는 70대 이상 사람들은 심장질환에 관련 있는 cortisol의 단계를 낮출 수 있다.

정답 TRUE

13 Isolation may cause a higher level of stress hormones at work.

○ K단락 두 번째 문장에서 '혼자 사는 노인들은 수면을 취할 때조차 높은 스트레스 호르몬 수준을 유지한다.'고 언급되어 있다. 업무 중 스트레스에 관해서는 직접적으로 제시하고 있지 않으므로 답은 NOT GIVEN이다.

고독은 업무 중의 스트레스 호르몬 단계를 더 많이 높인다.

정답 NOT GIVEN

READING PASSAGE 2

You should spend about 20 minutes on Questions 14-26 which are based on Reading Passage 2 below.

Space Flight Tourism

1 Falcon 1's successful launch on 28th of September was an outstanding achievement for the fledging space tourism industry. [14]When a rocket made by Space X in Hawthorne, California, reached an orbit of 500 kilometres from the Earth, it became possible for privately developed rocket too.

2 Two days after the launch, Virgin Galactic started a business with [15]the US National Oceanic and Atmospheric Administration which will be accepted by US scientists as a way of researching climate change using a spacecraft.

3 No doubt the civilian space flight industry is an exciting area and this was apparent at the International Aeronautical Congress [16]in Glasgow last month. It displayed slick promotional videos, and models of the "Nearly Ready" spacecraft in orbit to the people who would be investing money in the project.

4 However, in spite of increasing confidence, it is also necessary to be cautious: can a civilian spacecraft be safe like holiday airlines? Gerardine Goh, a lawyer at DLR, the German Aerospace Centre in Bonn and a member of Germany's delegation to the UN's Office of Outer Space Affairs reported that as [17]it is not global there needs to be enforceable regulations in place to guarantee the safety of a civilian spacecraft. She said "Ships should be equipped to be seaworthy, aircrafts should be equipped to be airworthy but there no legislation in place to ensure that a spacecraft is space worthy."

5 At the International Association for the Advancement of Space Safety, Goh is planning to press the UN to force civilian space operators to warrant which spacecrafts are designed and built to minimum safety standards. She says, "Mass commercial space flight does not currently have international safety regulations." And, "We deeply need a UN treaty which offers us this."

6 One way companies are planning to transport tourists into space is with a "mother ship" an aircraft which [18]carries a rocket at an altitude of 16 kilometres before launching it, says Goh. "But with launching the aircraft, the ICAO's air safety standards only apply to the mother ship and the rocket capsule until they are separated. After that, we do not have any safety standards for the capsule itself. It is a critical problem."

7 [19]From 16 kilometres to the Karman line, the point of 100 kilometres up where space is considered to start, the rocket will be travelling within a legal vacuum. Here, lawyers cannot agree on whether it is a plane or a rocket. Some insist that if you are in a well-equipped functioning rocket, more strict safety measures should try to be incorporated into the spaceship's design.

8 The other aspects of [20]the UN's 1967 treaty for outer space exploration may be discussed again if civilian space flight turns out to be successful. For example, countries must consider how to rescue and repatriate astronauts crashing or landing in their land. Also, governments have to decide if the money generated by the space flight industry will be enough to cover the cost of rescuing space tourists.

9 [21]Civilian space flight companies are very aware of the risks in this field as they have already had the experience of dealing with a tragedy. Unfortunately, three engineers were killed and another three were severely injured in 2007, when nitrous oxide rocket fuel suddenly exploded during fuel flow tests at a Scaled Composites facility in Mojave, California. The company is establishing WhiteKnightTwo, a carrier aircraft and SpaceShip Two, a six-seater rocket for Virgin Galactic. The facility was regulated by California's health and safety regulator, and it has now modified its technology to decrease the risks.

10 However, space flight's dangers are far from just fuel issues. According to [22]Laurent Gatheir of Dassault Aviation developing the VSH of a rocket powered sub-orbital tourist space plane, other critical safety factors are with depressurization risks, passengers close to the engine and the activities of flight trajectories including cosmic ray shielding.

11 Civilian space companies should incorporate the safety features into their designs. For instance, [23]the VSH will equip an ejector seat for all tourists and staff. It is a device for bailing out of the spacecraft with default of 40,000 feet (12 kilometres).

12 Goh's vision is essentially against the Federal Aviation Administration Office of Commercial Space Transportation (AST) and does not have any schemes to regulate civilian space flight safety until 2012. The Commercial Space Launch Amendments Act of 2004 mentions that [24]George Nield an AST chief said, the civilian space flight regulation must not "stifle" the developing technologies with inconvenient rules.

13 Before launching, a hands off approach to civilian space flight could be quite risky. Goh said, "A lack of safety standards and a lot of operational burdens will leave a commercial space flight in the dangerous activity categories in terms of insurance." It

means ²⁵insurance costs will be very high. ²⁶Critics who are developing safety standards also insist that the "at-your-own-risk" mentality that is applied to risky sports like scuba-diving should also be applied to civilian space flight.

outstanding a. 주요한   orbit n. 궤도   critical a. 결정적인   seaworthy a. (배가) 항진하기에 알맞은   repatriate v. ~을 귀환시키다   depressurization n. 억압   trajectories n. 궤도   stifle v. ~을 질식시키다

13 발사되기 전에, 민간 우주항공에 대해 수수방관하는 것은 꽤 위험할 수 있다. Goh는 "안전규정의 부족과 작업에 따른 높은 부담감은 상업용 우주비행을 보험에서 위험한 스포츠 카테고리로 분류하고 있다."고 말한다. 이것은 보험료가 무척 비싸진다는 것을 의미한다. 안전규정을 만들려는 비평가들 또한 스쿠버다이빙처럼 위험이 따르는 스포츠에 적용되는 "자기 자신의 책임"을 민간 우주비행에도 역시 적용해야 한다고 주장한다.

Questions 14-20

Complete the summary.

Choose **NO MORE THAN THREE WORDS** from the passage for each answer.

Write your answers in boxes **14-20** on your answer sheet.

On 28 September the emerging space tourism industry was enormous. In Hawthorne, California, a rocket was erected by **14** Space X. Climate change was monitored by **15** US scientists in US National Oceanic and Atmospheric Administration using its spacecraft. In Glasgow, at the international Aeronautical meeting, it is apparent that civilian space flight industry is growing, as it showed the **16** Nearly Ready spacecraft which promises sub-orbital flights. Although developing confirmation, non regulation is clear to guarantee **17** safety. A method for space business is cooperating with **18** mother ship conveyable at 16 kilometres in the skies. From 16 kilometres to 100 kilometres' travelling may be available, but lawyers definitely cannot agree with whether it is a **19** plane or a rocket. **20** UN's 1967 treaty need to be revisited if civilian space flight proves successful.

9월 28일, 우주관광산업의 출발은 대단했다. 캘리포니아 주의 Hawthorne에서 **14.** Space X에 의해 로켓이 만들어졌다. 기후변화는 우주선을 이용하여 미국가해양과 대기위원회의 **15.** 미국 과학자들에 의해 조사되었다. 글라스고우에서 민간 우주항공산업이 높은 단계에 있다는 사실이 국제항공회에서 명백해졌는데 거기서 **16.** '곧 준비완료' 라는 우주왕복선 모델을 선보이며 궤도 이전까지 진입을 약속했다. 비록 신뢰성이 향상되었지만, **17.** 안전을 보장하기 위한 규정은 확실하지 않았다. 우주사업에 대한 방법은 16km 상공까지 운반할 수 있는 **18.** 모선과 협력하여야 한다. 16km에서 100km까지의 여행은 가능할 수는 있지만, 변호인단들은 그것이 **19.** 비행기인지 로켓인지 확실히 합의하지 못했다. 민간 우주항공이 성공한다면 **20.** 유엔의 1967년 조약도 다시 논의할 필요가 있다.

14 ○ 키워드인 Hawthrone는 첫 번째 단락의 두 번째 문장에 있다.
~erected by Space X = ~made by Space X

정답 Space X

15 ○ 키워드인 US National Oceanic and Atmospheric Administration은 두 번째 단락의 첫 번째 문장에서 찾을 수 있다.
Climate change was monitored by US scientist = ~US scientists as a way of researching~

정답 US scientists

16 ○ 키워드인 In Glasgow를 세 번째 단락의 첫 번째 문장에서 찾을 수 있고, 정답은 다음 문장에 나온다.

정답 Nearly Ready

ACADEMIC READING

17 ○ 키워드인 non regulation is clear to guarantee를 네 번째 단락의 두 번째 문장에서 찾을 수 있다.
non regulation is clear to guarantee~ = it is not global and there needs to be~

정답 safety

18 ○ 키워드인 conveyable at 16 kilometres in the skies를 여섯 번째 단락의 첫 번째 문장에서 찾을 수 있다.
conveyable at 16 kilometres in the skies = carries a rocket at an altitude of 16 kilometres~

정답 mother ship

19 ○ 키워드인 From 16 kilometres to 100 kilometres' travelling을 일곱 번째 단락의 첫 번째 문장에서 찾을 수 있고 정답은 두 번째 문장에서 나온다.
lawyers definitely cannot agree whether it is a plane or a rocket. = lawyers cannot agree on whether it is a plane or a rocket.

정답 plane

20 ○ 키워드인 need to be revisited를 여덟 번째 단락의 첫 번째 문장에서 찾을 수 있다.
need to be revisited = may be discussed again

정답 UN's 1967 treaty

Questions 21-26

Complete each sentence with the correct ending **A-I** below.

Write the correct letter **A-I** in boxes **21-26** on your answer sheet.

A assisted some minimum safety standards may prevent that.
B emphasised a civilian space flight must not be under a severe regulation for technical advancement.
C hardly need a reminder of the danger with when considering past experiences.
D will protect a commercial space flight.
E try to develop a module of safety regulation applied to civilian space flight.
F made up for an ejector seat for tourist and the crew in case of a craft emergency in the skies.
G indicated main safety problems were with passengers' proximity to the power engine.
H believed that scuba-diving should be applied to civilian space flight.
I kept costs stratospheric.

A ~는 몇 가지 최소한의 안전기준이 그것을 예방할 수 있다고 주장했다.
B ~는 민간 우주비행이 기술 발전을 위해 심한 규정 하에 둘 필요는 없다고 강조했다.
C ~는 지난 경험을 통해서 운영의 위험에 대해 상기할 필요가 거의 없었다.
D ~는 상업적인 우주항공을 보호할 것이다.
E ~는 민간 우주비행에 적용되는 안전규정을 만들려고 한다.
F ~는 하늘에서 항공 긴급상황 시 많은 승무원과 관광객을 위한 탈출의자를 만들었다.
G ~는 파워엔진 근처에 있는 승객의 중요한 안전문제를 지적했다.
H ~는 스쿠버다이빙은 민간 우주항공에 적용되어야 한다고 믿었다.
I ~는 상한가로 올라갔다.

166

21 Civilian space flight companies [키워드] 민간 우주비행회사

◎ 키워드를 아홉 번째 단락의 첫 번째 문장에서 찾을 수 있다.
hardly need a reminder of the danger with operating through experience last = are very aware of the risks in this field as they have already had the experience of dealing with a tragedy.

정답 **C**

22 Laurent Gathier [키워드] 로랑 가티에

◎ 키워드를 열 번째 단락의 두 번째 문장에서 찾을 수 있다.
indicated main safety problems with passengers' proximity to the power engine = ~other critical safety factors are with depressurization risks, passengers close to the engine~

정답 **G**

23 VSH devised for a safety [키워드] 안전을 위해 고안된 VSH

◎ 키워드를 열한 번째 단락의 두 번째 문장에서 찾을 수 있다.
made up for an escaped seat for a member of a tourist and crew in case of a craft emergency in the skies = ~equip an ejector seat for all tourist and staff~

정답 **F**

24 AST chief George Nield [키워드] AST의장 조지 니일드

◎ 키워드를 열두 번째 단락의 두 번째 문장에서 찾을 수 있다.
emphasised a civilian space flight must not be under a severe regulation for technical advancement = ~the civilian space flight regulation must not "stifle" the developing technologies with inconvenient rules~
*stifle ~를 억누르다/억제하다

정답 **B**

25 Insurance costs [키워드] 보험료

◎ 키워드를 열세 번째 단락의 세 번째 문장에서 찾을 수 있다.
kept fares stratospheric = will be very high

정답 **I**

26 Critics [키워드] 비평가들

◎ 키워드를 열세 번째 단락의 네 번째 문장에서 찾을 수 있다.
try to develop a module of safety regulation applied to civilian space flight = ~developing safety standards~

정답 **E**

ACADEMIC READING

READING PASSAGE 3

You should spend about 20 minutes on Questions 27-40 which are based on Reading Passage 3 below.

Doctor's Rights and Drinks

1 New Yorker, [27, 34] John Davin started his campaign for election to Congress on 26th of September 1922. Actually, he was not a politician, but a doctor who practiced in a local city for 40 years at the top of his profession. Davin and other doctors with the same opinions were faced with the task of arguing their cases in front of the people. Also, they made a new political party, [28] the Medical Rights League, and decided that Davin should run as a candidate for the coming election. What did they want? Beer, or more precisely, a doctor who had the right to prescribe it.

2 The Congress had legislated the law prohibiting the sale of alcohol in January 1920. The aim was to transform a nation of drinkers and gamblers into one of hard-working, law-abiding, teetotal citizens. It was now illegal to sell or buy a drink that included [29] more than 0.5 per cent alcohol "for beverage purposes." Only Medical alcohol was allowed, but the conditions were so strict. Doctors could prescribe "liquor" when there was a "need to afford relief from a known ailment." Patients could not have more than a pint of liquor "within 10 days at any time." Doctors who needed to prescribe alcohol were approved for a permit. But the current law said nothing about beer, a traditional alcohol for ailments from anaemia to anthrax. So, could they prescribe beer or not?

3 As doctors were requesting permission to prescribe beer, someone had to make a decision. That person was Attorney General Mitchell Palmer, a staunch supporter of Prohibition. To the delight of doctors and dismay of prohibitionists, he urged "it was not the purpose of Congress to prohibit the use liquor for non-beverage usages." The Congress accepted medicinal alcohol for non beverage usages. It was for "beer and other malt liquors."

4 The Prohibitionists were very enraged. They had suspicions that doctors were in league with the brewers and that their intentions were more to disrupt Prohibition than for medicinal purposes. Although brandy and whisky might have some medicinal advantages, in their view, beer was not needed [31] at pharmacies. Congressman Andrew Volstead, who drafted the National Prohibition Act, criticized the decision saying "It is not a worthy argument that beer is medicine," "Everything in beer except the alcohol is similar to the beers that can be bought without any prescription." He immediately set up a supplementary bill that would further restrict medicinal alcohol and ban "medical beer" altogether.

5 Now, it was the doctors' turn out to be infuriated. How dare politicians presume to tell doctors what sort of things they could prescribe or how much. The merits of medicinal alcohol were suddenly a topic of national debate. For a couple of decades, doctors had been divided on the issue. Many insisted it was a treatment for all manners of disease. Others removed a worthless remedy left from the past. [32, 35]The American Medical Association (AMA), in 1971, denied the medicinal usage of alcohol, "Its value in therapeutics as a tonic, stimulant or food has no scientific basis."

6 However, as Prohibition hit home, [36]doctors' enthusiasm for alcohol improved. Articles admiring beer, wine and whisky spread among medical journals. One doctor suggested champagne worked wonders in cases of scarlet fever. Beer was [37]warranted to treat sleeplessness. One of the US's top doctors even insisted that when [33, 38]children with diphtheria developed secondary infections, alcohol could save them.

7 According to *JAMA*, the report said, [39]"Impressive particularly was the sincerity of the belief of a lot of physicians in the therapeutic effect of whisky within a limited number of diseases." "But equally impressive was the expressed belief of a limited number of physicians of necessity within a lot of disease." The contents ran from anaemia to uraemia, including influenza and indigestion, cancer, colds and heart disease.

---

prescribe v. ~을 규정하다   teetotal a. 완전한   anthrax n. (가축/사람의) 탄저열
staunch a. 견고한   dismay v. ~을 당황하게 하다   malt n. 맥아   enraged a. 분개한
brewers n. 양조업자들   supplementary a. 보충의   infuriated a. 격분한
therapeutics n. 치료학   stimulant n. 흥분제   diphtheria n. (병리)디프테리아
sincerity n. 성실

Questions 27-33

Do the following statements reflect the claims of the writer in Reading Passage 3?

*In boxes **27-33** on your answer sheet write*

YES   *if the statement reflects the opinion of the writer*
NO   *if the statement contradicts the opinion of the writer*
NOT GIVEN *if it is impossible to say what the writer thinks about this*

27 John Davin has been ready for election to Congress.

○ 문제의 키워드인 John Davin을 첫 번째 단락의 첫 번째 문장에서 찾을 수 있다. 그러나 John Davin이 의회선거를 위해서 그 이전부터 계속 준비해 왔다는 것을 문장으로는 알 수 없다. 다만, John Davin started his campaign for election to Congress~를 통해 '의회선거를 위해서 선거운동을 시작했다' 것만을 알 수 있다. 그러므로 답은 NOT GIVEN이다.

John Davin은 의회선거를 준비해 왔다.

정답 NOT GIVEN

ACADEMIC READING

28 The Medical Rights League was made to support the right to prescribe beer by Davin and like minded doctors.

　◯ 문제의 키워드인 Medical Rights League를 첫 번째 단락의 네 번째 문장에서 찾을 수 있다. Medical Rights League는 Davin과 동종의 의사들이 국민 앞에서 그들 입장(의사가 맥주를 처방할 수 있는 권리를 가진다는 것)을 밝히기 위해 만들어졌다.

의료권리동맹은 Davin과 같은 생각을 가진 의사들이 맥주를 처방할 수 있는 권리를 후원하기 위해서 만들어졌다.

정답 YES

29 It was illegal to sell or buy beverage that contained over 0.5 per cent alcohol.

　◯ 문제의 키워드인 over 0.5 per cent alcohol을 두 번째 단락의 세 번째 문장에서 찾을 수 있다. 문제상의 알코올 지수에 대한 기준이 동의어로 나와 있다. 즉, over(과도한)와 more than(~이상)로 서로 같은 의미이다.

알코올 성분이 0.5% 이상 함유되어 있는 음료를 팔거나 사는 것은 불법이었다.

정답 YES

30 Congress only granted beer as a medical alcohol.

　◯ 의회에서 beer와 other malt liquors의 두 가지 종류에 대해서 허가했지, beer만을 허가하지는 않았다.
*사회현상에 대한 문제에서 '절대적 의미'를 갖는 only는 NO/FALSE가 정답인 경우가 많다.

의회에서는 맥주만을 의료용 알코올로 허가했다.

정답 NO

31 As beer might have some benefit for medicinal use, it was in a pharmacy.

　◯ 문제의 키워드인 in a pharmacy를 네 번째 단락의 세 번째 문장에서 찾는다. 금지 법안자들은 브랜디와 위스키는 의학적으로 몇 가지 효과가 있지만 맥주는 약국에 있을 필요가 없다고 주장했다.

맥주가 의학용으로써 몇몇 이점을 가질지도 모르기 때문에, 맥주가 약국에 있었다.

정답 NO

32 The American Medical Association (AMA) has funded scientific basis.

　◯ 문제의 키워드인 AMA를 다섯 번째 단락의 여섯 번째 문장에서 찾을 수 있지만, 미국의학협회(AMA)에서 과학적 기반에 투자를 해오고 있다는 의미를 본문에선 알 수 없다.

미국의학학회에서는 과학적 기초에 자금을 투자해 왔다.

정답 NOT GIVEN

33 If children have diphtheria, alcohol may cure them.

　◯ 문제의 키워드인 children have diphtheria를 여섯 번째 단락의 마지막 문장에서 찾는다. 디프테리아에 걸린 아이는 맥주로 치유할 수 있다는 의미가 본문과 같다.

만약 아이들이 디프테리아 질환을 갖고 있다면, 알코올은 아이들을 치료할 수도 있다.

정답 YES

Questions 34-35

*Choose the appropriate letters **A-D** and write them in boxes **34-35** on your answer sheet.*

34 In 1922 the reason John Davin begun a campaign
   A was against beer and other malt liquors.
   B was to assert a doctor's right to prescribe beer.
   C was for the Medical Right League's duty.
   D was to oppose strong minded politicians.

1922년에 John Davin이 캠페인을 시작한 이유는 ~ 였다.
A 맥주와 다른 맥아주를 반대하기 위해서
B 맥주 처방을 위한 의사의 권리를 주장하기 위해서
C 의료권리동맹의 임무를 위해서
D 강력한 권리를 갖고 있는 정치인들에게 대항하기 위해서

◎ 문제의 키워드인 1922와 John Davin을 첫 번째 단락의 첫 번째 문장에서 찾을 수 있다. John Davin는 맥주 처방에 대한 의사의 권리를 행사하기 위해서 캠페인을 시작했다. 첫 번째 단락 마지막 문장에서 정답을 찾을 수 있다.

정답 B

35 In 1971, the American Medical Association (AMA)
   A decided beer is a worthless remedy.
   B declared beer has an effect as tonic.
   C decided beer won't be an evidence of medical basis.
   D assisted a patient with cancer.

1971년에 미국의학학회에서는 ~
A 맥주가 효과 없는 치료법이라고 결정했다.
B 맥주는 강장제로 효과가 있다고 단언했다.
C 맥주는 의학적 가치 근거가 없다고 결정했다.
D 암환자를 후원했다.

◎ 문제의 키워드인 1971과 AMA을 다섯 번째 단락의 여섯 번째 문장에서 찾을 수 있다. 미국의학학회(AMA)에서는 알코올 치료는 강장제(tonic), 흥분제(stimulant)처럼 과학적 근거가 없다는 입장을 취하고 있다.

정답 C

Questions 36-39

*Complete the summary below. Choose **ONE** word from Reading Passage 3 for each answer.*

*Write your answers in boxes **36-39** on your answer sheet.*

Once prohibition affected homes, doctors stimulated interests in **36** alcohol. Besides, doctors affirmed the effects of alcohol, beer was guaranteed to cure **37** sleeplessness. When children with **38** diphtheria transferred dual-infections, alcohol could save them. According to **39** JAMA, most physicians believed the effects of therapeutic usage of whisky in the treatment of a limited number of diseases to be remarkably impressive.

금지법안이 가정에 영향에 미치게 되자, 의사들은 36. 알코올에 대해 관심을 가졌다. 게다가, 어떤 한 의사는 알코올의 효능을 확증했고, 맥주는 37. 불면증을 치료하는데 보장되었다. 아이들이 38. 디프테리아에 2차로 감염되었을 때, 알코올은 아이들을 구할 수 있다. 39. JAMA에 따르면, 아주 인상적인 것은 대부분의 내과 의사는 몇몇 질병에서 위스키의 의약적인 효과를 믿고 있다.

ACADEMIC READING

36 ⊙ 키워드인 doctors와 interests in을 여섯 번째 단락의 첫 번째 문장에서 찾는다.
interest in = enthusiam for ~에 흥미가 있는

정답 alcohol

37 ⊙ 키워드인 guaranteed to cure를 여섯 번째 단락의 네 번째 문장에서 찾을 수 있다.
guaranteed to cure = warranted to treat ~을 치료하는데 보장하다

정답 sleeplessness

38 ⊙ 키워드인 children with와 transferred dual-infections를 여섯 번째 단락의 다섯 번째 문장에서 찾을 수 있다.
children with ~ transferred dual-infections = children with diphtheria developed secondary infections 2차 감염되어 발병된 된 아이는

정답 diphtheria

39 ⊙ 키워드인 According to와 remarkably impressive를 일곱 번째 단락의 첫 번째 문장에서 찾을 수 있다.
remarkablely impressive = impressive particulary 특히 인상적인 것은

정답 JAMA

Questions 40

*Choose the appropriate letter **A-D** and write it in box **40** on your answer sheet.*

40 This text is taken from
  A a medical text book for a beginner.
  B a critical research of the scientific basis of a beverage.
  C a magazine article about alcohol issues.
  D a document against government prohibition.

이 글은 ~에서 발췌되었다.
  A 초보자를 위한 의학 교과서
  B 음료의 과학적 기초에 관한 비판적인 연구
  C 과거 알코올 논쟁에 대한 잡지기사
  D 정부의 금지법에 대한 항의 서안

⊙ 출처에 대한 문제이다. 출처에 대한 내용은 첫 번째 단락에서 찾을 수 있다. 보통 주제와 글의 분위기는 두괄식 문형으로 서론에서 쉽게 찾을 수 있다. 맥주에 대한 의사(약)처방권리의 1920년대 시대의 상황과 역사를 진술하는 잡지기사라는 것을 알 수 있다.

정답 C

Academic Reading

Actual Test 3

Answer Sheet

1	B	11	D	21	B	31	chocolate
2	C	12	C	22	C	32	machines
3	F	13	A	23	A	33	Swiss
4	Monte Alto	14	FALSE	24	D	34	German
5	Dipteryx	15	NOT GIVEN	25	A	35	interdisciplinary
6	Chacra	16	NOT GIVEN	26	bacterial pneumonia / heart disease / stroke	36	TRUE
7	B	17	TRUE	27	(about) 70 (%)	37	NOT GIVEN
8	E	18	TRUE	28	A	38	TRUE
9	A	19	FALSE	29	C	39	FALSE
10	F	20	FALSE	30	B	40	FALSE

ACADEMIC READING

READING PASSAGE 1

You should spend about 20 minutes on Questions 1-13 which are based on Reading Passage 1 below.

Amazon Rainforest of Peru

A A cement maker proudly speaks about the brief history of the road: [9]this main road was part of an incentive programme supported by the US's fund to help local people to find economic alternatives to harvesting coca, from which cocaine is produced. Four years later, the road is a global vacuum from which timber from the Peruvian rainforest is taken to China. [13]Some wood will be polished into luxury parquet flooring for high quality homes in Shanghai and Beijing. More wood will be used in Chinese factories and made into patio furniture, decking or flooring in North America and Europe.

B Going down the street, muddy tracks show [4]the old forest known as *Monte Alto*, where local farmers have been using the sunlight that comes through the openings in the forest canopy to grow a variety of food crops, like cassava, sweet potatoes, bananas and plantains. [7]They are also growing a few cash crops like coffee and cacao. This also helps to fund essential services like schools and hospitals.

C As a tree ecologist and student studying about the timber trade, I am here researching a kind of *Dipteryx* known in the region as shihuahuaco [5](its international trade name is cumaru) and to research its movements from the Amazonian forest the Chinese factories. Although shihuahuaco is not particularly high profile, [3]ecologists call it a "keystone" tree, as [12]its large seeds are an essential food source for forest herbivores in the dry season, whilst its hollow rooms are utilized as [1]the nesting place of parrots and macaws. It is so hard that local residents use big shihuahuco trees as [2]a shelter when strong storms bring trees down.

D My trip began in the company of a great group of people who were logging from the sawmill town in Pucallpa. [11]A two day trip into the forest guided us beyond the road's end to a community called Esperanza, or "Hope." In the middle of a flourishing [6]Chacra – a farm typical of the area – there was a temporary logging camp. As well as their productive farming, the *chacra* had a family business called the Medinas which offered a refuge for birds, wild piglets and primates saved from logged areas. From there, I walked through the *Monte Alto* with my logging friends for 10 days, which they were soon to cut.

E The adult trees were colossal, reaching [8]heights of up to 50 metres and a width of 1.3 metres, towering above their huge buttresses which spread up to 5 metres around the main trunk. There were one or two such trees per hectare and most of them were put forward for the long voyage across the Pacific. Whilst we found approximately 250 seedlings and saplings, there were only two young trees which had reached the canopy and therefore could be expected to harvest into adults.

F I don't want to be sentimental about trees. On one of my last nights in the rainforest when speaking to the company's chief woodsman Pedro, I felt reassured about the situation. Pedro said, "At least there are the Medias *arbolitos*." "What, little trees?" I asked. The next day Pedro showed me the trees he was referring to. We walked up the hill and Pedro stopped in front of a very healthy looking young shihuahuaco growing in the sun. "When do you expect to harvest them?" I had to ask. I hope he wasn't planning to profile them in a few years.

---

muddy a. 진흙의   cassava n. 카사바   herbivores n. 초식동물들   sawmill n. 제재소
colossal a. 거대한   buttresses n. 버팀벽들   saplings n. 어린나무   sentimental a. 감정적인

곧 짤릴 운명에 있었다.

E 다 자란 나무들은 거대해서, 나무 몸통 주위의 5m까지 펼쳐진 거대한 버팀목을 넘어 길이 50m, 두께 1.3m로 성장했다. 이런 나무가 1헥타르당 1~2그루가 있었으며, 대부분은 태평양을 가로질러 긴 항해를 위해 운반되었다. 비록 우리는 250그루의 묘목과 어린 나무를 볼 수 있었으나, 단지 지붕모양으로 우거진 두 그루의 유목만이 있었고 성목으로 성장해서 벌목할 수 있는 기대를 가질 수 있었다.

F 나는 이 나무들에 대해 감상적이고 싶지 않다. 열대우림에서의 어느 마지막 밤, 벌목회사 사장인 Pedro와 대화할 때 나는 그 상황에 대해 안도감을 느꼈다. Pedro는 "적어도 Media의 arbolitos가 있어요."라고 말했다. 나는 "어떤, 어린 나무인가요?"라고 물었다. 다음 날, Pedro는 그가 말했던 나무를 나에게 보여줬다. 우리는 언덕에 올랐고 Pedro는 햇볕 속에서 자라고 있는 무척 건강하게 보이는 어린 shihuahuaco 앞에 멈췄다. "언제쯤 나무를 벨 예정인가요?" 나는 그가 몇 년 이내에 그것을 점찍어 두지 않기를 바랐다.

Questions 1-3

Choose **THREE** letters **A-F**.

Write your answers in boxes **1-3** on your answer sheet.

The list below gives some features of shihuahuaco.

Which **THREE** ways are mentioned by the writer of the text?

A   a field to grow varied sustainable food crops
B   a habitat for parrots and macaws
C   a shelter for natives against a natural disaster
D   a village of palm-thatch houses
E   a road to help local people for finding economic alternatives
F   an ecologist named it a keystone tree

아래 항목은 shihuahuaco의 몇 가지 특징을 보여 준다.

글의 저자가 언급한 shihuahuaco의 3가지(특징)는 무엇인가?

A 다양한 지속 가능한 농작물 재배를 위한 들판
B 앵무새와 마코앵무새의 서식지
C 자연 재앙을 피하는 원주민들의 은신처
D 야자수 집들이 있는 마을
E 경제적 대체산업을 찾기 위한 지역인들을 돕는 도로
F 생태학자가 shihuahuaco를 핵심나무라고 불렀다.

1 ➔ C단락의 두 번째 문장에서 shihuahuaco의 구멍이 '앵무새와 마코앵무새의 서식지'로 사용됨을 알 수 있다.
habitat = the nesting place

정답 B

2 ➔ C단락의 마지막 문장에서 '지역 주민들은 거센 폭풍으로 나무들이 쓰러질 때 거대한 shihuahuaco나무를 은신처로 사용한다'고 했다.

정답 C

ACADEMIC READING

3 ○ C단락의 두 번째 문장에서 '생태학자들은 shihuahuaco를 핵심나무라고 칭한다'고 언급하고 있다.

정답 F

Questions 4-6

Answer the questions below using **NO MORE THAN TWO WORDS** from the passage for each answer.

Write your answers in boxes **4-6** on your answer sheet.

4 What is the name given to the old forest of the Amazon?

아마존의 오래된 삼림을 무엇이라고 부르는가?

○ 키워드 the old forest를 B단락의 첫 번째 문장에서 찾을 수 있다.

정답 Monte Alto

5 What is called the international trade name of the cumaru?

국제무역 명칭이 cumaru라 불리는 것은 무엇인가?

○ 키워드 the international trade name of the cumaru를 C단락의 첫 번째 문장에서 찾을 수 있다. C단락의 첫 번째 문장에서 글을 쓴 주인공은 Dipteryx종을 공부하고 있으며, 그 나무가 그 지역에서는 shihuahuaco로 불리며 국제무역 명칭은 cumaru라고 설명하고 있다.

정답 Dipteryx

6 What is the typical farm land area that is used as a temporary logging camp?

임시 벌목캠프가 있는 전형적인 농장지대는 무엇인가?

○ 키워드 typical farm land area와 a temporary logging camp을 D단락의 세 번째 문장에서 찾을 수 있다. '지역의 전형적인 농업산림을 Chacra'라고 설명하고 있다.

정답 Chacra

Questions 7-13

Reading Passage 1 has six paragraphs labeled **A-F**.

Which paragraph contains the following information?

Write the correct letter **A-F** in boxes **7-13** on your answer sheet.

NB You may use any letter more than once.

7 the self-rescue measures there to cover essentials

필수품을 조달하기 위한 그곳의 자구책

○ B단락의 두 번째, 세 번째 문장, '지역 농부들은 또한 환금작물로 커피와 카카오와 같은 농작물을 재배해서, 교육과 의료서비스와 같은 필수적인 문제를 해결하고 있다.'에서 답을 찾는다.

정답 B

8 the dimensions of timber

목재의 크기

○ E단락의 첫 번째 문장에서 '길이 50m, 두께 1.3m'로 나무의 크기를 설명하고 있다.

정답 E

176

9 the road sponsored by the United State's fund to aid relief work schemes

구호사업 계획을 돕기 위한 미국의 재정적 후원으로 만들어진 도로

○ A단락의 첫 번째 문장에서 '이 도로는 코카인이 생산되는 식물인 코카를 재배하여 경제적 대체물을 찾는 지역 사람들을 돕고자 미국의 자본이 투입된 것이다.'라고 설명했다.

정답 A

10 an anecdote for the writer

저자의 개인적 일화

○ F단락에서 저자는 Pedro와의 대화를 통한 경험을 들려주고 있다.

정답 F

11 a short camping trip of the writer

저자의 단기 캠핑 여행

○ D단락의 두 번째 문장에서 이틀 동안의 숲 속 여행에 대해 서술하고 있다.

정답 D

12 practical sides of shihuahuaco

shihuahuaco의 실용적인 측면

○ C단락의 두 번째와 세 번째 문장에서 Shihuahuaco의 식량, 은신처로서의 역할에 대해 언급했다.

정답 C

13 the export of timber

목재 수출

○ A단락의 세 번째와 네 번째 문장에서 '목재들이 중국으로 수출되어 상하이와 베이징에서 고가의 저택의 사치스런 마루로 빛날 것이다. 또한 북미와 유럽에 파티오 가구로 장식되거나 바닥재로 사용될 것이다.'라고 설명하고 있다.

정답 A

READING PASSAGE 2

You should spend about 20 minutes on Questions 14-27 which are based on Reading Passage 2 below.

A shot for public health

1 Millions of elderly people in the US, Europe and elsewhere get injections for their annual flu shots this month. It is widely seen as a largely effective public health programme which halves the risk of dying over the winter people aged 65 or over. Actually for every 200 vaccinations one life is saved. However, there is overwhelming evidence that this claim is too good to be true, and we must look for additional ways to prevent the flu.

2 [23]According to the US Centres for Disease Control and Prevention (CDC), flu kills approximately 36,000 people [14]every winter in the US. Of them about 30,000 are aged 65 or over. [25]This is about 5% of the 650,000 winter deaths per year in this age group. [15, 26]Flu itself is never recorded as a cause of death: instead, it is leads to the elderly dying from other causes, like bacterial pneumonia, heart disease or a stroke.

3 [16]Most rich countries are concentrated on cutting this figure by vaccinating those who are at the highest risk, but how well does this actually work? The best way to carry out research is trials that compare those who are vaccinated against those who aren't, with applicants allocated randomly from each group. But as [17]flu shots are known to be an advantage, it would be unethical to deny some people vaccinations. Researchers compare those who choose to be vaccinated with those who don't. Then, they use the statistical methods of control to observe the differences between the two groups. One large [18]meta-analysis of such studies concluded that those who get flu shots are half as likely to die as their unvaccinated peers over the winter. Several other studies have come to a similar conclusion.

4 It sounds possibly a bit too good to be true. In 2005, [19]Lone Simonsen, a researcher at George Washington University and her colleagues, showed that the number of flu deaths among the elderly in the US has remained at about 5% of deaths in the group during winter. [21, 27]Vaccination coverage has skyrocketed from about 15% in 1980 to about 70% today. So how could flu vaccination be preventing half of the deaths in winter, when the flu accounted for only 5% of those deaths back in 1980, when most people were not vaccinated?

178

5   Also, in 2006 epidemiologist Lisa Jackson and her colleagues at the Centre for Health Statistics in Seattle, analysed a Seattle medical database [22]using the same statistical methods as the previous studies. [20]It showed that the maximum benefit of having the flu shot happened in the months before the season of flu even started.

6   Jackson insisted that the studies failed to give an account of ill and weak elderly people who had died but were less inclined to be vaccinated, making vaccination seem more valuable than it actually is.

7   But the debate was not over. Last year Kristin Nichol and her colleagues from the University of Minnesota published a dissertation using slightly different statistical methods and included records from tens of thousands of patients in three cities over 10 years. [24]It came to the same incredible conclusion that vaccination was preventing about half of all deaths in winter. Researchers like Simonsen, Jackson and myself estimated Nichol's methods. Also, we believe this finding is subject to the sort of bias already identified by Jackson.

8   Last week Simonsen and Nichol discussed the issue at the Interscience Conference on Antimicrobial Agents and Chemotherapy in Washington DC. Nichol accepted that although there might still be some bias in her latest survey, flu deaths are estimated indirectly, especially counting extra deaths beyond those expected in winter. Researchers may have underestimated the number of people who have died as a result of the flu.

9   In conclusion, we need to improve our statistical methods for measuring the effectiveness of the flu vaccine. This issue has much wider implications as similar methods are used to analyse other areas in which randomized trials are not possible. For example, the effectiveness of cholesterol-lowering statins for pneumonia patients is also analysed in this way.

---

injections n. 주사액들   overwhelming a. 압도적인   allocated a. 할당된   skyrocket v. 급상승하다   hindering a. 방해하는   dissertation n. 논문   bias n. 편견   implication n. 영향

ACADEMIC READING

Questions 14-20

Do the following statements reflect the claims of the writer in Reading Passage 2?

*In boxes **14-20** on your answer sheet write*

- **TRUE** — if the statement agrees with the information
- **FALSE** — if the statement contradicts the information
- **NOT GIVEN** — if there is no information on this

14 About 3,600 people are dying from the flu every winter in the US.

○ 키워드는 every winter in the U.S이며, 두 번째 단락의 첫 번째 문장에서 찾을 수 있다. 본문은 36,000명으로 나와 있으므로 정답은 FALSE다.

미국에서 약 3,600명이 매년 겨울 독감으로 목숨을 잃는다.

정답 FALSE

15 Although flu itself is seldom a disease that causes death, it can make the people age quicker.

○ 문제의 키워드는 flu itself is seldom a disease that causes death이며, 두 번째 단락의 네 번째 문장에서 찾을 수 있다. 그러나 노화를 촉진할 수 있다는 내용을 본문에선 찾을 수 없다.

독감 자체가 좀처럼 사망에 이르게 하는 병은 아니지만, 노화를 빠르게 촉진할 수 있다.

정답 NOT GIVEN

16 Lots of rich countries have successfully carried out a high quality vaccination programme.

○ 문제의 키워드는 Lots of rich countries이며, 세 번째 단락의 첫 번째 문장에서 찾을 수 있으나, 성공적으로 최고의 양질의 백신을 생산해 왔다는 의미는 본문에서 알 수 없다. 단지, 높은 위험이 있는 이들에게 접종하는 것이 목적이라고만 나와 있다.

많은 선진국에서 성공적으로 양질의 백신 프로그램을 실행해 왔다.

정답 NOT GIVEN

17 Flu shots should be useful for prescription but it may be immoral to hold back vaccination.

○ 키워드는 Flu shots should be useful이며, 세 번째 단락의 세 번째 문장에서 찾을 수 있다.
Flu shots should be useful = flu shots are known to be an advantage
immoral = unethical : 비윤리적

독감주사는 처방에 효과적이므로 백신을 제한하는 것은 비윤리적일 수도 있다.

정답 TRUE

18 From meta-analysis those who get the flu shot are fifty per cent less likely to die than their unvaccinated peers.

○ 키워드는 From meta-analysis이며, 세 번째 단락의 여섯 번째 문장에서 찾을 수 있다.
are fifty per cent less likely to die = are half as likely to die

메타분석으로부터 독감주사를 맞은 사람들은 예방접종을 받지 않은 집단보다 50% 정도 생명을 잃을 것 같다.

정답 TRUE

19 **Lone Simonsen** indicated how many people died from flu deaths among the young.

○ 키워드는 Lone Simonsen이며, 네 번째 단락의 두 번째 문장에서 찾을 수 있다. 본문에서는 Lone Simonsen ~ showed that the number of flu deaths among the elderly~로 대상이 노인층으로 나와 있어 젊은 층을 조사했다는 문제의 내용과 다르다.

Lone Simonen은 젊은층에서 독감으로 얼마나 많은 사람들이 사망하는지 조사했다.

정답 FALSE

20 The time for the highest level of efficacy of the flu shot turned out within the weeks previous to the flu season.

○ 키워드는 The time for the highest level of efficacy of the flu shot turned out이며, 다섯 번째 단락의 두 번째 문장에서 찾을 수 있다. 본문에서는 몇 달 전 (in the months before~)에 독감주사를 맞는 것이 좋다고 나와 있으므로 문제와 기간이 다르다.

독감주사를 맞는 최적의 시기는 독감 계절이 시작되기 몇 주 전이다.

정답 FALSE

Questions 21-25

Classify the following statements as being

A US Centre for Disease Control and Prevention (CDC)
B George Washington University in Washington DC
C Centre for Health Statistics in Seattle
D University of Minnesota in Minneapolis

미국질병관리예방센터
워싱턴 DC의 조지워싱턴대학
시애틀의 건강통계센터
미니애폴리스의 미네소타대학

*Write the appropriate letters **A-D** in boxes **21-25** on your answer sheet.*

NB You may use any letter more than once.

21 Vaccination extent has maximised. [키워드]

○ 키워드를 네 번째 단락의 세 번째 문장에서 찾는다.
Vaccination extent has maximised. = vaccination coverage has skyrocketed

예방접종의 범위가 넓어졌다.

정답 B

22 Seattle medical database was analysed using a statistical method. [키워드]

○ 키워드를 다섯 번째 단락의 첫 번째 문장에서 찾는다.

Seattle건강통계는 통계학적 방법을 사용하여 분석되었다.

정답 C

23 Around 83 per cent of flu related fatalities are in the over 65 age group. [키워드]

○ 키워드를 두 번째 단락의 첫 번째와 두 번째 문장에서 찾는다.
About 83 per cent of lethality with flu is over 65. = ~ flu kills approximately 36,000 people every winter in the US. Of them about 30,000 are aged 65 or over. (30,000/36,000×100 = 83%)

독감 관련 사망자의 83%는 65세 이상의 노인층이다.

정답 A

ACADEMIC READING

24 Vaccination was able to prevent about fifty per cent of all winter deaths. [키워드]

○ 키워드를 일곱 번째 단락의 세 번째 문장에서 찾는다.
Vaccination was able to prevent about fifty per cent of all winter deaths.
= ~ vaccination was preventing about half of all deaths in winter.

예방접종은 겨울에 목숨을 잃은 사람들 중에 약 절반 가량을 예방할 수 있었다.

정답 D

25 The flu death account for five per cent of annual winter deaths in the age group of 65 or over. [키워드]

○ 키워드를 두 번째 단락의 세 번째 문장에서 찾는다.

독감으로 인한 사망은 65세 이상 연령층에서 겨울철 사망의 5%를 차지한다.

정답 A

Questions 26-27

Complete the sentences below with taken from Reading Passage 2.

Use **ONE OR TWO WORD** for each answer.

Write your answers in boxes **26** and **27** on your answer sheet.

26 What is ONE of several diseases recorded as a cause of death if the elderly have the flu?

○ 키워드 diseases와 a cause of death if the elderly with flu을 두 번째 단락의 마지막 문장에서 찾을 수 있다.

노인이 독감에 걸리면 사망하게 되는 여러 질환 중의 하나는 무엇인가?

정답 bacterial pneumonia / heart disease / stroke 중 택 1

27 What percentage of the vaccination coverage is recently maximised by the research of Lone Simonsen?

○ 키워드 vaccination coverage와 maximised by research of Lone Simonsen을 네 번째 단락의 두 번째와 세 번째 문장에서 찾을 수 있다.
~ Lone Simonsen ~ Vaccination coverage has skyrocketed ~ to about 70% today.

Lone Simonsen 조사에 의하면 예방접종 범위는 몇 퍼센트까지 늘어났는가?

정답 (about) 70 per cent(%)

READING PASSAGE 3

You should spend about 20 minutes on Questions 28-40 which are based on Reading Passage 3 below.

High-tech Switzerland

1 For a nation with a [36]history of making sophisticated clocks, it is not surprising that Switzerland is the best place for precision and high-tech research. The country is so proud of two Federal Institutes of Technology, like the CERN of particle physics laboratory and a core of IBM research facilities. Also, there are two big pharmaceutical companies called Roche and Novartis. Also, who can forget Switzerland's [37]world famous chocolate industry?

2 British citizens are able to work in Switzerland visa-free and the country offers salaries of up to £72,000 per year for highly-skilled experienced researchers with the option of skiing in the lunch break. It is easy to know why Switzerland appeals to so many. In what fields are these great opportunities available?

Computing Clout

3 IBM is one of the global companies that has established a research hub in Switzerland. [28, 38]The Ruschlikon lab located in the south of Zurich draws researchers from around the world, with 80% of them coming from abroad.

4 [39]This lab is a leader in digital storage technology and semiconductor and optical electronics for on-line networks. [29]Projects to build a top-class nanotechnology research centre in the place are on-going and will be completed by 2014.

5 Irene Holenweger Koeb, a manager in IBM human resources, says that the lab is looking for a wide range of disciplines including physics, chemistry and mathematics. Also, it is a thriving bioscience group working on the application of nanotechnology to life sciences and other areas. Most of the positions only accept applicants with a Ph.D. but the lab also hires approximately 100 applicants with Bachelors and Masters degrees each year.

6 Paul Hurley, a researcher in IBM's systems software group, is enjoying the flexible atmosphere of his work. There is a relaxed atmosphere in the office at IBM and meetings often take place over lunch or a coffee break.

7 As a lot of employees are not Swiss nationals, the company offers a lot of support and also has a policy of paying relocation

ACADEMIC READING

expenses. Koeb says that it is important to gradually ease employees into their new workplace.

8 German lessons which are paid for by IBM, are offered to new employees working in Zurich. The standard of German is different to the German spoken in Zurich. Whilst Hurley has attended the classes, he says it a little bit more practice is needed to notice the "Swiss-isms."

Raising the Chocolate Bar

9 [31]Switzerland is known for chocolate. Jose Rubio of Lindt's human resources department says "Our company has 44 nationalities and 18 languages."

10 Scientists are able to find jobs within quality management, research and development and in the factory working conditions. [32]The work of R&D is to help improve new recipes and products as well as designing and building new machines for making them. You are able to hone your skills in a well managed company and have the pleasant task of testing the products to make sure they meet the company's high standards.

11 Rubio says that [33]a foreign staff must speak at least one of the official Swiss languages. [34, 40]Most of the positions need a good level of German, as it is vital when working with Swiss coworkers in the production lines.

12 The ETH in German-speaking Zurich has a sister institution, which is the Federal Institute of Technology in French-speaking Lausanne (EPFL). With over 250 research groups and 10,000 students and faculties, [35]it is focused on interdisciplinary scientific research. The institute's technology transfer programmes ensure that practical tools and methods make it out of the lab and into industry.

---

precision n. 정확   pharmaceutical a. 제약의   thriving a. 번성하는   hone v. ~을 숫돌로 갈다   vital a. 중추적인   interdisciplinary a. 많은 학문 분야에 관계가 있는

용부담에 따른 정책도 역시 갖고 있다. 근무자들이 새로운 작업환경에 점차적으로 쉽게 만드는 것이 중요한 일이라고 Koeb는 말한다.

8 IBM에서 부담하는 독일어 수업은 Zurich(취리히)의 신입직원들에게 제공된다. 표준화된 독일어와 Zurich에서 사용되는 독일어는 다르다. Hurely가 그 수업을 듣긴 헜지만 그는 '스위스식'을 알아차리는 데는 다소 많은 연습을 요구한다고 말한다.

초콜릿 바의 성장

9 스위스는 초콜릿으로 유명하다. "우리 회사는 44개 국적과 18개 언어를 갖고 있다."고 Lindt 인사부장인 Jose Rubio는 말한다.

10 과학자들은 품질관리, 연구개발 그리고 공장의 작업환경 분야에서 일을 찾을 수 있다. R&D(연구개발)분야의 일은 새로운 요리법과 제품들뿐만 아니라 그것을 만들기 위해 새로운 기계를 설계하고 만드는 것을 향상시키도록 돕는다. 당신은 잘 관리된 회사에서 기술을 연마할 수 있으며 회사의 높은 기준에 따라갈 수 있는 제품을 테스트할 수 있는 즐거움을 갖는다.

11 외국인 직원은 적어도 스위스 공용어 가운데 하나 정도는 구사할 수 있어야 한다고 Rubio는 말한다. 대부분 직종에는 능숙한 독일어를 요구하며, 특히 생산라인에서 스위스 동료와 일을 할 때는 필수적이다.

12 독일어를 사용하는 취리히의 ETH는 자매연구기관이 있는데, 그곳은 프랑스어를 사용하는 Lausanne의 기술연방연구소(EPFL)이다. 250개가 넘는 연구 그룹과 10,000명의 학생과 교수단을 갖추었고, ETH연구소는 학제 간 과학연구에 초점이 맞춰져있다. 연구소의 기술이전프로그램은 효율적인 도구와 방법들이 연구실 밖으로 나와 산업에서 사용된다고 확신한다.

Questions 28-30

Choose the appropriate letters **A-D** and write them in boxes **28-30** on your answer sheet.

28 Ruschliko lab located in Zurich attracts
- **A** almost 80 per cent of research staff from overseas.
- **B** 80 per cent of research staff domestically.
- **C** at least 80 per cent of engineers from abroad.
- **D** 80 per cent of staff with a PhD from overseas.

○ 키워드 Ruschlikon lab located in Zurich는 세 번째 단락의 두 번째 문장에서 찾을 수 있다. 해외에서 온 연구원들이 80%에 이른다고 언급하고 있다.

Zurich의 Ruschliko 연구실은 ~을 끌어들인다.
- A 거의 80%의 해외 연구진들
- B 80%의 국내 연구진들
- C 최소 80%의 해외 기술자들
- D 80%의 해외 박사 연구원들

정답 A

29 The lab has a plan to complete in 2014
- **A** founding a top-class Ruschlikon lab.
- **B** making a world-famous chocolate industry.
- **C** founding the best nanotechnology research centre.
- **D** researching digital storage marketing.

○ 키워드 The lab has a plan to complete in 2014는 네 번째 단락의 두 번째 문장에 있다. 2014년에 나노기술연구센터가 완공될 예정이라고 나와 있다.

실험실은 2014년에 ~을 완성하는 계획을 갖고 있다.
- A 최고 수준의 Ruschlikon실험실을 설립하기
- B 세계적으로 명성 있는 초콜릿 산업을 만들기
- C 최고의 나노기술연구센터를 설립하기
- D 디지털 저장 시장을 연구하기

정답 C

30 According to information in the text, the main purpose of the writer is
- **A** to survey various high-tech research in Switzerland.
- **B** to introduce attractive research centres in Switzerland.
- **C** to recruit a variety of human resources in Switzerland.
- **D** to understand the world-famous chocolate in Switzerland.

○ 저자의 주된 목적을 찾는 문제로 주제와 관련된 사항은 두괄식이 원칙이므로 서론 부분에서 찾을 수 있다. 저자는 스위스 연구센터의 매력을 알리고 있다. 이와 관련된 문장은 1~2단락에서 찾는다.

글의 정보에 따르면, 저자의 주요 목적은 ~이다.
- A 스위스의 다양한 첨단기술 연구를 조사하기 위해서
- B 스위스의 매력적인 연구센터를 소개하기 위해서
- C 스위스의 다양한 인력자원을 모집하기 위해서
- D 스위스의 세계적 명성인 초콜릿을 이해하기 위해서

정답 B

ACADEMIC READING

Questions 31-35

Complete the summary below. Choose **NO MORE THAN TWO WORDS** from Reading Passage 3 for each answer.

Write your answers in boxes **31- 35** on your answer sheet.

Raising the chocolate bar

Switzerland famous for **31** chocolate, attracted scientists in quality management, research and development. Those working in R&D aid to improve new version of recipes, products and design and build on **32** machines. Foreign staff should fluently speak one of **33** Swiss official tongues in the least. Especially, a number of workplaces need to have an advanced level of **34** German. With over 250 research groups and 10,000 students and faculty, it emphasises **35** interdisciplinary scientific research.

초콜릿 바의 성장

31. 초콜릿으로 유명한 스위스는 품질관리, 연구개발 분야에서 과학자들을 끌어들였다. 연구개발분야에서 일하는 사람들은 새로운 요리법과 제품들을 개선하는 것을 돕고 32. 기계들을 설계하고 개발한다. 외국인 직원들은 적어도 33. 스위스 공용어 가운데 한 개는 유창하게 말할 수 있어야 한다. 특히, 대부분의 일터에서 고급 수준의 34. 독일어를 필요로 한다. 250여 개의 연구단체와 10,000여 명의 학생들과 교수단을 갖추고 있으며, 35. 학제 간 과학연구를 강조한다.

31 ○ 아홉 번째 단락의 첫 번째 문장을 찾는다.
Switzerland is familiar with = Switzerland is known for

정답 chocolate

32 ○ 열 번째 단락의 두 번째 문장을 찾는다.
R&D aid to improve new version of recipes, products and design and build on machines = The work of R&D is to help ~

정답 machines

33 ○ 열한 번째 단락의 첫 번째 문장을 찾는다.
Foreign staff should fluently speak one of Swiss official tongues in the least. = a foreign staff must speak at least one of the official Swiss languages

정답 Swiss

34 ○ 열한 번째 단락의 두 번째 문장을 찾는다.
a number of workplaces need to have an advanced level of German = Most of the positions need a good level of German

정답 German

35 ○ 열두 번째 단락의 두 번째 문장을 찾는다.
it emphasises interdisciplinary scientific research = it is focused on interdisciplinary scientific research

정답 interdisciplinary

Questions 36-40

Do the following statements reflect the claims of the writer in Reading Passage 3?

In boxes 36-40 on your answer sheet write

> **TRUE**　　　*if the statement agrees with the information*
> **FALSE**　　*if the statement contradicts the information*
> **NOT GIVEN**　*if there is no information on this*

36 Switzerland has a reputation for history of making precise clockwork.

○ 키워드 history of making precise clockwork는 첫 번째 단락 첫 번째 문장에서 찾을 수 있다.
history of making clockwork = history of making sophisticated clocks

스위스는 정밀한 시계를 만드는 역사로 평판이 나 있다.

정답 TRUE

37 Coffee in Switzerland is world-famous.

○ 키워드 world-famous는 첫 번째 단락의 마지막 문장에서 찾을 수 있다. 그러나 문제의 '커피산업'에 대한 정보는 알 수 없다.

스위스의 커피산업은 세계적으로 유명하다.

정답 NOT GIVEN

38 Four-fifths of the staff at the Ruschlikon in Zurich are from overseas

○ 키워드 The Ruschlikon in Zurich는 세 번째 단락의 두 번째 문장에서 찾을 수 있다.
Four-fifths of the staff ~ are from overseas = 80% of them coming from abroad

Zurich의 Ruschlikon의 직원들 4/5는 외국에서 왔다.

정답 TRUE

39 The Ruschlikon lab is a traiblazer in only the field semiconductors in digital storage technology.

○ 키워드 The Ruschlikon lab is a traiblazer ~ technology는 네 번째 단락의 첫 번째 문장에서 찾을 수 있다. 본문에선 Ruschliko 연구소는 디지털 저장 기술과 반도체 그리고 광학전자공학에 앞서 있다고 언급하므로 문제와 본문간의 내용이 다르다.

Ruschlikon실험실은 디지털 저장기술 내에서 반도체에서 중요한 선구적인 역할을 하고 있다.

정답 FALSE

40 Most study fields need a high level of English.

○ 키워드 Most study fields need는 열한 번째 단락에서 찾을 수 있다. 본문에선 독일어 능통자를 원한다는 의미이므로 문제의 내용과는 다르다.

대부분의 연구분야에서 영어 능통자를 필요로 한다.

정답 FALSE

Academic Reading

Actual Test 4

Answer Sheet

1	swine flu pandemic	11	YES	21	A	31	E
2	swine H$_1$N$_1$ virus	12	NO	22	C	32	A
3	pandemic virus	13	YES	23	D	33	C
4	Summer	14	i	24	NOT GIVEN	34	Doushantuo Formation
5	Australia	15	v	25	Yes	35	Lack of oxygen
6	Chile	16	vi	26	No	36	Darwin's Lost World
7	Argentina	17	ii	27	NOT GIVEN	37	oxygen
8	seasonal virus	18	iv	28	NOT GIVEN	38	complex life
9	Tamiflu	19	ix	29	C	39	transformation of the planet
10	NOT GIVEN	20	vii	30	B	40	carbon dioxide

ACADEMIC READING

READING PASSAGE 1

You should spend about 20 minutes on Questions 1-13 which are based on Reading Passage 1 below.

THE SWINE FLU PANDEMIC

1 The swine flu pandemic has become more problematic. The White House will meet with state representatives on the 9th of July to talk about the preparation for the autumn flu season in the [1, 10]US, whilst the UK has focused their response on the H_1N_1 virus to cope with widespread infection.

2 Meantime, the southern hemisphere is going into the middle of the winter flu season, and the swine H_1N_1 virus [2]seems to be replacing the seasonal flu viruses that have been circulating until now. This is related to the seasonal flu vaccine which several companies are still producing. It could cause some problems when the northern hemisphere flu season comes at the end of this year.

3 The flu pandemics of 1918, 1957 and 1968 showed a high level of seasonal change and also released mild form of the H_1N_1 virus which circulates through the existing flu virus, H_3N_2. So, nobody knows how the H_1N_1 virus is going to behave. If it is not exchanged with the seasonal virus the milder H_1N_1 and H_3N_2 – the world is facing the prospect of catching all three viruses at once. It would be a complicated scenario, such as both seasonal and pandemic vaccines would be wanted and patients from different age groups would be affected. Although, based on what is happening in the southern hemisphere, it does not seem that this will be the case.

4 In the northern hemisphere, swine flu has spread to the extent that [3, 11]over 98% of flu cases genotyped in the US towards the end of June were caused by the pandemic virus. This is to be expected. Whilst the [4]seasonal flu viruses generally die out during the summer season, the pandemic virus can be more powerful as [4]fewer people have built up immunity to it.

5 The state of Victoria in [5]Australia reported this week that the H_1N_1 virus is now considered for [5]99% of all flu cases. There are reports of a similar situation in South America. In [6]Chile, the H_1N_1 virus is also much stronger than other seasonal viruses. [6]"98% of the flu cases we now take are caused by H_1N_1," Jeanette Vega, Chile's under-secretary of public health, said last week about a pandemic peak in Cancun, Mexico. "The seasonal vaccine is not used."

유행성 신종 플루

1 신종 플루가 점점 더 문제가 되고 있다. 미 백악관은 가을 독감철 대비에 관해서 이야기하기 위해 7월 9일, 주 하원의원들을 만날 예정이고, 반면에 영국은 확산된 감염에 대처하기 위해 H_1N_1 바이러스에 대한 대응에 초점을 맞추고 있다.

2 그 사이, 남반구는 겨울 독감철 중반기에 접어들었고, 신종 플루 바이러스가 여태까지 반복되어 왔던 계절 독감 바이러스를 대신하는 것처럼 보인다. 이것은 몇몇 회사에서 여전히 생산하고 있는 계절 독감 백신과 관련이 있다. 북반구의 독감철이 올해 말에 올 때 문제가 발생할 수도 있다.

3 1918년, 1957년, 1968년의 유행성 독감은 계절 변화의 높은 단계를 보여 주었고, 이미 존재하던 H_3N_2 독감 바이러스를 통해 순환하는 H_1N_1 바이러스의 약한 형태를 나타냈다. 그래서 H_1N_1 바이러스가 어떻게 행동할지 아무도 알지 못한다. 만일 그것이 계절 바이러스, 즉 더 약한 H_1N_1과 H_3N_2와 교환되지 않는다면, 전 세계는 이 세 가지 바이러스에 모두 걸릴 수 있는 상황에 직면한다. 이것은 복잡한 시나리오가 될 것이다. 이를테면, 즉 계절성과 유행성 백신 예방이 모두 필요해지며 다른 연령대의 환자들이 영향을 받을 것이다. 그럼에도 불구하고, 남반구에서 발생된 것으로 보아 이러한 현상이 일어나지 않을 수도 있을 것으로 보인다.

4 북반구에서는 신종 플루가 확산되고 있다. 미국에서는 6월 말까지 유전자형 독감 사례의 98% 이상이 유행성 바이러스에 의해 발생되었다. 이런 상황은 예상되었다. 계절 독감 바이러스가 일반적으로 여름에는 소멸되는 반면에, 유행성 바이러스는 더욱 영향력이 강하여 면역력을 가진 사람이 더 적다.

5 호주의 Victoria 주는 모든 독감의 99%가 H_1N_1 바이러스로 인한 것으로 생각된다고 이번 주에 발표했다. 남미에서도 비슷한 상황에 대한 보고가 있다. 칠레에서는 H_1N_1 바이러스가 다른 계절 바이러스보다 훨씬 강력하다. "지금 우리가 걸린 독감의 98%는 H_1N_1에 의해 발생되었다." 칠레의 국민보건부 서기인 Jeanette Vega는 지난주 Mexico의 Cancun지역에서 전염이 정점에 도달했을 때 말했다. "계절성 백신은 쓸모가 없다."

6 In the [7]Argentine capital Buenos Aires, Juan Manzur, the health minister, reported last week about the emergency situation in that [7, 12]90% of the flu in a result of the H_1N_1 virus.

7 During this winter in the northern hemisphere, it is an important matter. "If the pandemic virus greatly attacks the seasonal viruses in a regular flu season, the seasonal viruses [8]are likely to be exchanged by the new virus, like in the 1968 pandemic," says [8]Ab Osterhaus in the University of Rotterdam in the Netherlands.

8 In previous pandemics, the virus has changed, producing negative side effects. So far for H_1N_1, there have only been a few ominous signs.

9 The mutation of the virus's polymerase enzyme has been replicated efficiently from a sample taken in Shanghai. Ron Fouchier at the University of Rotterdam says that this could spread if it makes the virus more contagious, but the virus may also improve pathogenicity.

10 Also last week, two cases of the H_1N_1 virus with [9]resistance to the main antiviral drug, [13]Tamiflu, were found in people using the drug. Another was found in a girl who had never take the drug, suggesting Tamiflu – resistant to the H_1N_1 virus might already be in circulation.

pandemic a. 유행하는   hemisphere n. 반구   genotyped a. 유전자   immunity n. 면역성   ominous a. 불길한   enzyme n. (생화학)효소   replicated a. 복제   efficiently ad. 효율적으로   pathogenic a. 병원의   resistance n. 저항   antiviral a. 항바이러스성의

Questions 1-9

Complete the summary below.

Choose **NO MORE THAN THREE WORDS** from the passage for each answer.

Write your answers in boxes **1-9** on your answer sheet.

There is currently severe problem of **1** swine flu pandemic in the world, especially both the US and the UK are making strenuous efforts to solve the problem.

In the meantime, during the middle of winter flu season, **2** swine H_1N_1 virus is likely to substitute the seasonal flu viruses in the southern hemisphere. Also, over 98 per cent out of flu cases genotyped in the US were generated by **3** pandemic virus. Whilst seasonal flu viruses are usually fade out in **4** Summer, the pandemic virus has the advantage that few people have immunity to it.

ACADEMIC READING

There are reports that the H_1N_1 virus accounts for more than 90 per cent of all flu cases in countries, such as **5** Australia, **6** Chile and **7** Argentina.

According to Ab Osterhaus, **8** seasonal virus in a regular flu season can be replaced by the pandemic virus. New viruses were found to be resistant to the antiviral drug, **9** Tamiflu.

연구보고서는 신종 플루 바이러스가 5. 호주 6. 칠레 7. 아르헨티나 같은 나라에서 독감 사례들 중에 90퍼센트 이상을 차지한다고 보고한다.

Ab Osterhaus에 따르면, 일반 독감철에 8. 계절 바이러스가 유행성 바이러스에 의해 대체될 수도 있다고 한다. 항바이러스성 약인 9. Tamiflu에 저항성을 가지는 새로운 바이러스가 발견되었다.

1 ➡ 키워드 both the US and the UK은 첫 번째 단락에서 찾을 수 있다. 문제의 전치사 (of) 다음에 동명사/명사(구)가 위치할 수 있으므로 이와 관련된 답을 본문에서 찾는다.
both the US and the UK = US, whilst the UK

정답 swine flu pandemic

2 ➡ 키워드 the middle of winter flu season과 is likely to substitute는 두 번째 단락에서 찾을 수 있다.
is likely to substitute = seems to be replacing

정답 swine H_1N_1 virus

3 ➡ 키워드 over 98 per cent out of flu cases genotyped in the US were generated by는 네 번째 단락에서 찾을 수 있다.
over 98 per cent out of flu cases genotyped in the US were generated by = over 98% of flu cases genotyped in the US

정답 the pandemic virus

4 ➡ 키워드 seasonal flu viruses usually fade out과 = few people have immunity to it은 네 번째 단락에서 찾을 수 있다.
seasonal flu viruses usually fade out = seasonal flu viruses generally die out
few people have immunity to it = fewer people have built up immunity to it

정답 the summer

5, 6, 7

➡ 키워드 more than 90 per cent of flu cases와 countries는 다섯 번째와 여섯 번째 단락에서 찾을 수 있다.
countries = Australia, Chile, Argentina

정답 Australia, Chile, the Argentine

8 ➡ 키워드 Ab Osterhaus와 can be replaced by는 일곱 번째 단락에서 찾을 수 있다.
can be replaced by = are likely to be exchanged by

정답 seasonal virus

9 ➡ 키워드 to be resistant to the antiviral drug는 열 번째 단락에서 찾을 수 있다.

정답 Tamiflu

Questions 10-13

Do the following statements reflect the claims of the writer in Reading Passage1?

In boxes **10-13** on your answer sheet write

YES if the statement reflects the opinion of the writer
NO if the statement contradicts the opinion of the writer
NOT GIVEN if it is impossible to say what the writer thinks about this

---

10 The UK and the US had discussed and worked together on the swine flu pandemic in the past.

영국과 미국은 과거 신종 플루에 대해 함께 토론하고 연구해 왔었다.

○ 키워드 The UK and the US는 첫 번째 단락의 두 번째 문장에서 찾을 수 있다. 미국과 영국이 지난 과거에 swine flu pandemic에 대해서 공동으로 연구하고 회의한 것에 대해서는 언급되지 않았기 때문에 답은 NOT GIVEN이다.

정답 NOT GIVEN

---

11 Over 98 per cent of flu cases in the US were motivated by the pandemic virus.

미국의 독감 중 98% 이상이 유행성 바이러스에 자극을 받았다.

○ 키워드 Over 98 per cent of flu cases in the US were motivated by는 네 번째 단락의 첫 번째 문장에서 찾을 수 있다. 본문에서도 미국에서 98% 이상의 독감 사례는 pandemic virus에 의해 유발되었다고 언급되었으므로 답은 YES이다.
Over 98 per cent of flu cases in the US were motivated by
= Over 98% of flu cases genotyped in the US ~ were caused by

답 YES

---

12 In Argentina, 60 per cent of the flu virus in circulation is the H_1N_1 virus.

아르헨티나에서는 순환성의 독감 바이러스의 60%는 신종 바이러스 H_1N_1이다.

○ 키워드 In Argentina는 여섯 번째 단락의 첫 번째 문장에서 찾을 수 있다. 본문에선 아르헨티나의 독감의 90%를 신종 플루 H_1N_1으로 추정하고 있다. 문제와 정보가 다르므로 답은 NO이다.

정답 NO

---

13 Tamiflu is the crucial antiviral medicine which is resistant to the H_1N_1 virus.

타미플루는 신종 바이러스 H_1N_1에 대항하는 주요 항바이러스성 의약품이다.

○ 키워드 Tamiflu는 열 번째 단락의 첫 번째 문장에서 찾을 수 있다.
crucial = main (주요/탁월한)

정답 YES

ACADEMIC READING

READING PASSAGE 2

You should spend about 20 minutes on *Questions 14-28* which are based on Reading Passage 2 on the following pages.

Questions 14-20

Reading Passage 2 has nine paragraphs, *A-I*.

Choose the correct heading for paragraph *B-I* from the list of headings below.

Write the correct number, i-ix, in boxes *14-20* on your answer sheet.

List of Headings		한글
i	The scientific value of the rocks	i 암석의 과학적 가치
ii	The craters of the moon	ii 달의 분화구
iii	The mission to collect material on the moon	iii 달의 물질을 수집하는 임무
iv	The impact of the rocks discovered	iv 발견된 암석의 영향력
v	The surprise evidence about the lunar	v 달에 관한 놀라운 증거들
vi	The history of the early solar system	vi 초기 태양계의 역사
vii	The unknown questions left for future	vii 미래를 위해 남겨진 알려지지 않은 질문들
viii	NASA's lunar rock collection	viii 나사의 달 암석 수집
ix	Study of lunar history	ix 달의 역사에 대한 연구

Example	Answer
Paragraph **A**	iii

14 Paragraph **B**

　○ B단락의 첫 번째 문장, '운석은 과학적 보물로 그 당시 알려졌으며 또한 실망시키지 않았다'에서 암석의 과학적 가치를 추론할 수 있다.　　　　　　　정답 i

15 Paragraph **C**

　○ C단락의 세 번째 문장, 초기 달이 많은 양의 녹은 바위로 덮여 있었다는 증거는 놀라움이었다.　　　　　　　정답 v

16 Paragraph **E**

　○ E단락의 첫 번째 문장에서 초기 태양계에 대한 급진적인 재평가를 하게 했다고 설명하고 있다.　　　　　　　정답 vi

17 Paragraph **F**

▶ F단락은 달의 모든 분화구들이 같은 나이를 가지고 있다는 발견과 그 근거들을 설명하고 있다.

정답 ii

18 Paragraph **G**

▶ G단락의 첫 번째 문장에 '화학적 분석과 동위원소 연대기를 위해 달에서 가져온 샘플들 없이는, 어느 누구도 지구의 역사에 대한 이러한 중요한 발견을 결코 하지 못했을지도 모른다.'에서 발견된 암석의 영향력을 알 수 있다.

정답 iv

19 Paragraph **H**

▶ H단락의 첫 번째 문장에서 광물샘플 연대측정기술 등으로 달의 역사에서 몇 가지 중요한 연대를 재검토했던 연구들에 대해 언급하고 있다.

정답 ix

20 Paragraph **I**

▶ I단락의 첫 번째 문장에서 'Apollo에서 채취한 달의 샘플은 좀 더 총체적인 상황에 대한 질문 중 단지 일부를 이야기하는 것으로 끝나지는 않는다.'에서 답을 찾을 수 있다.

정답 vii

Mission to Collect Materials on the Moon

A [24]Whilst the world watched in excitement as Neil Armstrong and Buzz Aldrin landed on the moon, planetary scientists were focused on something else. For them, the value of the mission was in the cargo they brought back to earth. By the time Armstrong and Aldrin climbed into the lunar for the last time, they had gathered 22 kilograms of moon rocks, completely filling a small suitcase. Over five Apollo crews brought back a total collection of 382 kilograms of material containing 2,200 samples.

B [14]The rocks were known at the time as a scientific treasure and they did not disappoint. Paul Spudis, a geologist of the Lunar and Planetary Institute in Houston, Texas, said "Our ideas about planetary formation and evolution must be rewritten after the discoveries made by the Apollo crews." Harold Urey, a Nobel prizewinner, and one of the advocates of lunar exploration, had predicted that the moon was composed of primitive meteoritic material. But his conclusion was wrong. Some of the rocks looked just like the rocks on earth.

C Many clues that the [25]lunar rocks contained have taken a couple of years [25]to effectively analyse. Also, some of the

달의 물질들을 수집하기 위한 임무

A 세계가 닐 암스트롱과 버즈 올드린이 달에 착륙하는 것을 흥분 속에 지켜보는 동안에, 행성학자들은 다른 현상에 주목했다. 그들에게 있어, 우주비행의 가치는 비행사들이 지구에 가지고 돌아올 화물 속에 담겨 있는 것이었다. 마지막으로 암스트롱과 올드린이 달에 올라갈 때까지, 그들은 22kg의 달의 암석을 수집했고, 작은 가방을 가득 채웠다. 5명 이상의 아폴로 대원들은 2,200개의 샘플이 들어 있는 총합 382kg의 달의 암석을 가지고 돌아왔다.

B 당시 암석은 과학적 보물로 알려졌으며 또한 실망시키지 않았다. 텍사스 주 휴스턴에 있는 Lunar and Planetary Institute의 지리학자인 Paul Spudis는 "행성의 모양과 진화에 대한 우리의 생각은 아폴로 대원들의 발견 이후부터 재기록되어야 한다."라고 말한다. 달 탐사 지지자 중 한 사람이며 노벨상 수상자인 Harold Urey는 달이 원시적인 운석 물질로 이루어져 있다고 예견했다. 그러나 그의 의견은 잘못되었다. 몇몇 암석은 지구의 암석과 많이 닮아 있었다.

C 달의 암석에 포함된 많은 열쇠들을 실질적으로 분석하기 위해 수년이 걸렸다. 몇 가지 결론들은 아직도 뜨겁게 논의되고 있다. 초기 달이 많은

conclusions are still debated. [15]A big surprise was the evidence that the early moon was covered by a lot of molten rock. The moon's mountainous regions are made of anorthosite, a rare rock on Earth that forms when light, aluminum-rich minerals floats to the top of lava.

D Nowadays, the smart money is on the idea that the moon was created as a result of something that occurred around 50 million years after the solar system was created, when the Earth was in its infancy. From this hypothesis, earliest Earth ran into a planet that was a similar size to Mars and debris from the collision went into orbit around Earth which rapidly came together to form the moon.

E [16]The "giant impact" scenario led to a radical re-evaluation of the history of the early solar system. Before Apollo, planetary scientists watched the collection of objects orbiting the sun like a clockwork mechanism in which collisions were rare and trivial. Now, it is accepted as being a far more active environment, shuffling, colliding or ejecting. This history of all the inner planets has been shaped by collisions and nowhere is that history more visible than the moon.

F [17]Another surprise was the rocks from the moon's largest impact craters indicate that [26]all craters are roughly the same age, [26]between 3.8 and 4 billion years old. It never coincided. The moon — and by extension, Earth must have been caused by a devastating barrage half a billion years after the solar system formed. To causing this process, something big must have been going back to the outer solar system, but what? Surprisingly, this episode in the history of the solar system has come to be known as the last heavy bombardment, and ended at roughly the same time as the first signs of life on Earth.

G [18,27]These key discoveries about our planet's history may never have been made without [22,27]the samples taken from the moon for chemical analysis and isotopic dating. So do the Apollo rocks hide any more secrets? All 2,200 samples have been researched, and Randy Korotev, a lunar geochemist at Washington University in St Louis, Missouri, says that it is unlikely that there will be anything groundbreaking left to find from them. However, they may yet keep some more delicate secrets. Korotev says "We are steadily developing better tools and asking better questions." Especially, the instruments for dating mineral samples have been more delicate, enabling researchers to study the age of ever smaller samples, like tiny mineral grains within a rock.

H [19]These techniques have stimulated a rethink of some key dates in lunar history in the past two years. A team at the Swiss Federal Institute of Technology dated the formation of the moon's magma oceans. Also, by inference, the creation of the moon itself is estimated to have happened between 20 and 30 million years later than we originally thought, at approximately 4.5 billion years ago. Alexander Nemchin with five colleagues in Cutin University of Technology in Perth, Western Australia also estimated that a lunar zircon was around 4.417 billion years old when the last of the magma oceans solidified.

I [20]The Apollo rock samples are not finished answering some of the bigger picture questions. What will we discover on the opposite side of the moon's surface that we are unable to see from Earth? Can we put together a detailed history of the lava flows that formed the basalts of the lunar seas? Can we discover any samples from deep inside the moon? These are all seen as very good reasons for coming back to the moon. The big picture needs more samples, more data and more contexts. According to [23]Gary Lofgren, a curator of NASA's lunar rock collection at Johnson Space Centre in Huston, "There's no lack of target and scientific questions. It's not just about the moon but about the solar system's history. This is the lesson that we have learned from Apollo."

---

geologist n. 지질학자 predicted a. 예견된 primitive a. 근원적인 infancy n. 유아기 hypothesis n. 가설 debris n. 먼지 collision n. 충돌 orbit n. 궤도 trivial a. 사소한 shuffling a. 질질 끄는 colliding a. 충돌하는 ejecting a. 배출하는 craters n. 분화구들 coincided a. 동시에 일어나는 devastating a. 파괴하는 barrage n. 탄막사격 bombardment n. 폭격 isotopic a. (화학)동위소의 geochemist n. 지구화학자 delicate a. 섬세한

H 지난 2년간 이러한 기술들은 달의 역사에서 몇 가지 중요한 연대를 재검토할 수 있도록 자극했다. 스위스 연방기술연구소의 어느 한 팀에서는 달의 마그마 해양의 형성연대를 측정했다. 또한, 우리가 원래 생각했던 것보다 2천만~3천만 년 후인 대략 45억 년 전에 달이 생겼다고 추정한다. 그리고 호주 서부의 퍼스지역에 있는 Curtin 기술대학의 Alexander Nemchin와 다섯 동료들은 달의 지르콘(지르코늄 원광)의 연대를 마지막 마그마 해양이 굳어진 때인 약 44억 1700만 년으로 측정했다.

I 아폴로에서 채취한 암석 샘플은 전체적인 모습에 대한 질문에 대답하는 것을 여전히 멈추지 않았다. 지구에서 결코 볼 수 없는 달의 표면 반대편에서 우리는 무엇을 찾을 수 있는 것인가? 달의 바다에서 현무암을 형성한 화산유암의 자세한 역사를 우리가 구성할 수 있는가? 우리는 달의 깊숙한 내부로부터 샘플을 발견할 수 있는가? 이러한 것들이 달에 되돌아가야 하는 강력한 이유가 된다. 큰 그림은 더 많은 샘플, 자료 그리고 내용물들을 요구한다. "과학적 질문과 목적에는 부족한 것이 없다. 이런 상황은 달에 대한 것만이 아니라 태양계의 역사에 대한 것이며, 이것은 아폴로에서 우리가 배웠던 교훈이다."라고 휴스턴에 있는 존슨우주센터의 나사 달 암석 수집관장인 Gary Lofgren은 말한다.

Questions 21-23

Choose the correct letter, **A**, **B**, **C** and **D**.

Write the correct letter in boxes **21-23** on your answer sheet.

21 The scenario "giant impact" is mainly concerned with
  A ways of finding the history of the early solar system.
  B the history of the early solar craters.
  C the origin of the earth.
  D ways of learning about orbiting the sun.

➡ 키워드 giant impact를 E단락의 첫 문장에서 찾을 수 있다.

'거대한 효과'라는 시나리오는 ~에 주로 관련이 있다.
A 초기 태양계의 역사를 알 수 있는 방법
B 초기 태양의 분화구의 역사
C 지구의 기원
D 태양의 공전을 아는 방법

정답 A

ACADEMIC READING

22 The samples taken from the moon help
  A planetary scientists have made for dating mineral.
  B geochemists to study some craters.
  C planetary scientists to make key discoveries about the earth's history.
  D geologists to predict the moon's primitive material.

  ○ 키워드 the samples taken from the moon을 G단락의 첫 문장에서 찾을 수 있다. G단락의 첫 번째 문장에 '화학적 분석과 동위원소 연대기를 위해 달에서 가져온 샘플들 없이는, 어느 누구도 지구의 역사에 대한 이러한 중요한 발견을 결코 만들지 못 했을지도 모른다.'에서 답을 찾을 수 있다.

달에서 가져온 샘플들은 ~을 도와주었다.
A 행성학자들이 광물의 연대를 측정하는 것을
B 지구화학자들이 몇몇 분화구를 연구하는 것을
C 행성학자들이 지구의 역사에 대해 중요한 발견을 하는 것을
D 지질학자들이 달의 원시적인 물질에 대해서 예견하는 것을

정답 C

23 Gary Lofgren's quote says that, when we try to remember things,
  A the remaining big picture questions will never come true.
  B the history of the lava flows will be returned.
  C plenty of targets and scientific questions will be collected.
  D the earth's development will be the milestone in the solar system's history.

  ○ 키워드 Gary Lofgren's를 I단락의 일곱 번째 문장에서 찾을 수 있다. I단락의 여덟 번째와 아홉 번째 문장에 '이런 상황은 달에 대한 것이 아니라 태양계의 역사에 대한 것이며, 이것은 Apollo 우주선에서 우리가 배웠던 교훈이다.'에서 답을 찾을 수 있다.

Gray Lofgren의 인용문에는, 우리가 상황을 기억하려 애쓰는 것에 대해서 ~라고 쓰여 있다.
A 현존하는 큰 그림에 대한 질문들은 결코 실현되지 못 할 것이다.
B 화산유암의 역사는 재순환된다.
C 풍부한 목적과 과학적 질문들은 축적될 것이다.
D 지구의 성장은 태양계의 역사 내에서 중요한 이정표가 될 것이다.

정답 D

Questions 24-28

Do the following statements reflect the claims of the writer in Reading Passage1?

In boxes **24-28** on your answer sheet write

  YES   if the statement reflects the opinion of the writer
  NO   if the statement contradicts the opinion of the writer
  NOT GIVEN if it is impossible to say what the writer thinks about this

24 The rocks which Neil Armstrong and Buzz Aldrin collected were more valuable than those of Russian astronauts.

  ○ 문제에서 키워드인 Neil Armstrong and Buzz Aldrin은 A단락의 첫 번째 문장에서 찾을 수 있다. 그러나 문제의 내용을 본문에선 알 수 없기 때문에 답은 NOT GIVEN이다.

Neil Armstrong과 Buzz Aldrin이 수집한 암석들은 러시아의 우주비행사들이 얻은 것보다 더 가치가 있었다.

정답 NOT GIVEN

25 The lunar rocks taken are critical to beginning to understand the history.

  ○ 키워드 The lunar rocks taken과 to understand the history는 C단락의 첫 번째 문장에서 찾을 수 있다.
  to understand the history = to effectively analyse

달에서 채취한 암석은 달의 역사를 이해하는 결정적인 시발점이다.

정답 YES

26 All craters on the moon are of a similar age, up to 5 billion years old.

달 표면의 모든 분화구는 연대가 최대 약 50억 년으로 비슷하다.

○ 키워드인 All craters와 up to 5 billion years old는 F단락의 첫 번째 문장에 나온다. 본문에선 38억~40억 년 전으로 되어 있다. 문제의 내용과 내용이 다르므로 답은 NO이다.

정답 NO

27 The main clues for discovering the earthquake are given by the samples taken from the moon.

지진 발견의 중요한 단서는 달에서 채취한 샘플들로 알 수 있다.

○ 문제에서 키워드인 The main clues of discovering과 the samples taken from the moon는 G단락의 첫 번째 문장에서 찾을 수 있다. 본문에선 문제의 지진(the earthquake)에 대한 직접적인 정보를 알 수 없기 때문에 답은 NOT GIVEN 이다.

정답 NOT GIVEN

28 The half of the moon's surface that we can never see is related to the solar system's history.

우리가 결코 볼 수 없는 달 표면의 절반은 태양계의 역사와 관련이 있다.

○ 문제에서 키워드인 The half of the moon's surface는 어떠한 단락에서 찾을 수 없다. 문제에 대한 직접적인 정보를 본문에서 알 수 없으므로 답은 NOT GIVEN 이다.

정답 NOT GIVEN

READING PASSAGE 3

You should spend about 20 minutes on Questions 29-40 which are based on Reading Passage 3 on the following pages.

Organism's Appearance

1. As Darwin discovered his evolution theory, the earliest known fossils were left in rocks which he called the Silurian age. Older rocks seemed to contain no fossils. The apparently sudden appearance of subtle animals like trilobites was not inconsistent with Darwin's thoughts of gradual evolution.

2. "If my theory will be true, it is unquestionable that before the lowest Silurian stratum was deposited ... the world swarmed with living creatures. To the question why we do not find records of these vast primordial periods, I can give no satisfactory answer," [32]Darwin wrote in the first edition of *On the Origin of Species*. His puzzle is known as Darwin's dilemma.

3. Of course, we have discovered a lot of fossils from the earliest periods. Rocks of 3.8 billion years old have signs of life, and the first recognizable bacteria to come out in rocks of 3.5 billion years old. During the Ediacaran, approximately one billion years ago, Multi-cellular plants with red and green algae appeared and approximately 575 million years ago was found in the first multi-cellular animals.

4. Even so, there are many perplexing questions. Why did animals evolve so late in the day? And why did the ancestors of modern animals apparently evolve in a geological blink of an eye during the early Cambrian period between 542 and 520 million years ago? Recently, a series of discoveries could help to explain these long-lasting mysteries. These discoveries suggest that the earliest animals evolved much earlier than we thought, perhaps over 850 million years ago. However, the really extraordinary part is that these early animals may have completely changed the planet, paving the way for the larger and more complex animals to follow them.

5. Several aspects of the biggest discoveries have come from [34]an ancient seabed in China, called the [34]Doushantuo Formation, where unusual conditions conserved some extraordinary fossils. During the last part of the Ediacaran period, layers between 550 and 580 million years old include tiny spheres made of from one to dozens of different cells — just like animals' first embryos. A couple of things have suggested that they are the property of giant bacteria, but a series of studies over the past decade have left little doubt that they are really animal embryos.

6. [30]Leiming Yin, a researcher at the Nanjing Institute of Geology and Paleontology in China, reported discovering embryos

encased inside hard, spiky shells unlike anything produced by bacteria in 2007. Furthermore evidence of shells that apart from the deficiency of conserved embryos on the inside are identical, can be seen in rocks as old as 632 million years – the appearance of the Ediacaran period - suggesting that the animal embryos themselves go back this far.

7   Other more tentative discoveries push the appearance of animals back even further. [29]Roger Summons, a researcher in the Massachusetts Institute of Technology and his colleague Gordon Love studied brownish, oily sandstone cores drilled from 4 kilometres below the desert of Oman. The oily remains of dead organisms drifted down to the depths of ancient oceans, where they [35]decomposed slowly because of the lack of oxygen. No visible fossils are present but within that oil are molecular fossils –chemicals taken from the ancient organisms. In layers that are 635 to 713 million years old, [33]Summons and Love discovered 24-isopropylcholestane (24-IPC), a stable form of a kind of cholesterol that these days are only discovered in the cell membranes of certain sponges. "The sponges biomass must have been so substantial," says Love, now at the University of California, Riverside. "They were ecologically outstanding."

Fuel of Life

8   With the oceans [37]changed, the stage was finally set for the evolution of more complicated body forms. The idea that increasing oxygen levels played a major role in the explosion of life during the Cambrian period is far from new, but most of the researchers attribute the increase in oceanic oxygen to the increase in the atmosphere. If Butterfield is right, it was basically because of animals taking over from bacteria. "These geochemical signatures [of oxygenation] are not causing the evolution of animals," he insists. "They're consequences of the dawn of animals."

9   "He is right," says Brasier. In fact, he thinks the link between [38]complex life and the transformation of the planet [39]runs even deeper. [36]In *Darwin's Lost World*, a book published earlier this year, Brasier suggests that the improved burial of carbon resulting from [36]the rising of large cells and groups of cells – perhaps with plants, like seaweed – [40]sucked carbon dioxide out of the atmosphere, setting off the series of ice ages that aided the first animals to wrestle for control of the oceans with bacteria. "Rather than being the cause of animal evolution, the ice ages may well have been the response to it," he says.

subtle a. 희박한   trilobites n.(고생물)삼엽충   stratum n. 지층   swarmed a. 떼를 짓는   primordial a. 최초의   algae n. 바닷말   perplexing a. 당황하게 하는   extraordinary a. 비상한   embryos n. (식물)배   encased a. ~로 둘러싸인   spiky a. 길고 끝이 뾰족한   deficiency n. 부족   tentative a. 시험적인   consequences n. 결과들

ACADEMIC READING

Questions 29-33

Look at the following statements Questions 29-33 and the list of researchers below.

Match each statement with the correct researcher(s), **A-E**.

Write the correct letter, **A-E**, in boxes **29-33** on your answer sheet.

NB You may use any letter more than once.

List of Researchers

A   Darwin
B   Leiming Yin
C   Summons and Love
D   Elizabeth Turner
E   Brasier

---

29   studied brownish, oily sandstone cores. [키워드]

○ 일곱 번째 단락의 두 번째 문장에서 'Massachusetts 공과대학의 연구원인 Roger Summons와 그의 동료인 Gordon Love는 Oman의 사막 아래 4km 깊이에서부터 구멍을 뚫어 갈색을 띠고, 오일 성분이 있는 사암을 핵을 분석했다.'에서 답을 찾을 수 있다.

Summons and Love는 갈색을 띠고, 오일 성분이 있는 사암의 핵을 연구했다.

정답 C

30   announced embryos on the inside surrended by hard, spiky shells. [키워드]

○ 키워드를 여섯 번째 단락의 첫 번째 문장에서 찾는다.
surrounded = encased

Leiming Yin은 내부가 단단하고 뾰족한 껍질로 둘러싸인 배를 발표했다.

정답 B

31   claimed that the expanded burial of carbon resulted in the series of ice ages. [키워드]

○ 키워드를 마지막 단락의 세 번째 문장에서 찾는다.
expanded burial = improved burial

Brasier는 확대된 탄소 매장량이 결과적으로 일련의 빙하시대에서 야기한다고 주장했다.

정답 E

32   wrote in the first edition of On the Origin of Species. [키워드]

○ 두 번째 단락의 두 번째 문장에서 답을 찾을 수 있다.

Darwin은 「종의 기원」 초판에서 적었다

정답 A

33   discovered 24-isopropylcholestane. [키워드]

○ 일곱 번째 단락의 다섯 번째 문장에서 '6억 3500만 년~7억 1300만 년 사이의 층에서, Summons과 Love는 해면의 세포막에서만 발견된 지금의 cholesterol의 안정화된 형태인 24-isopropylcholestane(24-IPC)을 발견했다.'에서 답을 찾는다.

Summons and Love는 24-isoprcpylcholestane을 발견했다.

정답 C

Questions 34-36

Complete the sentences below.

Choose **NO MORE THAN THREE WORDS** from the passage for each answer.

Write your answers in boxes **34-36** on your answer sheet.

34 What is an ancient seabed in China, conserving some weird fossils?

> 키워드 an ancient seabed in China를 다섯 번째 단락의 첫 번째 문장에서 찾을 수 있다.
> weird fossils = extraordinary fossils

몇 가지 특이한 화석을 보존한 중국의 고대 해저를 무엇이라고 하는가?

정답 Doushantuo Formation

35 What made organisms decompose in the depths of ancient oceans?

> 키워드 organisms decompose를 일곱 번째 단락의 세 번째 문장에서 찾을 수 있다.
> organisms decompose = decomposed slowly

고대 해저에서 유기체는 무엇 때문에 사멸되었는가?

정답 Lack of oxygen

36 What was written by Brasier to swell burial of carbon resulting from the rise of large cells and groups of cells?

> 키워드 Brasier to swell burial of carbon resulting을 아홉 번째 단락의 세 번째 문장에서 찾을 수 있다.
> swell burial of carbon resulting = the rising of large cells and groups of cells-perhaps

거대세포와 세포들의 그룹들의 증가로 인한 탄소의 매장을 증가시켜야 된다는 Brasier의 저서는 무엇인가?

정답 Darwin's Lost World

Questions 37-40

Complete the summary below.

Choose **NO MORE THAN TWO WORDS** from the passage for each answer.

Write your answers in boxes **37-40** on your answer sheet.

Fuel of life: (본문 여덟, 아홉 번째 단락 참조)

From the oceans fluctuated, **37** oxygen of increasing levels which played a vital part in the increase of oceanic oxygen in the atmosphere. Actually, Brasier considers the connection of **38** complex life and **39** transformation of the planet goes deeper. According to *Darwin's Lost World*, he claims that carbon burial was getting more inhaled **40** carbon dioxide outside of the atmosphere, caused the series of ice ages that was supported with the first organism generated from bacteria.

대양의 불규칙한 변동으로부터, 증가하는 37. 산소의 양은 대기 중의 바다에서 중요한 역할을 한다. 실제, Brasier는 38. 복잡한 생명체와 39. 지구의 변형의 연관성이 좀 더 심도 있게 진행된다고 고려하고 있다. Darwin's Lost World에 따르면, 그는 매장된 탄소가 지구 밖의 40. 이산화탄소를 점점 더 흡수하고 있으며, 박테리아에서 진행된 유기체 근원으로 도움을 얻을 수 있는 연속된 빙하기의 원인이 됐다고 주장한다.

ACADEMIC READING

37
- 키워드를 여덟 번째 단락의 첫 번째 문장에서 찾는다. 정답은 두 번째 문장에 나와 있다.
fluctuated = changed

정답 oxygen

38, 39
- 키워드를 아홉 번째 단락의 두 번째 문장에서 찾는다.
goes in more depth = runs even deeper

정답 complex life / transformation of the planet

40
- 키워드를 아홉 번째 단락의 세 번째 문장에서 찾는다.
more inhaled = sucked

정답 carbon dioxide

Academic Reading

Actual Test 5

Answer Sheet

1	B	11	FALSE	21	J	31	money
2	F	12	NOT GIVEN	22	NOT GIVEN	32	medicine
3	A	13	FALSE	23	FALSE	33	developing countries
4	E	14	C	24	TRUE	34	ethical, legal responsibilities
5	C	15	F	25	FALSE	35	(the) Nuremberg code
6	H	16	A	26	TRUE	36	strict
7	G	17	K	27	B	37	genuine altruism
8	D	18	I	28	A	38	money, medicine
9	FALSE	19	B	29	drugs	39	ethical quandaries
10	TRUE	20	L	30	their own disorders	40	B

READING PASSAGE 1

You should spend about 20 minutes on Questions 1-13 which are based on Reading Passage 1 below.

Parasitic Worms' Efficacy

A Parasitic worms, like hookworms, whipworms, pinworms and flukes that plague humans are enough to make most of us shudder. [3, 9]Except John Turton, in the middle of 1970s, whilst working at the UK's Medical Research Council Laboratories in Surrey, he intentionally infected himself with hookworms in an attempt to alleviate his chronic hay fever. It worked. During two summer seasons whilst he held the parasites, his allergy diminished.

B In regions where parasitic worm infections are rife, when the remedy was emerged, Turton's vital experiment came. [10]In 1913 W. Herrick, a doctor from Columbia University in New York, found a very different link between parasitic worms, or helminthes, and allergies. [1]Lab workers analysed the gut-dwelling roundworm *Ascaris* that often caused tenderness and swelling around the fingers, and more severely asthma after longer exposure.

C [5, 11]Researchers have been trying to make sense of these contradicting findings since the 1970s in the hope of being able to use the power of parasites to help free people of their allergies, without making things worse. They know they are playing with fire. After all, helminthes are responsible for some truly horrible diseases and cause great suffering around the world. However, as the effects of helminthes on the human body become clearer, it looks like their healing powers may have potential benefits.

D Not surprisingly, no researchers have been willing to take the risk of deliberately infecting themselves as Turton had done. Instead, most studies are dependent on populations in countries where people are already infected. [8]This research tends to emphasis on three commonly diagnosed allergic conditions: asthma, eczema and hay fever. The results have been confusing, but now researchers are beginning to have a better understanding.

E For instance, a study conducted in Taiwan showed that people infected with Enterobius vermicularis, a pinworm that is one of the most common gut parasites in the world, were less likely to have hay fever than the rest of the general population. But the results from Ecuador show a different story. Hay fever was not more common in children living in urban areas than it was in children living in rural areas. [4]The parasite was equally common in both groups, so the researchers concluded that something else must be responsible for the prevalence of hay fever.

F [2]Knowing about eczema has proved as difficult to interpret. For instance, a study in Uganda discovered that eczema was less common among babies whose mothers had been infected with helminthes whilst being pregnant. But, another study this time in Ethiopia, discovered that children with *Trichuris* worms, and whipworms that infest the large intestine, were more likely to have eczema than uninfected children.

G Regarding asthma, Herrick's discovery that it can be started by contact with the *Ascaris* was confirmed in the 1970s. But, hookworms decreased the extremity of asthma in a group of Ethiopians and similar benefits have been seen in Brazilian asthma sufferers infected with the *Schistosoma mansoni*, the flatworm responsible for schistosomiasis, which damages internal organs. What are we to make of all this? [7, 12]The outstanding link between allergies and parasites is the human immune system. Allergies are caused by an overactive immune response, and helminthes have strategies to dampen down our immune response to stimulate their survival. After all, they have evolved alongside humans for several thousands of years.

H [6]In people with no allergies, foreign material entering the body stimulates the release of cytokines, molecules that sound the alarm to get the attention of other immune cells. As immune cells set to attack the intruder, another set of molecules is released to prohibit the immune response from overreacting. One of the main molecules responsible for keeping reactions in check is interleukin-10, which inhibits the release of certain cytokines. [13]People with allergies tend to have lower than normal levels of interleukin-10, so their immune responses frequently get out of hand. In contrast, people infected with helminthes have above average levels of the molecule, and research on schistosomiasis patients indicates that this is at least partially because of the worms that set free chemicals that trigger the production of interleukin-10 in their host.

---

plague v. 괴롭히다   shudder v. 전율하다   alleviate v. ~을 완화시키다
chronic a. 만성적인   rife a. 왕성한   helminthes n. 기생충   asthma n. 천식
deliberately ad. 신중하게   eczema n. (병리) 습진   prevalence n. 널리 행하여짐
interpret v. ~을 해석하다   intestine n. (신체) 장   intruder n. 침입자

ACADEMIC READING

Questions 1-8

Reading Passage 1 has eight paragraphs, **A-H**.

Which paragraph contains the following information?

Write the correct letter, **A-E**, in boxes **1-8** on your answer sheet.

NB   You may use any letter more than once.

1   Lab workers' duties   실험실 직원들의 임무

● B단락 세 번째 문장에서 실험실 직원들은 손가락을 부어오르거나 무르게 하는 등의 회충을 분석한다고 설명하고 있다.

정답 B

2   Contrary results between surveys   통계조사상의 상반된 결과

● F단락의 첫 번째 문장에서 습진에 대한 알려진 사실은 해석하기가 어렵다고 판명되었다고 주장하면서 우간다와 에티오피아의 상반되는 결과를 비교하고 있다.

정답 F

3   A voluntary attempt against allergy   알레르기 치료를 위한 자발적인 시도

● A단락의 두 번째 문장에서 John Turton은 만성 건초열을 완화하기 위해 십이지장충을 자신에게 직접 의도적으로 감염시켰다고 말하고 있다.

정답 A

4   The same results between surveys   통계조사상의 같은 결과

● E단락의 네 번째 문장에서 연구원들은 시골과 대도시에서 생활하는 아이들의 기생충 감염 수치를 비교했지만 같은 결과를 얻었다고 설명했다.

정답 E

5   A powerful remedy for allergies   알레르기에 대한 강력한 치료

● C단락의 첫 번째 문장에서 '1970년 이래로, 연구원들은 더 악화되는 것 없이 알레르기성 질환을 완화할 수 있게 도와주는 기생충의 효력을 이용할 수 있기를 바라며 이러한 반대되는 발견을 이해할 수 있도록 노력해 왔다.'에서 답을 찾는다.

정답 C

6   Understanding of immune responses   면역반응의 이해

● H단락의 첫 번째 문장에서 이질적인 물질이 신체 안으로 들어오면 사이토카인이 방출되어 다른 면역 세포가 활동한다고 말하며 면역반응이 어떻게 일어나는지에 대해 설명하고 있다.

정답 H

7   Critical connection between allergies and parasites   알레르기와 기생충 간의 결정적 연관성

● G단락의 네 번째 문장에서 '알레르기와 기생충 사이에서의 두드러지는 연관성은 인간의 면역 체계이다.'에서 답을 찾을 수 있다.

정답 G

8 Three most commonly allergies

    ◐ D단락 세 번째 문장에서 세 가지 일반적인 알레르기는 천식, 습진, 건초열임을 알 수 있다.

세 가지 일반적인 알레르기

정답 D

Questions 9-13

Do the following statements reflect the claims of the writer in Reading Passage1?

In boxes 9-13 on your answer sheet write

    TRUE   *if the statement agrees with the information*
    FALSE   *if the statement contradicts the information*
    NOT GIVEN *if there is no information on this*

9 John Turton infected himself with hookworms by mistake

    ◐ 키워드 John Turton과 hookworms는 A단락의 두 번째 문장에서 찾을 수 있다. 문제의 내용과는 다르게 본문에서 intentionally(의도적으로)라고 표현되어 있으므로 답은 FALSE이다.

John Turton은 실수로 십이지장충을 자신의 몸에 직접 주사했다.

정답 FALSE

10 Dr Herrick has found a different feature between worms and allergies

    ◐ 키워드 Dr Herrick과 a different feature는 B단락의 두 번째 문장에서 찾을 수 있다.
a different feature = a different link

Dr Herrick은 기생충과 알레르기 사이에 다른 특징을 찾아냈다.

정답 TRUE

11 Researchers have not known the healing potential of parasites since the 1970s.

    ◐ 키워드 Researchers와 since the 1970s는 C단락의 첫 번째 문장에서 찾을 수 있다. 본문에서 치료 효과에 대한 확실성을 입증하기 위해서 연구해 왔다고 표현하고 있어 답과 내용이 서로 다르므로 FALSE이다.

연구원들은 1970년 이래로 지금까지 기생충의 잠재력인 치료 효과를 알지 못했다.

정답 FALSE

12 Allergies have the same appearance as parasites.

    ◐ 키워드인 Allergies과 parasites은 G단락의 네 번째 문장에서 찾을 수 있다. 그러나 본문에서 '알레르기와 기생충 사이에서의 결정적인 연관성은 인간의 면역 체계이다.' 라고만 나와 있으므로 답은 NOT GIVEN이다.

알레르기 반응 물질은 기생충과 외형이 같다.

정답 NOT GIVEN

13 People with allergies may have higher than ordinary levels of interleukin-10.

    ◐ 키워드 People with allergies와 interleukin-10은 H단락의 네 번째 문장에서 찾을 수 있다. 본문에서는 더 낮은 경향이 있다고 나와 있으므로 답은 FALSE이다.

알레르기 반응을 가진 사람은 interleukin-10의 일반적인 단계에서 더 높게 나타날 수 있다.

정답 FALSE

ACADEMIC READING

READING PASSAGE 2

You should spend about 20 minutes on Questions 14-28 which are based on Reading Passage 2 below.

The Nagymaros Dam

1   [14]When Janos Vargha, a biologist from the Hungarian Academy of Sciences, began a new career as a writer with a small monthly nature magazine called *Buvar*, it was 9 years after the story behind the fall of the Berlin Wall had started to unfold. During his early research, he went to a beauty spot on the river Danube outside Budapest known as the Danube Bend to interview local officials about plans to build a small park on the site of an ancient Hungarian capital.

2   [15]One official mentioned in passing that this tree-lined curve in the river, a popular tourism spot for Hungarians, was monotonous. Also, it was to be submerged by a giant hydroelectric dam in secret by a much-feared state agency known simply as the Water Management.

3   [16, 22, 28]Vargha investigated and learned that the Nagymaros dam (pronounced "nosh-marosh") would cause pollution, destroy underground water reserves, dry out wetlands and wreck the unique ecosystem of central Europe's longest river. Unfortunately, nobody objected. "Of course, I wrote an article. But there was a director of the Water Management on the magazine's editorial board. The last time, he went to the printers and stopped the presses, the article was never published. I was frustrated and angry, but I was ultimately interested in why they cared to ban my article," he remembers today.

4   [17, 27]He found that the Nagymaros dam was part of a joint project with neighbouring Czechoslovakia to produce hydroelectricity, irrigate farms and enhance navigation. They would build two dams and re-engineer the Danube for 200 kilometres where it created the border between them. [23]"The Russians were working together, too. They wanted to take their big ships from the Black Sea right up the Danube to the border with Austria."

5   Vargha was soon under vigorous investigation, and some of his articles got past the censors. He gathered supporters for some years, but he was one of only a few people who believed the dam should be stopped. He was hardly surprised when the Water Management refused to debate the project in public. After a public meeting, the bureaucrats had pulled out at the last minute. [18]Vargha knew he had to take the next step. "We decided it wasn't enough to talk and write, so we set up an organization, the Danube Circle. We announced that we didn't agree with censorship. We would act as if we were living in a

democracy." he says.

6 [24]The Danube Circle was illegal and the secret publications it produced turned out to be samizdat leaflets. In an extraordinary act of defiance, it gathered 10,000 signatures for a petition objecting to the dam and made links with environmentalists in the west, inviting them to Budapest for a press conference.

7 The Hungarian government enforced a news blackout on the dam, but articles about the Danube Circle began to be published and appear in the western media. In 1985, the Circle and Vargha, a public spokesman, won the Right Livelihood award known as the alternative Nobel prize. Officials told Vargha he should not take the prize but he ignored them. The following year when Austrian environmentalists joined a protest in Budapest, they were met with tear gas and batons. [19, 25]Then the Politburo had Vargha taken from his new job as editor of the Hungarian version of *Scientific American*.

8 The dam became a focus for opposition to the hated regime. Communists tried to hold back the waters in the Danube and resist the will of the people. Vargha says, "Opposing the state directly was still hard." "Objecting to the dam was less of a hazard, but it was still considered a resistance to the state."

9 Under increasing pressure from the anti-dam movement, the Hungarian Communist party was divided. Vargha says, "Reformists found that the dam was not very popular and economical. It would be cheaper to generate electricity by burning coal or nuclear power." "But hardliners were standing for Stalinist ideas of large dams which mean symbols of progress." [20]Environmental issues seemed to be a weak point of east European communism in its final years. During the 1970s under the support of the Young Communist Leagues, a host of environmental groups had been founded. Party officials saw them as a harmless product of youthful idealism created by Boy Scouts and natural history societies.

10 [21, 26]Green idealism steadily became a focal point for political opposition. In Czechoslovakia, the human rights of Charter 77 took up environmentalism. The green-minded people of both Poland and Estonia participated in the Friends of the Earth International to protest against air pollution. Bulgarian environmentalists built a resistance group, called Ecoglasnost, which held huge rallies in 1989. Big water engineering projects were potent symbols of the old Stalinism.

monotonous a. 단조로운   frustrated a. 실패된   irrigate v. 물을 대다   enhance v. 강화하다   bureaucrats n. 관료주의자들   samizdat n. 소연방 시대 때의 지하 출판(물)   defiance n. 저항   blackout n. 정전   baton n. 지팡이, 바통   regime n. 정권   hazard n. 위험

ACADEMIC READING

Questions 14-21

Complete the summary using the list of words and phrases, **A-L**, below.

Write the correct letter, **A-L**, in boxes **14-21** on your answer sheet.

The story of the fall of the Berlin Wall had started to unfold 9 years earlier. Janos Vargha visited the river Danube out of Budapest to discuss a matter of **14** constructing a park small-scale with executives. However, unfortunately, the tree-lined curve in the river was **15** swallowed up by a colossal dam which caused a lot of fear. He noticed the negative impact of the Nagymaros dam would be **16** severe on the ecosystem around the main river. Besides, the dam was engineering public works, generating hydroelectricity, irrigating farmlands and developing sailing trade which was **17** combined with border of Czechoslovakia.

After one public meeting, Vargha **18** established the Danube Circle for showing the autonomy of the people in a democracy. Despite of every effort, he who would eventually become the editor of the Hungarian edition was **19** discharged by the Politburo. Fortunately, with plenty of pressure from the anti-dam movement, east European communism's final symbol was opposed by the **20** environmentalist. Overall, between political processing and environmentalists have been on a **21** collision of views.

베를린 장벽 붕괴에 대한 이야기가 9년 전 밝혀지기 시작했다. Janos Vargha는 14. 작은 규모의 공원 건립에 대한 문제로 관리관들과 토론할 목적으로 부다페스트 외곽의 다뉴브 강을 방문하였다. 그러나, 불행하게도, 강에 나무가 늘어선 커브가 무서움을 유발하는 거대한 댐에 의해서 15. 잠식되어 갔다. 그는 Nagymaros 댐의 부정적인 영향력이 강 주변의 생태계에 16. 심각한 문제를 야기할 수 있다고 주목했다. 게다가, 댐은 공공 사업을 설계하고 수력 에너지를 발생시키며 농지에 관개하고 체코슬로바키아 국경에서 17. 협력하는 해상무역을 발전시키고 있었다.

한 번의 공청회가 있는 후에, Vargha는 민주주의 국민의 자치권을 표명할 다뉴브 서클 조직을 18. 세웠다. 모든 노력에도 불구하고, 헝가리판 편집장이 될 그는 Politburo(구소련공산당정치부)에 의해서 19. 해임되었다. 운이 좋게도, 댐 건설에 반대하는 운동의 거대한 압력으로 동유럽 공산당 정부의 최후의 상징은 20. 환경운동가들에 의해서 반대되었다. 결국, 정치적 과정과 환경주의자들은 21. 충돌의 국면에 놓이게 되었다.

A severe	**B** discharged	**C** constructing a park of small-scale
D passed	**E** reformist	**F** swallowed up
G separated	**H** favourable	**I** established
J collision	**K** combined	**L** environmentalist

14 ● 키워드 Janos Vargha와 to discuss a matter of _____ with executives를 첫 번째 단락의 첫 번째와 두 번째 문장에서 찾는다.
to discuss with executives = to interview local officials

정답 C

15 ● 키워드 the tree-lined curve in the river와 by a colossal dam을 두 번째 단락의 첫 번째와 두 번째 문장에서 찾는다.
swallowed up = submerged by

정답 F

16 ● 키워드 the Nagymaros dam과 on the ecosystem around the main river를 세 번째 단락의 첫 번째 문장에서 찾는다.
severe = wreck

정답 A

17 ○ 키워드 the dam과 border of Czechoslovakia를 네 번째 단락의 첫 번째 문장에서 찾는다.
combined with border of Czechoslovakia = a joint project with neighbouring Czechoslovakia

정답 K

18 ○ 키워드 Vargha와 the Danube Circle을 다섯 번째 단락의 다섯 번째와 여섯 번째 문장에서 찾는다. 'Vargha는 다뉴브 서클을 창설하였다.'에서 답을 찾는다.

정답 I

19 ○ 키워드 the editor of the Hungarian edition과 the Politburo을 일곱 번째 단락의 다섯 번째 문장에서 찾는다. discharged = taken from

정답 B

20 ○ 키워드 east European communism's final symbol과 was opposed by the를 아홉 번째 단락의 다섯 번째 문장에서 찾는다. '환경 문제는 최후에 있는 동유럽 공산주의의 약점인 듯했다.'에서 답을 찾는다.

정답 L

21 ○ 키워드 political processing과 environmentalists을 마지막 단락의 첫 번째 문장에서 찾는다. collision = opposition

정답 J

Questions 22-26

Do the following statements reflect the claims of the writer in Reading Passage 2?

*In boxes **22-26** on your answer sheet write*

> **TRUE**　　　　*if the statement agrees with the information*
> **FALSE**　　　*if the statement contradicts the information*
> **NOT GIVEN**　*if there is no information on this*

22 Janos Vargha predicted that the Nagymaros dam would be wreck the natural atmosphere before it was built.

Janos Vargha는 Nagymaros 댐이 준공되기 전에 댐이 자연환경에 악영향을 줄 것이라고 예견했다.

○ 키워드 Janos Vargha과 Nagymaros dam은 세 번째 단락의 첫 번째 문장에서 찾을 수 있다. 본문에는 Vargha가 단지 Nagymaros 댐의 그동안의 부정적 실태에 대해서만 조사하고 배웠다고만 언급되어 있다. 그가 '예견했는지는' 본문에서 알 수 없으므로 답은 NOT GIVEN이다.

정답 NOT GIVEN

23 The Nagymaros dam's project was managed by the Russians only.

Nagymaros 댐의 계획은 러시아인들에 의해서만 운용되었다.

○ 키워드 The Nagymaros dam's project와 the Russians는 네 번째 단락의 세 번째 문장에서 찾을 수 있다. 본문에서 '러시아인들도 관련되었다.'로 표현되어 문제와 본문 간의 의미가 다르므로 답은 FALSE이다.
*사회현상에 대한 문제에서 '절대적 의미'를 갖는 only는 NO/FALSE로 답이 나오는 경향이 있다.

정답 FALSE

ACADEMIC READING

24 The Danube Circle was an unauthorised group for opposing the dam.

○ 키워드 The Danube Circle은 여섯 번째 단락의 첫 번째 문장에서 찾을 수 있다.
unauthorized = illegal, opposing the dam = objecting to the dam

다뉴브 서클은 댐에 반대하는 비합법적인 단체이다.

정답 TRUE

25 The Politburo accepted Vargha as editor of the Hungarian edition.

○ 키워드 The Politburo, Vargha, the Hungarian edition은 일곱 번째 단락의 마지막 문장에서 찾을 수 있다. 문제는 taken from(해임/경질하다)과 다르므로 답은 FALSE이다.

Politburo는 Vargha를 헝가리 편집장으로 임명했다.

정답 FALSE

26 The human rights Charter 77 in Czechoslovakia accepted green thoughts.

○ 키워드 The human rights Charter 77과 green thoughts는 마지막 단락의 두 번째와 첫 번째 문장에서 찾을 수 있다.
accepted = took up, green thoughts = environmentalism

체코슬로바키아의 인권 법 77조항은 환경보호주의자의 이념을 받아들였다.

정답 TRUE

Questions 27-28

Choose the correct letter, **A**, **B**, **C** or **D**.

Write the correct letter in boxes **27-28** on your answer sheet.

27 In this passage, the Nagymaros dam's main purpose was
  A related to the Russian Water Management.
  B to develop a source of electronic power, farming and sail.
  C to connect the Black Sea and the Danube.
  D to develop a beauty spot on the river Danube.

○ 키워드 the Nagymaros dam's main purpose(나지마로스 댐의 주된 목적)을 네 번째 단락의 첫 문장에서 찾을 수 있다.
to develop a source of electronic power = to produce hydroelectricity

본 글에서, Nagymaros 댐의 주된 목적은
A 러시아 수질(운영)관리와 관련 있다.
B 전력과 농경 그리고 해상의 원천을 개발하는 것이다.
C 흑해와 다뉴브를 연결하는 것이다.
D 다뉴브 강의 아름다운 장소를 개발하는 것이다.

정답 B

28 Vargha claims that opposing the dam was
  A to preserve precious ecosystem around the river Danube.
  B to protest against air pollution.
  C to supply plenty of water for fishing and aquaculture in the river Danube.
  D to preserve the site of an ancient Hungarian capital.

○ 키워드 Vargha claims를 세 번째 단락의 첫 번째 문장에서 찾을 수 있다. Vargha는 조사 결과 댐이 환경을 파괴할 수 있음을 알게 되었고, 이를 반대하기 시작했다.

Vargha는 댐 반대는 ~라고 주장한다.
A 다뉴브 강 주위의 소중한 생태계를 보존하기 위해서
B 공기 오염을 막기 위해서
C 다뉴브 강 내의 어업과 양식업어 필요한 풍부한 물 공급을 하기 위해서
D 고대 헝가리 수도 지역을 보존하기 위해서

정답 A

READING PASSAGE 3

You should spend about 20 minutes on Questions 29-40 which are based on Reading Passage 3 on the following pages.

Human Guinea Pig

1 [29, 40]There are 50 million people in the world being used as guinea pigs in clinical trials testing experimental drugs. Apart from potentially risking part of their lives, applicants must pass a severe series of tests just to be able to participate in some trials. However, acceptance means more tests, negative side effects and a considerable disturbance to their daily lives. So what's in it for them? [30, 37]As journalist Alex O'Meara explains in *Chasing Medical Miracles*, some participate out of genuine altruism, whilst some are looking for cures for their own disorders. O'Meara having diabetes himself volunteered for a risky transplant of insulin-producing cells from the liver, and his story spread through the book.

2 [31]O'Meara knows people choose to participate for life's great motivator: money. Clinical trials are a huge business, making up to $24 billion annually, and the cash they offer as compensation has become a sought-after way to make extra money. This exchange of money often involves people who are sick and vulnerable, and emphasises the dark ethical waters in which current clinical trials are mired.

3 [32]At intervals, the ill feel compelled to join a trial to get medical care. Some unethical researchers, desperate to recruit the large numbers needed to make their researches statistically valid, take advantage of this. It can be difficult for ill people to take that, at best, they are taking experimental medicine and at worst they are taking nothing at all.

4 [38]Desperation for money or medicine is never a basis for unbiased decision-making. How can a researcher be sure a person is giving their true consent? And if a person gets better as a result of taking an experimental drug, what happens when their drug supply finishes after the trial?

5 [33, 39]These ethical quandaries have influenced healthcare in developing countries where clinical trials are a prospering industry. According to Adriana Petryna in *When Experiments Travel*, in spite of the fact that drug companies are moving their trials to developing countries, only 10% of drug research addresses disorders that influence the world's poor. Such diseases make up to 90% of the global disease burden. [34]Establishing ethical and legal responsibilities is also becoming

harder, she reports. With an increased number of subcontractors included in trials, it is clear that no one is overly concerned about patient welfare.

6 ³⁵From this theory, international human rights frameworks, such as the Nuremberg Code should ensure that participants are not taking any positive effect. In reality, largely poor and illiterate populations are being exploited. ³⁶Besides, ethical regulations in poor countries are rarely strict, therefore researchers can get away with recruiting people into HIV trials knowing that they will die without the experimental drug.

7 O'Meara also reports about drug company's greed and the inability of regulators to control the rapidly increasing number of trials. The US Food and Drug Administration inspects less than 1% of the 350,000 registered trial sites. Drug firms are managing non-profit organizations that are undertaking just 30% of trials. However, in spite of their faults, clinical trials are still an essential tool of modern medicine.

guinea pig n. 실험대상   severe a. 심각한   altruism n. 애타주의   diabete n. 당뇨병
transplant v. ~을 이식하다   vulnerable a. 상처받기 쉬운   mired a. 진흙 속에 박힌
quandary n. 궁지   prosper v. 번창하다   greed n. 탐욕

Questions 29-36

Complete the summary below.

*Choose **NO MORE THAN THREE WORDS** from the passage for each answer.*

*Write your answers in boxes **29-36** on your answer sheet.*

For testing experimental 29 drugs, there are 50 million people being used as guinea pigs for remedies to 30 their own disorders in clinical trial in spite of the risks through the world. Actually, that means people are both eager for life's considerable milestone of 31 money to make up insufficient labour pay in their lives and 32 medicine to participate in a trial. These ethical dilemmas have influenced health problems in 33 developing countries which drug companies encouraged their trials.

From these situations between **34** ethical and legal responsibilities, international human rights frameworks like **35** (the) Nuremberg code should inform people of poverty of the poor countries which have a lack of **36** strict ethical regulations.

34. 윤리와 법적인 책임 사이의 이러한 상황들로부터,
35. 뉘른베르크 강령과 같은 국제 인권 체제는 36. 엄격한 윤리적 규정이 결여된 가난한 나라의 궁핍한 사람들에게 영향을 미쳐야 한다.

29 ● 키워드 testing experimental과 50 million people은 첫 번째 단락의 첫 번째 문장에서 찾을 수 있다.
testing experimental = clinical trials testing experimental

정답 drugs

30 ● 키워드 remedies to는 첫 번째 단락의 다섯 번째 문장에서 찾을 수 있다.
remedies = cures

정답 their own disorders

31 ● 키워드 eager for life's considerable milestone of와 to make up insufficient labour pay in their lives는 두 번째 단락의 첫 번째 문장에서 찾을 수 있다.
eager for life's considerable milestone of = life's great motivator: money

정답 money

32 ● 키워드 to participate in a trial은 세 번째 단락의 첫 번째 문장에서 찾을 수 있다. to participate in a trial = to join a trial

정답 medicine

33 ● 키워드 ethical dilemmas와 which drug companies encouraged their trials는 다섯 번째 단락의 첫 번째와 두 번째 문장에서 찾을 수 있다.
ethical diemmas = ethical quandaries
encouraged their trials = moving their trials

정답 developing countries

34 ● 키워드 these situations between A and B는 다섯 번째 단락의 네 번째 문장에서 찾을 수 있다. '윤리적(ethical)이며 합법적인 책임(legal responsibilities)을 따지는 것은 더 힘들어진다.' 에서 답을 찾는다.

정답 ethical, legal responsibilities

35 ● 키워드 international human rights frameworks like는 여섯 번째 단락의 첫 번째 문장에서 찾을 수 있다. '이론상으로, 뉘른베르크 강령과 같은 국제 인권 체계에서 임상 실험 참여자들은 어떠한 혜택도 취할 수 없다고 규정해야 한다.' 에서 답을 찾는다.

정답 (the) Nuremberg code

36 ● 키워드 the poor countries와 a lack of은 여섯 번째 단락의 세 번째 문장에서 찾을 수 있다. '게다가, 가난한 나라의 윤리적 규정(ethical regulations)들은 거의 엄격하지 않으므로, 연구원들이 실험용 의약품이 없으면 죽을 거라고 사람들에게 말하면서 HIV 임상실험에 사람들을 모집할 수 있다.'
of the poor countries which have a lack of = in poor countries are rarely strict

정답 strict

ACADEMIC READING

Questions 37-39

Complete the summary below.

Choose **NO MORE THAN TWO WORDS** from the passage for each answer.

Write your answers in boxes **37-39** on your answer sheet.

37 Whilst some choose to cure for themselves, some participated due to ---------------.

  ○ 키워드 cure for themselves와 participated이다. 이 두 단어는 본문 첫 번째 단락의 다섯 번째 문장에서 찾을 수 있다.

일부가 자신의 질병에 대한 치료법을 찾는 동안 일부는 순수한 애타심으로 참여한다.

정답 genuine altruism

38 Hopeless for either --------------- or --------------- does not work for fair decision-making.

  ○ 키워드 Hopeless와 work for fair decision-making이다. 이 두 단어는 본문 네 번째 단락의 첫 번째 문장에서 찾을 수 있다.
  Hopeless = Desperation, fair decision-making = unbiased decision-making

돈 혹은 의약품에 대한 포기가 공정한 의사 결정에 작용하지 않았다.

정답 money, medicine

39 Drug companies invest a lot of money in developing countries, causing ---------------.

  ○ 키워드 Drug companies와 developing countries이다. 이 두 단어는 본문 다섯 번째 단락의 두 번째와 첫 번째 문장에서 찾을 수 있다. '이러한 윤리적인 곤혹감은 임상 실험들이 발달한 개발도상국의 의료 서비스에 영향을 준다.' 에서 답을 찾는다.

제약 회사는 개발도상국에 막대한 자금을 투자하였으며, 그것은 윤리적인 당혹감의 원인이 되었다.

정답 ethical quandaries

Questions 40

Complete the correct letter, **A**, **B**, **C** or **D**.

Write the correct letter in box **40** on your answer sheet.

40 Which of the following phrases best describes the main aim of Reading Passage 3?

  A to warn that guinea pigs are likely to have financial problems
  B to describe how clinical trial was rapidly increasing and how serious it was
  C to suggest that Nuremberg Code is needed in other countries
  D to examine how drug companies promoted the use of guinea pigs

  ○ 문제의 요지는 주된 목적이므로, 이것은 첫 번째 단락에서 찾을 수 있다. human guinea pig에 대한 의학적 시술의 남용과 심각성을 서술하고 있다'

본 글의 주된 목적을 잘 묘사하고 있는 어구는 무엇인가?

A 기니피그가 재정적 문제를 갖게 될 가능성에 대해서 경고하고 있다.
B 임상 실험이 어떻게 급속도로 증가하고 있으며 얼마나 심각한지를 묘사하고 있다.
C 뉘른베르크 강령이 다른 나라에 필요하다고 제안하고 있다.
D 어떻게 제약회사가 기니피그의 활용을 홍보하는지 조사하고 있다.

정답 B

Academic Reading

Actual Test 6

Answer Sheet

1	NOT GIVEN	11	B	21	NO	31	iv
2	TRUE	12	E	22	YES	32	i
3	FALSE	13	G	23	YES	33	viii
4	NOT GIVEN	14	(the) yellow crescent	24	NO	34	ii
5	TRUE	15	enforcement	25	NOT GIVEN	35	vi
6	TRUE	16	ribs	26	D	36	drinking
7	TRUE	17	trauma	27	C	37	three-quarters
8	C	18	live cancer	28	A	38	11
9	A	19	eyes, liver	29	iii	39	dehydration
10	F	20	bear farming	30	vii	40	delayed drinkers

ACADEMIC READING

READING PASSAGE 1

You should spend about 20 minutes on *Questions 1-13* which are based on Reading Passage 1 below.

Extraterrestrial National Park

1 The message to visitors at many beauty spots is "TAKE only pictures, leave only footprints." Although you won't see the actual place, Apollo11 astronauts Neil Armstrong and Buzz Aldrin took their giant leap for mankind on the moon. It will be the first extraterrestrial national park.

2 [1, 8]It may still be some years off, but the imminent reality of space tourism is already stimulating some archaeologists to begin to plan how to protect historic sites in space. With further moon missions planned, the fear is that the principle sites like Apollo11's landing place may be in danger. According to Beth O'Leary, a researcher in New Mexico State University in Las Cruces, "Technologically, probably the most important event in human history was to land on another celestial body," "It's like the discovery of fire, or the first stone tools. They should be protected and conserved."

3 [2]In September 1959 since the Soviet Union's Luna2 crashed into the moon, a total of 40 expeditions have touched down on the moon's surface. [3]22 of them were launched by the US with the six, crewed Apollo missions launching between 1969 and 1972. [9]The Apollo missions alone left behind 23 large artefacts including the descent and ascent stages of the lunar module landing equipment, the stage three Saturn rockets used to fly them there, and the lunar rovers or "moon buggies" the astronauts used to explore when they arrived.

4 [4]As well as these, there are also smaller artefacts and personal items scattered around, such as Neil Armstrong's boots and portable life-support system, scientific instruments and their power generators. Of course, the iconic US flag planted in the moon's surface is there too. [5]There are also the footprints and rover tread paths. In spite of the passing of the years, these remains are carved into the dust, since the moon has no wind or rain to wash them away.

5 [10]P.J. Capelotti, an anthropologist at Penn State University in Abington, has mapped out five "lunar parks." These are the areas where the majority of the artefacts are concentrated and will be used as a basis for future preservation efforts. "Although nobody's saying that the whole moon has to be off-limits, people are starting to make plans for tourism and mineral extraction, or for putting a base there, needing to be aware of them and work around them."

6   More technological developments are also on their way. [11]NASA's LCROSS mission plans to crash an SUV-sized rocket into one of the moon's poles later this year with the hope of finding water there. At the same time, teams competing for the Google Lunar X Prize for the first privately funded robot to reach the moon have been offered a $ 5 million bonus if they take a picture of artefacts like the Apollo11 landing equipment. Already, a question to be reported is how national governments and private companies should cooperate to ensure that artefacts are protected. There is some evidence that the US government is interested in working alongside other governments.

7   [12]A space-flight company called TransOrbital, based in Palo Alto, California, presented its plans for sending a commercial mission to the moon by the end of the 1990s. [6]These plans include making detailed maps of the moon and landing a capsule containing personal items, like business cards and cremated ashes. The US National Oceanic and Atmospheric Administration stipulated that TransOrbital's rockets must crash well away from any historic US artefacts when its flight was over. [7]Although ultimately TransOrbital were unable to fund the mission, it might try again in the near future.

8   [13]According to Phil Stooke, a planetary cartographer of the University of Western Ontario in London, he agrees Luna2 also has great significance. "It crashed, but that impact site is every bit as historic as Apollo11." Another one is Luna9, the first spacecraft to land sending back pictures. "They must be preserved."

9   On the remaining Apollo sites, Stooke is searching how electronics, metal and paints have degraded after years of exposure to solar radiation and extremes of temperature. Also, he suggests that another Apollo site could be turned into a biological research centre, analysing the DNA and bacteria left behind from astronauts' life-support packs.

10   Once a consensus has been reached as to which sites are worthy of conservation, and guidelines have been built up to protect them from being damaged by future missions, the next question will be how future space tourists should be allowed to interact with them. Capelotti says, "Looking at grey dust is going to hold its attraction for only so long," "People are going to make pilgrimages to these sites."

11   There is a suggestion to build domes over historic sites, or perhaps even hotels, with the artefacts displayed in the "lobby." Another idea is to build up a raised railway track over the sites, so visitors could look at them without touching them. Capelotti says, "If Walt Disney was developing it, he would put a monorail

ACADEMIC READING

around all five 'lunar parks,' so you could do the entire Apollo tour."

---

extraterrestrial a. 대기권 밖의　archaeologist n. 고고학자　celestial a. 하늘의
descent n. 하강　ascent n. 상승　pilgrimage n. 성지순례

11 유적지에 돔이나 심지어 '르비'에 인공물들을 전시하는 호텔들을 건설하자는 제안이 있다. 또 다른 의견은 유적지를 건너는 높은 철도를 건설해서, 관광객들이 그곳을 밟지 않고 볼 수 있게 하자는 것이다. Capelotti는 "만약 Walt Disney가 이곳을 개발했다면, 그는 5개의 모든 '달 공원' 주위에 모노레일을 깔았을 것이고, 이것으로 당신은 모든 아폴로호 관광을 할 수 있게 된다."고 말한다.

Questions 1-7

Do the following statements reflect the claims of the writer in Reading Passage 1?

In boxes **1-7** on your answer sheet write

TRUE	*if the statement agrees with the information*
FALSE	*if the statement contradicts the information*
NOT GIVEN	*if there is no information on this*

1 Archaeologists have established links between space tourism and Apollo11.

　▶ 키워드 Archaeologists는 두 번째 단락의 첫 번째 문장에서 찾을 수 있다. 우주 관광과 아폴로 11호 사이의 관계는 본문에선 알 수 없으므로 답은 NOT GIVEN이다.

고고학자들은 우주 관광과 아폴로 11호를 관계지어 왔다.

정답 NOT GIVEN

2 Of the 40 expeditions that landed on the lunar, the US embarked on more than half of them.

　▶ 숫자 키워드인 Of the 40 expeditions는 세 번째 단락에서 찾을 수 있다. 그중 22회가 미국에 의해 시도되었다고 했으므로 미국이 반 이상 시도했다는 진술은 사실이다.

달에 접촉한 40회의 탐험 중에서 미국이 반 이상 시도했다.

정답 TRUE

3 Between 1969 and 1972, there were not remarkable issues in the Apollo missions.

　▶ 숫자 키워드인 Between 1969 and 1972는 세 번째 단락에서 찾을 수 있다. 이 기간 동안 6명을 태운 아폴로 탐사가 있었으므로 문제와 달라 답은 FALSE이다.

1969년과 1972년 사이에 아폴로 우주비행에 주목할 만한 사건은 없었다.

정답 FALSE

4 Neil Armstrong made up his mind to exploit the natural resources of the moon.

　▶ 키워드 Neil Armstrong은 네 번째 단락의 첫 번째 문장에서 찾을 수 있다. 그러나 문제의 내용을 본문에선 알 수 없다.

Neil Armstrong은 달의 천연자원을 발굴하기로 결심하였다.

정답 NOT GIVEN

222

5 Astronauts' traces marked on the surface of the moon remain unchanged due to the lack of wind and rain.

> 키워드 Astronauts' traces와 due to the lack of wind and rain은 네 번째 단락의 세 번째와 네 번째 문장에서 찾을 수 있다.
> traces = the footprints and rover tread paths
> wind and rain = wash them away

달 표면에 새겨진 우주인들의 자취들은 바람과 비가 없어 변하지 않고 남아 있다.

정답 TRUE

6 Commercial space-flight companies planned to place both business cards and ashes on the moon.

> 키워드 both business cards and ashes는 일곱 번째 단락에서 찾을 수 있다. 본문에서 TransOrbital이라는 비행 회사는 달에 명함과 유해 같은 것을 발송하는 비행을 계획했다.

상업 우주 항공 회사는 명함과 유해를 달에 발송하는 것을 계획했다.

정답 TRUE

7 In spite of financial problems, TransOrbital plan to launch their mission again in the foreseeable future.

> 키워드 TransOrbital과 launch their mission again in the foreseeable future는 일곱 번째 단락의 마지막 문장에서 찾을 수 있다.
> mission again = try again

재정적인 문제에도 불구하고, TransOrbital사는 가까운 미래에 비행을 다시 시도할 것을 계획한다.

정답 TRUE

Questions 8-13

Complete each sentence with the correct ending, **A-H**, below.

Write the correct letter, **A-H**, in boxes **8-13** on your answer sheet.

A	left various artefacts on the moon's surface.
B	discovered water supported by NASA's LCROSS mission scheme.
C	aimed to launch a project to preserve relic sites in space.
D	funded a robot to reach the moon.
E	promoted commercial business on the moon.
F	designed the lunar parks for cultural industries resources.
G	had a similar historic impact to Apollo11.
H	made detailed maps of the moon and personal items.

A	달 표면에 다양한 인공 구조물을 남겨 두는 것
B	NASA의 LCROSS 비행 계획으로 물을 발견하는 것
C	우주의 역사적인 지역을 보호하는 방법에 대한 계획을 수립하는 것
D	달에 도달하기 위한 로봇에 투자하는 것
E	달에 산업을 촉진하는 것
F	문화 산업 자원을 목적으로 달 공원을 만드는 것
G	아폴로 11호와 같은 유사한 역사적 영향력을 가지는 것
H	달의 자세한 지도와 개인 소지품을 만드는 것

ACADEMIC READING

8 Archaeologists

○ 본문에서 Archaeologists는 두 번째 단락의 첫 번째 문장에서 찾을 수 있다.
launch a project to preserve relic sites in space = begin to plan how to protect historic sites in space

정답 C

9 The Apollo missions

○ 본문에서 The Apollo missions는 세 번째 단락의 세 번째 문장에서 찾을 수 있다.
left various artefacts on the moon's surface = left behind 23 large artefacts

정답 A

10 Anthropologist P.J. Capelotti

○ 본문에서 P.J Capelotti는 다섯 번째 단락의 첫 번째 문장에서 찾을 수 있다.
designed the lunar parks for cultural industries resources = mapped out five "lunar parks"

정답 F

11 SUV-sized rocket into the moon's pole

○ 본문에서 SUV-sized rocket은 여섯 번째 단락의 두 번째 문장에서 찾을 수 있다.
discovered water = finding water there

정답 B

12 TransOrbital

○ 본문에서 TransOrbital은 일곱 번째 단락의 첫 번째 문장에서 찾을 수 있다.
promoted commercial business on the lunar = its plans for sending a commercial mission to the moon

정답 E

13 The impact site of Luna2

○ 본문에서 Luna2는 여덟 번째 단락의 첫 번째 문장에서 찾을 수 있다.
had a similar historic impact to Apollo11 = impact site is every bit as historic as Apollo11

정답 G

READING PASSAGE 2

You should spend about 20 minutes on Questions 14-28 which are based on Reading Passage 2 below.

Asiatic black bear

1 [14, 21]Known as a moon bear, Jasper is an Asiatic black bear with a yellow crescent on his chest. The bear came to the Animals Asia Moon Bear Rescue Centre in Chengdu, China, from a bear farm in 2000.

2 When Jasper arrived, rescuers had to cut Jasper out of a tiny "crush cage." [22, 26]Bear bile has been used in traditional Chinese medicine and fetches a high price. The wholesale price is approximately 4000 yuan (approximately $ 580) per kilogram with each bear producing up to 5 kilograms every year in China. But it comes at a high price.

3 Jasper normally spent 15 years in a cage. Other bears spend up to 25 years without moving in cages no bigger than their bodies. [23]Bears are milked for bile twice a day. In China, farmers use a catheter inserted into the gall bladder or permanently open wound. In Vietnam, Farmers use long hypodermic needles.

4 The Animals Asia has rescued 260 bears from Chinese bear farms over the past 10 years. These bears are lucky. The official number of reared bears in China is 7,000, but the Animals Asia fears the real figure is close to 10,000.

5 In spite of the obvious cruelty, bear farming is legal in China. Whilst the Convention on International Trade in Endangered Species lists Asiatic black bears as being at the highest level of endangerment, China grants them only second-level protection allowing them to be farmed. Although some have reported there are 15,000 bears, its figure is not a true estimate of the remaining wild population in China.

6 [15]Bear farming is also practiced in Vietnam where it is illegal but remains common due to a lack of enforcement. There are approximately 4,000 bears on Vietnamese farms but even more in Laos, Cambodia and Korea.

7 Bear farming is justified on the grounds that it satisfies the local demand for bile in China, therefore decreasing the number of bears are taken from the wild. Since 1989 farmers have been allowed to breed bears in captivity and hunting wild bears has been illegal. In spite of this, a lot of wild bears are still poached for their gall bladders or to restock the farms. [16]Sometimes bears arrive at the rescue centre with missing ribs after being caught in the wild.

8 [17]Those bears that arrived at the centre have suffered from severe physical and psychological trauma. Rescued bears can't be set free into the wild due to the long-term damage caused by their incarceration. They all need surgery to get rid of damaged gall bladders and many need additional surgery and long-term medical care because of missing claws or paws, infected necrotic wounds along with broken and missing teeth caused by biting at bars or because farmers break them to make the bears less of a hazard. [18]Also, many have liver cancer as a result of being continually milked for bile and suffer from litany of other ailments including blindness, arthritis, peritonitis, weeping ulcers and ingrown claws.

9 On the other hand, with the horrors of bear farming, the rehabilitation process is amazing and inspiring to witness. It takes around a year to rehabilitate a bear. Although some have to be kept alone for the rest of their lives, most can eventually be housed with other bears. The transition in personality from animals who are violent and fearful to ones who are trusting, inquisitive and completely at ease with people is truly remarkable, Robinson says, "I have visited the rescue centre and it changed my life." That is how powerful the bears' stories are.

10 In spite of the rescue programme, bear bile extraction remains a cause of wanton and remorseless abuse. [19, 24]It is difficult to change attitudes when bear bile has been used in Chinese medicine for over 3,000 years to cope with "heat related" ailments, such as eye conditions, liver disease. These days, it is used to treat conditions from hangovers to haemorrhoids. There is some evidence from western medicine that a synthetic version of the active ingredient in bear bile, ursodeoxycholic acid, is able to treat a range of disorders including hepatitis C. But traditional Chinese medicine still insists on using natural bear bile which is often contaminated with pus, blood, urine and faeces. Although healthy bear bile is free flowing and orangey-green, veterinarians describe bile leaking from the diseased gall bladders of rescued bears as "black sludge."

11 The half-moon bear rescue project raises a number of critical questions. For instance, why do bears show large individual differences in response to persecution, and variations in recovery? Rescued bears are powerful ambassadors, but should so much time and money be invested in saving the lives of individuals who will not make any direct contributions to saving their species? How can people from outside China work to free bears whilst respecting their Chinese colleagues and remaining sensitive to cultural traditions?

12 Efforts to quit bear farming will continue. [20, 25, 27]Soon after Robinson established the Animals Asia in 1998, she negotiated an agreement with the Chinese government to work towards the eradication of bear farming. All farmers are cruel, but the very worst are identified for closure by the government and the farmers have their licences revoked. It is bears from these farms that come to the rescue centre. The Animals Asia compensates the farmers so that they can begin another business or retire. More than 40 farms have so far been closed, and China has not issued any new licences since 1994.

---

crescent n. 초승달 fetch v. ~을 데리고 오다 insert v. 삽입하다 poach v. 밀렵하다 gall n. 답즙 bladder n. 방광 restock v. 보충하다 severe a. 심각한 trauma n. 정신적 외상 incarceration n. 감금 necrotic a. 괴저성의 hazard n. 위험 litany n. 장황한 설명 ailment n. 병 rehabilitation n. 회복 inquisitive a. 호기심이 강한 wanton a. 고의적인 remorseless a. 무정한 hangover n. 숙취 veterinarian n. 수의사

12 곰 사육을 금지하는 노력은 계속되고 있다. Robinson이 1998년에 Animals Asia를 설립한 뒤로, 그녀는 곰 사육을 금지하는 방향으로 중국 정부와 협상했다. 모든 농장주들이 잔인했지만 가장 나쁜 농장주들은 정부에 의한 폐쇄가 확인되었고 농장주들의 허가증이 취소되었다. 보호센터에 오는 곰들은 바로 이러한 농장들로부터 온다. Animals Asia는 농장주들에게 다른 사업을 시작하거나 은퇴를 할 수 있게 보상을 해 주고 있다. 지금까지 40개 이상의 곰 사육 농장들이 문을 닫았으며, 중국은 1994년 이후 어떠한 새로운 허가증을 발행하지 않았다.

Questions 14-20

Complete the summary below.

Choose **NO MORE THAN THREE WORDS** from the passage for each answer.

Write your answer in boxes **14-20** on your answer sheet.

In 2000 Jasper, an Asiatic black bear, in China, was called a moon bear due to embedding **14** (the) yellow crescent on the chest. Whilst bear farming is illegal, it is prevalent because of weak **15** enforcement in Vietnam. Since 1989 hunting wild bears has been illegal in China, breeding bears in the farmland is not prohibited, at intervals, bears are delivered to the rescue centre without **16** ribs by poachers.

Most bears arrived at the centre have experienced **17** trauma of both physical and psychological problems to be continued. Besides, **18** liver cancer is caused by extracting the bile from bear's gall. Over 3,000 years Chinese has made use of the bile for healing illness like both **19** eyes and liver. In 1998 the Animals Asia was established by Robinson. She made an agreement against bear farming. Actually, she negotiated with Chinese government to eliminate **20** bear farming.

ACADEMIC READING

14 ➲ 키워드 In 2000 Jasper, an Asiatic black bear와 on the chest는 첫 번째 단락의 첫 번째 문장에서 찾을 수 있다. 반달곰으로도 알려진 Jasper는 '가슴에 노란색 초승달이 있는' Asiatic black bear(아시아 흑곰)이다.

정답 (the) yellow crescent

15 ➲ 키워드 in Vietnam은 여섯 번째 단락의 첫 번째 문장에서 찾을 수 있다.
prevalent = remain common, weak = lack of

정답 enforcement

16 ➲ 키워드 bears are delivered to the rescue centre without은 일곱 번째 단락의 마지막 문장에서 찾을 수 있다.
are delivered to = arrive at, without = with missing

정답 ribs

17 ➲ 키워드 both physical and psychological problems는 여덟 번째 단락의 첫 번째 문장에서 찾을 수 있다.
experienced = suffered

정답 trauma

18 ➲ 키워드 extracting the bile from bear's gall은 여덟 번째 단락의 마지막 문장에서 찾을 수 있다.
extracting the bile = milked for bile

정답 liver cancer

19 ➲ 키워드 Over 3,000 years와 healing illness는 열 번째 단락의 두 번째 문장에서 찾을 수 있다.
healing illness = "heat related" ailments

정답 eyes, liver

20 ➲ 키워드 she negotiated with Chinese government는 열두 번째 단락의 두 번째 문장에서 찾을 수 있다.
eliminate = remove

정답 bear farming

Questions 21-25

Do the following statements reflect the claims of the writer in Reading Passage 2?

*In boxes **21-25** on your answer sheet write*

    YES   *if the statement reflects the opinion of the writer*
    NO   *if the statement contradicts the opinion of the writer*
    NOT GIVEN *if it is impossible to say what the writer thinks about this*

21 Jasper is an Asiatic black bear and it had grown in the wild.

Jasper는 아시아 흑곰이며 야생에서 자랐다.

➲ 키워드 an Asiatic black bear과 grown in the wild는 첫 번째 단락의 첫 번째 문장과 두 번째 문장에서 찾을 수 있다. 본문에서 Jasper는 곰 사육 농가에서 잡혀 왔다고 했으므로 (또한 우리에서 15년을 보냈다고 했으므로) 문제와 본문 간의 내용이 달라서 답은 NO이다.

정답 NO

22 Chinese is accustomed to use the bear bile as traditional medicine from the old times.

　● 키워드 Chinese is accustomed to use the bear bile과 as traditional medicine은 두 번째 단락의 두 번째 문장에서 찾을 수 있다.
　is accustomed to use = has been used

중국인들은 웅담을 전통적 의약으로 사용해 왔다.

정답 YES

23 The bile from bear's gall is extracted every day.

　● 키워드 is extracted는 세 번째 단락의 세 번째 문장에서 찾을 수 있다.
　extract = milk: ~을 추출하다

웅담은 매일 추출된다.

정답 YES

24 Even though bear bile use has spread among Chinese, it had no effect on them.

　● 키워드 bear bile use has spread among Chinese는 열 번째 단락의 두 번째 문장에서 찾을 수 있다.

웅담이 중국인들에게 널리 보급이 되었지만, 약효는 없었다.

정답 NO

25 In 1998 Robinson has reported the Animals Asia to the United Nations.

　● 키워드 In 1998 Robinson과 the Animals Asia은 열두 번째 단락의 두 번째 문장에서 찾을 수 있다. '1998년 로빈슨은 유엔에 Animals Asia 센터를 보고했다.' 라는 문제의 내용을 본문에선 알 수 없으므로 답은 NOT GIVEN이다.

1998년 Robinson은 유엔에 the Animals Asia 센터를 보고했다.

정답 NOT GIVEN

Questions 26-27

Choose the correct letter, **A**, **B**, **C** and **D**.

Write the correct letter in boxes **26-27** on your answer sheet.

26 The writer reports that bear bile have been prevalent in China due to
　A working a sense of beauty for women.
　B using traditional medicine and a little expense.
　C delaying the ageing and relieving mental fatigue.
　D using traditional medicine and its price being skyrocketing.

　● 키워드 bear bile have been prevalent in China은 두 번째 단락의 두 번째 문장에서 찾을 수 있다.
　its price being skyrocketing = fetches a high price

저자는 ~ 중국에서 웅담이 널리 퍼져 있다고 보도하고 있다.
A 여성들의 미적 감각에 효과가 있어서
B 전통 의약으로 활용되며 비용이 저렴해서
C 노화를 지연시키고 정신적인 피로를 이완시켜 주어서
D 전통 의약으로 활용되며 가격이 치솟아서

정답 D

ACADEMIC READING

27 Jill Robinson founded the Animals Asia in 1998 in order to
- **A** protect animals in Asian zoo.
- **B** promote the bear rescue project to the United Nations.
- **C** protect the bear and prohibit brutal farming in Asia.
- **D** support bear farms.

Jill Robinson는 1998년 Animals Asia 기관을 ~ 건립했다.
A 아시아 동물원의 동물을 보호하기 위해서
B UN에 곰 구출 계획을 홍보하려고
C 곰을 보호하고 아시아의 야만적인 사육을 막기 위해서
D 곰 사육 농장을 후원하기 위해서

○ 키워드 Jill Robinson founded the Animals Asia in 1998은 열두 번째 단락의 두 번째 문장에서 찾을 수 있다.
prohibit brutal farming = work towards the eradication of bear farming

정답 C

Questions 28

From the list below choose the most suitable title for Reading Passage 2.

*Write the appropriate letter **A-E** in boxes 28 on your answer sheet.*

- **A** Cruel bear bile business
- **B** Increasing the bear bile supply
- **C** Traditional Chinese medicine
- **D** Rescue project forward
- **E** Bear farming enforcement

A 잔인한 웅담 사업
B 웅담 공급의 증가
C 전통 중국 약제
D 사전 계획의 보호
E 웅담 농업의 강화

○ 본 문제는 주제[the most suitable title]를 찾는 문제이다. 주제는 첫 번째 단락 ~ 두 번째 단락(두괄식)에서 알 수 있다. 아시아(중국) 전통 요법과 거래 가격 폭리로 인한 만연화된 웅담 사업이 적절하다.

정답 A

READING PASSAGE 3

You should spend about 20 minutes on *Questions 29-40* which are based on Reading Passage 3 on the following pages.

Questions 29-35

Reading Passage 3 has eight sections, **A-H**.

Choose the correct heading for sections **B-H** from the list of headings below.

Write the correct number, *i-viii*, in boxes **29-35** on your answer sheet.

List of Headings

i	The opposite of Adolph's view
ii	Adolph's studies to guarantee in the book
iii	The utmost limits for survival
iv	Positive evidence of Adolph's research
v	A barren landscape for marching
vi	Noakes' stance on humans of drinking
vii	A simple solution for developing performance
viii	Misjudgment of Salazar's thought

i	Adolph의 견해에 대한 반대
ii	저서에서 확언하는 Adolph의 연구
iii	생존에 대한 극한성
iv	Adolph의 연구에 대한 긍정적인 증거
v	행진에 혹독한 환경
vi	음료를 마시는 인간에 대한 Noakes의 입장
vii	성과 향상을 위한 단순한 해결안
viii	Salazar의 생각의 오판

Example   *Answer*
Section **A**   **v**

29 Section **B**

○ B단락의 첫 번째와 두 번째 문장에서 '그가 뜨겁고, 건조한 상태가 인체에 미치는 영향에 대해 생각한 첫 번째 사람은 아니었다.' 와 '아른거리는 신기루를 향해 기어가다 사막에서 길을 잃은 여행자의 모습은 아마도 사막 여행 그 자체만큼 오래되었을 것이다.' 에서 답을 찾을 수 있다.

정답 iii

30 Section **C**

○ C단락의 첫 번째 문장을 보면 알 수 있다. Adolph의 발견은 시합 중에 물을 마시는 것이 경기를 향상시켜 준다는 것이다.

정답 vii

31 Section **D**

○ D단락은 Adolph의 주장을 뒷받침할 수 있는 근거로 인체는 체온이 높을 때 땀 배출을 통해 수분을 증발시키고 다시 수분을 보충하기 위해서는 수분 공급이 필요하다는 내용이다.

정답 iv

ACADEMIC READING

32 Section E

○ E단락의 첫 번째 문장에서 '그러나 이것에 대한 완전한 반대 의견도 있었다.'에서 앞 단락 Adolph의 견해에 대한 반대 의견을 제시하고 있다.

정답 i

33 Section F

○ F단락의 세 번째 문장에서 모든 사람들은 Salazar가 잘못된 행동을 했다는 것을 알아냈다. 즉, Salazar가 경기 전 경기 중에 충분한 물을 섭취하지 않아 탈진하고 거의 죽을 뻔했다고 나타낸다.

정답 viii

34 Section G

○ G단락의 첫 번째 문장에서 Adolph는 이런 사실을 인정했었지만, 그의 저서에서 사실을 서술해 놓은 몇 줄로 증명하기엔 너무 분명하다고 생각했다.

정답 ii

35 Section H

○ H단락의 첫 번째 문장에서 Noakes는 인간은 "지연된 음료 마시는 사람"이라고 지적한 것과 같이 인간은 사냥 습성으로 인해 편할 때까지 마시는 것을 미룬다고 설명했다.

정답 vi

Colorado Desert

A Particularly in the summer, California's lower Colorado desert is a harsh place. It's a barren landscape of rocks and rattlesnakes that little grows in but creosote bushes and cactus. Midday temperatures can reach 43℃ and searing winds and afternoon sun combine to suck moisture from the body. This is not the place for a midday march, but that is precisely what Edward Adolph had in mind when, in the summer of 1942, he took a group of soldiers and researchers there. Adolph, a physiologist at the University of Rochester in New York state, wanted to investigate how people could live and work efficiently in the desert and how to get the best out of them.

B 29He wasn't the first to consider the effects of hot, dry conditions on the human body. The image of the traveler lost in the desert, crawling towards a shimmering mirage, is probably as old as desert travel itself. But earlier researchers mainly focused on survival. According to Timothy Noakes, an exercise physiologist at the University of Cape Town and master of some of the world's toughest ultra-marathons, "They never looked at performance." Adolph was the first to test the presumptions most of the people still have about what to do if forced to make any sort of effort in unbearable heat. He discovered most were

Colorado 사막

A 캘리포니아의 더 낮은 곳에 위치한 Colorado 사막은 혹독한 장소이며, 특히 여름철엔 더하다. 이곳은 크레오소트 관목과 선인장을 제외한 어떤 생물도 성장할 수 없는 바위와 방울뱀들의 황무지이다. 한낮의 기온은 최고 43도를 육박하며 메마른 바람과 오후의 태양은 몸의 수분을 흡수할 정도로 이글거린다. 이곳은 한낮에 행진하기에 적합한 장소는 아니지만, 1942년 여름에 Edward Adolph가 병사들과 연구원들을 그곳에 데리고 갔을 때 염두에 두었던 곳이다. 뉴욕의 Rochester대학의 물리학자인 Adolph는 사람들이 어떻게 사막에서 효율적으로 생활하고 일을 할 수 있으며, 사막에서 최선을 다하게 하는 방법을 얻을 수 있는지 조사하고 싶었다.

B 그는 뜨겁고, 건조한 상태가 인체에 미치는 영향을 생각한 첫 번째 사람은 아니었다. 아른거리는 신기루를 향해 기어가다 사막에서 길을 잃은 여행자의 모습은 아마도 사막 여행 그 자체만큼 오래되었을 것이다. 그러나 초기 연구원들은 주로 생존에 초점을 맞추었다. "그들은 결코 연기를 보지 않았다."라고 Cape Town대학 실험물리학자이며, 세계에서 가장 힘든 울트라 마라톤의 베테랑인 Timothy Noakes는 말했다. Adolph는 만약 견딜 수 없는 열에서 어떤 노력을 할 경우 무엇을 해야 할지에 관해 대부분의 사람들이 가지고 있는 가정을 최초로 실험한 사람이었다. 그

232

myths. For example, Stripping to T-shirt and shorts is not the best way to treat dehydration. Although long sleeves and long trousers may feel hotter, they'll slow the loss of water. Nor is there any point in rationing water when supplies are low. Postponing drinking it only makes you unhappier sooner. Adolph wrote "It is better to drink the water and have it inside you than to carry it."

C 30, 36The most critical of Adolph's discoveries was the simplest: drinking during exercise enhances performance. Nowadays, we take this for granted, but generations of coaches and distance runners were taught that drinking during exercise was for wimps. Some claimed it would only make you thirstier. Others said it could even trigger a heart attack. The author of *Marathon Running* in 1909 advised, "Don't buy into the habit of drinking and eating in a marathon race," "Some outstanding runners do, but it is not helpful." Adolph tested these old assumptions by splitting his soldiers into two groups. When the average afternoon high was up to 42℃, both marched through the desert for 8 hours. The soldiers in one group were allowed to drink as much water as they needed and the others weren't allowed any water. The results were obvious, the drinkers outperformed the non-drinkers, but the men in both groups back out once they had sweated off 7 to 10% of their body weight.

D 31To Adolph, this made perfect sense. On days when the temperature is hotter than the average person's skin temperature – approximately 33℃ the only way for the body to cool itself is by the evaporation of sweat, and he could estimate how much moisture that required. 37A brisk walk could easily need three quarters of a litre or more, of evaporative cooling each hour. Adolph's research was launched by the North Africa campaign, and he finished in 1943. But he came back to the desert every summer and supplemented his experiments with tests in his heated lab. His discoveries stayed secret until 1947, when published *Physiology of Man in the Desert*. It went almost entirely unnoticed. In the late 1960s, marathon runners were still advised not to drink water during races. 38Until 1977, runners in international competitions were prohibited from drinking water in the first 11 kilometres and after that were allowed water only every 5 kilometres.

E 32However, there was a complete reversal of opinion. A study began to warn of the dangers of running a marathon without enough water and suddenly runners were told they must drink during the race – and if they didn't feel like it they should force themselves or risk heatstroke. In 1978, Alberto Salazar, one of America's great distance runners, ran a 7.1-mile race in temperatures of 29℃. At mile six, he was in second place. He said later, "The last thing I remember, and I was watching Bill Rodgers pull away from me. It was dreamlike. Bill was floating away, and I wasn't able to follow the energy to go after him. In the next mile, I faded from second to tenth, but I do not have any memory of being passed by anyone."

F [39]Salazar almost died. At the finish, his body temperature was 42℃ and he was saved only as a result of a quick-thinking member of the medical crew promptly dumping him into a tub of iced water. [33]Everyone "found" what Salazar had done wrong: Salazar hadn't drunk enough before or during the race. He therefore became dehydrated and nearly killed himself. Even Salazar accepted this. "Dehydration is insidious," he would later say. At first glance, Adolph's discoveries seem to support this. His notes about his dehydrated soldiers are a litany of sorrow. "Their only desire is to stop and to rest," he wrote of one man, after 13.4 waterless kilometres in 40℃ heat. "He had an unsocial attitude, began to lag and finally stopped," he wrote of another, who managed 29.8 kilometres at 34℃.

Both 1970s and 1980s runners and coaches assumed that collapsing athletes like Salazar were simply extreme cases of the same thing. Dehydration and heat collapse were virtually synonymous in many minds. "Drink early and often," athletes were told it and not just when thirsty. However, as Noakes points out, none of Adolph's dehydrated soldiers suffered heatstroke. "They just got very angry and stopped walking." What's more, they recovered quickly when allowed to rest and drink. "They were able to walk almost immediately after drinking water," Adolph wrote in one case. In another: "exhaustion relieved by water." Salazar's brush with death wasn't the result of drinking too little: on a very hot day he had simply tried to run a world-class race. Under these kinds of conditions, heat is the enemy, not dehydration.

G [34]Adolph had accepted this but thought it too clear to guarantee more than a few lines in his book. He had conducted most of his tests on marches, not because he wasn't interested in the effects of running in the heat, but because when he made his soldiers run, even at a slow jog their body temperature soared by 2.5℃ in 30 minutes. "There is no doubt that men are limited in the physical work they can do in the desert," he wrote. The advocates of drinking-early-and-often had also overlooked Adolph's discovery that even soldiers who were able to drink what they wanted still tended to dehydrate, and only made up their deficiencies at mealtimes. Adolph disregarded this as a "peculiarity of dehydration," but Noakes believes he had stumbled upon a quirk of human evolution.

H [35, 40]Humans, Noakes observed are "delayed drinkers." He supposes that this is a consequence of early humans hunting and chasing game for long distances under the African sun. There are good reasons for not stopping to drink during a hunt, not least the expectation of the prey escaping. There's also the fact that we are not built like camels and other animals that are able to drink deeply and quickly. That makes us better runners – and running hunters – but means we cannot drink as much as we can sweat, so we delay our thirst until it's comfortable to drink, says Noakes. Adolph never used the word evolution in his book but he would have understood Noakes's point.

rattlesnakes n. 방울뱀들   searing a. 타는 듯한   shimmer v. 빛나다   presumption n. 가정   dehydration n. 탈수   trigger v. ~를 일으키다   evaporation n. 탈수   supplement v. 보충하다   synonymous a. 동의어의   advocate v. ~을 변호하다   deficiency n. 결핍   peculiarity n. 특징   quirk n. 별난 점

30분 이내에 2.5도까지 올라갔기 때문이다. "사람들이 사막에서 할 수 있는 물리적 일은 제한이 있다는 것은 의심의 여지가 없다."라고 그는 기록했다. 물을 일찍, 자주 마시는 것을 옹호하는 사람들은 원하는 것을 마신 병사들도 탈수 증상이 있고 단지 식사 시간에 부족분을 보충했다고 주장한 Adolph의 발견을 무시했다. Adolph는 이런 현상을 '탈진의 특이한 성질'로 무시했지만 Noakes는 그가 인간 진화의 급변을 우연히 발견했다고 믿었다.

H Noakes가 관찰한 인류는 "지연된 음료 마시는 사람"이다. 그는 이것을 초기 인류가 아프리카 태양 아래서 장거리 사냥과 목표물을 쫓은 결과라고 가정한다. 사냥하는 도중에 물을 마시지 않은 충분한 이유가 있는데, 특히 사냥감이 도망가리라는 예상 때문이다. 인간은 물을 깊이 빨리 마실 수 있는 낙타와 다른 동물들과는 다르게 만들어졌다. 이것은 인간을 더 나은 경주자들 즉 달리는 사냥꾼들로 만들었지만 이것은 인간이 땀을 흘릴 수 있을 정도로 충분한 양의 물을 마시지 않는다는 것을 의미하며, 때문에 인간은 물을 마시기 편할 때까지 갈증을 연장한다고 Noakes는 말한다. Adolph는 그의 저서에서 진화라는 단어를 사용하지는 않았지만, Noakes의 의견을 이해했을 것이다.

Questions 36-40

Complete the sentences below.

Choose **NO MORE THAN TWO WORDS** from the passage for each answer.

Write your answers in boxes **36-40** on your answer sheet.

36 Adolph found out that a critical way for improving a marathon race is -------------- during performance.

➤ 키워드 Adolph found out과 a critical way는 C단락의 첫 번째 문장에서 찾을 수 있다.
Adolph found out that a critical way = The most critical of Adolph's discoveries

Adolph는 마라톤 경기 향상의 결정적인 방법이 시합 중 음료를 마시는 것이라는 사실을 알아냈다.

정답 drinking

37 During walking, the body needs approximately -------------- of a litre moisture per hour.

➤ 키워드 During walking과 of a litre moisture per hour는 D단락의 세 번째 문장에서 찾을 수 있다.
of a litre moisture per hour = a litre or more of evaporative cooling each hour

걷는 동안 신체는 시간당 4분의 3리터 정도의 물을 필요로 한다.

정답 three-quarters

ACADEMIC READING

38 International competitions didn't allow water within racing --------------- kilometres.

○ 키워드 International competitions와 didn't allow water within은 D단락의 마지막 문장에서 찾을 수 있다.
not allowed water within = prohibited from taking water in the first 11 kilometres

국제 경기에서 11Km 내에서는 음료수를 허용하지 않았다.

정답 11

39 Salazar nearly died at the end of the race as a result of ---------------.

○ 키워드 nearly died는 F단락의 첫 번째 문장에서 찾을 수 있다.
nearly died = almost died

달리기의 마지막에서 Salazar는 탈수로 인해 거의 죽을 지경에 처했다.

정답 dehydration

40 In this final section, Noakes indicates humans are part of the concept of ---------------.

○ 키워드 Noakes와 humans는 마지막 H단락의 첫 번째 문장에서 찾을 수 있다.

이 글의 마지막 부분에서 Noakes는 사람을 지연된 음료 마시는 사람의 개념으로 나타냈다.

정답 delayed drinkers

Academic Reading

Actual Test 7

Answer Sheet

1	i	11	YES	21	C	31	E
2	vi	12	YES	22	A	32	B
3	iii	13	NOT GIVEN	23	E	33	G
4	viii	14	Europe	24	D	34	D
5	v	15	(a) windscreen	25	B	35	pleasure
6	NO	16	(the) bonnet	26	C	36	sheep
7	YES	17	(a) giant airbag	27	B	37	Green Revolution
8	NOT GIVEN	18	(the) windscreen	28	A	38	Organic farming
9	NO	19	z-shaped	29	C	39	obesity (or overweight)
10	NO	20	(a) colossal incentive	30	A	40	(a) virus

ACADEMIC READING

READING PASSAGE 1

You should spend about 20 minutes on **Questions 1-13** *which are based on Reading Passage 1 on the following pages.*

Questions 1-5

Reading Passage 1 has six sections, **A-F**.

Choose the correct heading for sections **B-F** from the list of headings below.

Write the correct number, i-viii, in boxes **1-5** on your answer sheet.

List of Headings	
i	a significant role to creatures
ii	spectrum's previous models
iii	a distinction of hydrogen bonds
iv	nature's mysteries in the small place
v	the effect of spectrum on liquid water
vi	molecular composition of water
vii	water based on infrared light
viii	one-body structure of water

i	생명체에 주는 중요한 역할
ii	스펙트럼의 이전 모델
iii	수소 결합의 특징
iv	작은 공간에서의 자연의 신비
v	액체 상태의 물에 대한 스펙트럼의 효과
vi	물의 분자 구성
vii	적외선에 바탕을 둔 물
viii	한 가지 화학구조를 갖는 물

Example	Answer
Section **A**	iv

1 Section **B**

◉ B단락의 첫 번째 문장 '물의 기이하지만 필수적인 특질들은 거기서 멈추지 않는다.'에서 답을 찾을 수 있다.

정답 i

2 Section **C**

◉ C단락의 세 번째 문장에서 물의 분자 구성은 두 개의 수소 원자와 한 개의 산소 원자로 구성되었다고 설명하고 있다.

정답 vi

3 Section **D**

◉ D단락의 첫 번째 문장 '수소 결합들은 분자 내의 원자들과 함께 연결된 결합보다 더 약하며, 계속적으로 깨지고 재형성되지만, 각각의 수소 결합으로 분자 결합과 연결되기 위해 분자들이 구조화될 때 가장 강해진다.'에서 답을 찾을 수 있다.

정답 iii

4 Section **E**

> E단락의 첫 번째 문장 '대부분의 물리학자들은 물이 일반적인 조건하에서 단일의 구조로 돌아간다고 가정했었다.' 에서 답을 찾을 수 있다.

정답 viii

5 Section **F**

> F단락의 첫 번째 문장 '그들의 관심을 촉발시킨 특성은 액체 상태의 물에 대한 전통적인 모델에 의해 예견되지 못하는 흡수 스펙트럼에서의 최정점에 관한 것이었다.' 에서 답을 찾을 수 있다.

정답 v

The Mysteries of Water

Section A
From the nature of dark matter and the origin of the universe to the research for a theory of everything, we come across many mysteries. Whilst these are all puzzles on a grand scale, there is another not quite so grand but equally confusing mystery of the physical world that you can observe from the comfort of your own kitchen. Simply fill a tall glass with chilled water, throw in an ice cube and leave it to stand. The fact that the ice cube floats is the first oddity. And the mystery deepens if you take a thermometer and measure the temperature of the water at various depths. [6]At the top, near the ice cube, you'll find it to be around 0℃, but at the bottom it should be about 4℃. That's why water is denser at 4℃ than it is at any other temperature which is another strange feature that sets it apart from other liquids.

Section B
[1]Water's odd but essential qualities don't stop there, for ice is less dense than water, and water is less dense at its freezing point than it is when it is slightly warmer. It freezes from the top down rather than the bottom up. [7]So even during the ice ages, life kept going on to flourish on lake floors and in the deep ocean. Also, water has an extraordinary capacity to absorb up heat, and this helps smooth out climatic changes that could otherwise lay waste to ecosystems. However, in spite of water's enormous importance to life, no single theory had been able to satisfactorily explain its mysterious qualities – until now. If we can believe physicists Anders Nilsson at Stanford University, California, and Lars Pettersson of Stockholm University, Sweden, we could at last be getting to the bottom of many of these anomalies.

Section C
Their disputed ideas expand on a theory proposed more than a century ago. [8]According to Wilhelm Roentgen, the man who discovered the X-ray, claimed that the molecule in liquid water packs together not in just one way, as today's textbooks would

have us believe, but in two different ways. ²The way its molecules are composed of two hydrogen atoms and one oxygen atom and how they interact with one another is essential to the understanding of water's mysteries. ⁹The oxygen atom has a slight negative charge whilst the hydrogen atoms share a compensating positive charge. Through this process, the hydrogen and oxygen atoms of neighbouring molecules are drawn to one another, forming a link called a hydrogen bond.

Section D

³Hydrogen bonds are even weaker than the bonds that link the atoms within molecules together, so keep going to break and reform, but they are at their strongest when molecules are organized so that each hydrogen bond lines up with a molecular bond. ¹⁰The shaping of a water molecule is such that each H_2O molecule is surrounded by four neighbours organized in the shaping of a triangular pyramid better known as a tetrahedron. At least, that's the way the molecules organize themselves in ice. From the conventional view, liquid water has a similar, although less hard, structure, in which extra molecules are able to pack into some of the open gaps in the tetrahedral arrangement. It explains why liquid water is denser than ice – and it seems to comply with the results of various experiments that beams of X-rays, infrared light and neutrons are bounced off samples of water.

Section E

⁴Some physicists had suggested that water placed under certain extreme conditions may separate into two different structures, but most had assumed it resumes a single structure under normal conditions. ¹¹And then, 10 years ago, a change found by Pettersson and Nilsson called this idea into question. They were using X-ray absorption spectroscopy to research the amino acid glycine. The peaks in the X-ray absorption spectrum can shed light on the accurate nature of the target substance's chemical bonds on its structure. Critically, the researchers had got hold of a new, high-power X-ray source with which they could make more sensitive and precise measurements than had ever been possible. ¹²They soon knew that the water containing their glycine sample was producing a far more interesting spectrum than the amino acids did. Nilsson recalls, "What we saw there was sensational, so we had to get to the bottom of it."

Section F

⁵The characteristic that sparked their interest was a peak point in the absorption spectrum that is not anticipated by the traditional model of liquid water. Actually, in a paper published in 2004 concludes that at any given moment 85% of the hydrogen bonds in water must be weakened or broken. This is far more than the 10% anticipated by the textbook model. The hints of this finding are dramatic: it claims that a total rethink of the structure of water is

needed. So, both Nilsson and Pettersson turned to other X-ray experiments to confirm these claims. Their first move was to enlist the aid of Shik Shin of the University of Tokyo who specialises in a technique called X-ray emission spectroscopy. The main thing about these spectra is that the shorter the wavelength of the X-ray in a substance's emission spectrum is, the looser the hydrogen bonding must be.

The team struck gold: the two peak spectrum of discharged X-ray might correspond to two separate structures. [13]The researchers insisted that the spike of the longer-wavelength X-ray, indicated the proportion of tetrahedrally organized molecules, whilst the shorter-wavelength peak reflects the proportion of disordered molecules. Critically, the shorter-wavelength peak in the X-ray emissions was the more intense of the two, suggesting that the loosely bound molecules must be more outstanding within the sample, an assertion that fitted the team's previous models. What's more, they also recognised that this peak shifts to an even shorter wave length, as if the water was heated, the other peak remains more or less fixed.

---

oddity n. 괴벽   enormous a. 거대한   anomaly n. 변칙   compensating a. 보상된
absorption n. 흡수   emission n. 발산   assertion n. 주장

Questions 6-13

Do the following statements reflect the claims of the writer in Reading Passage 1?

In boxes **6-13** on your answer sheet write

> **YES**   *if the statement reflects the opinion of the writer*
> **NO**   *if the statement contradicts the opinion of the writer*
> **NOT GIVEN**   *if it is impossible to say what the writer thinks about this*

6 Water's temperature of top and bottom is generally the same.

➤ 키워드 top and bottom을 Section A단락의 여섯 번째 문장에서 찾을 수 있다. 본문에서는 상층부의 온도는 약 0도이고 하층부는 약 4도로 온도의 차이가 난다고 설명하고 있으므로 문제와 내용이 서로 다르기 때문에 답은 NO이다.

정답 NO

7 During the ice ages, there was life in the deep ocean because of warmth.

➤ 키워드 During the ice ages와 the deep ocean을 Section B단락의 세번째 문장에서 찾을 수 있다. 본문에서 빙하기 시대에 생명체들이 호수 밑과 깊은 바다에서 번식했다는 내용이 일치하므로 답은 YES이다.

정답 YES

ACADEMIC READING

8 Wilhelm Roentgen discovered X-rays for water molecules.

○ 키워드 Wilhelm Roentgen와 X-rays을 Section C단락의 두 번째 문장에서 찾을 수 있다. 본문에서는 Wilhelm Roentgen은 X선을 발견했다고만 언급되어 있다.

Wilhelm Roentgen은 물 분자를 목적으로 X선을 발견했다.

정답 NOT GIVEN

9 Both hydrogen and oxygen's atoms are similar to a positive charge.

○ 키워드 hydrogen and oxygen's atoms와 positive charge을 Section C단락의 네 번째 문장에서 찾을 수 있다. 본문에서는 수소가 양(+)전하인 반면에 산소는 음(-)전하라고 나와 있으므로 답은 NO이다.

수소와 산소의 원자는 양(+)전하로 유사점이 있다.

정답 NO

10 A single H_2O molecule is composed entirely of five-angled shape.

○ 키워드 A single H_2O molecule를 Section D단락의 두 번째 문장에서 찾을 수 있다. 본문에서는 삼각뿔의 피라미드 모양으로 정렬된 4개의 이웃한 분자라고 말하고 있으므로 답은 NO이다.
A single H_2O molecule = each H_2O molecule

한 개의 물 분자는 완전한 5각형의 모양으로 구성되어 있다.

정답 NO

11 Pettersson and Nilsson were scrutinising the amino acid glycine by using X-ray absorption spectroscopy.

○ 키워드 Pettersson and Nilsson과 the amino acid glycine과 X-ray absorption spectroscopy를 Section E단락의 두 번째와 세 번째 그리고 네 번째 문장에서 찾을 수 있다. 내용이 일치하므로 답은 YES이다.
scrutinizing = research

Pettersson과 Nilsson은 X선의 흡수 분광법을 이용해 아미노산 글리신을 조사했다.

정답 YES

12 The water including glycine was making superior spectrum to the amino acid.

○ 키워드 The water including glycine과 spectrum과 the amino acid를 Section E단락의 여섯 번째 문장에서 찾을 수 있다. 본문에서 물리학자들이 glycine 표본이 포함된 물이 amino acid보다 한 층 더 흥미로운 스펙트럼을 생산한다는 사실을 알게 되었다는 것을 알 수 있다.
[(라틴어계 비교급) A + be동사 + superior to B : A는 B보다 더 월등하다]
The water including glycine = the water containing their glycine sample

글리신이 포함된 물이 아미노산보단 탁월한 스펙트럼을 만들었다.

정답 YES

13 The shorter-wavelength is subjected to the longer-wavelength.

○ 키워드 The shorter-wavelength은 Section F단락에서 찾을 수 있다. 본문에선 엑스레이 방출에서 더 짧은 파장 길이의 정점이 더 격렬해졌다고만 나와 있어 문제의 내용이 본문에 언급되어 있지 않기 때문에 답은 NOT GIVEN이다.

단파장이 장파장에 속한다.

답 NOT GIVEN

READING PASSAGE 2

You should spend about 20 minutes on Questions 14-28 which are based on Reading Passage 2 below.

Vehicle Safety Systems

1 Although drivers and their passengers are encased in the event of a crash, people hit by a car have no protection. Now that could change thanks to a new system that built into a vehicle will enhance a pedestrian's safety. [14, 26] Every month about 3,400 pedestrians are killed in traffic accidents on the roads in the US, and a similar number die in Europe. [15] Some 30% of the injuries included in this group are caused by an impact with a windscreen or its frame.

2 [16, 21, 27] A European-wide collaboration led by Roger Hardy of the Cranfield Impact Centre at Cranfield University close to Bedford in the UK has devised an experimental system for cars that aims to cut this death toll and decrease the risk of injuries. [17] When the system registers that the car is about to hit a pedestrian, it automatically raises the rear of the bonnet (hood), releasing a giant airbag in front of the windscreen.

3 [22] "The raised bonnet absorbs some of the energy of the impact, decreasing the risk of severe injury to the pedestrian," says Hardy, whose project forms part of the European Union-funded Integrated Project on Advanced Protection Systems (APROSYS). "If it's a large pedestrian or on a small town car, the airbag also offers a cushioning effect around the stiff peripheral regions of the windscreen," he says. The airbag system used by Hardy was enhanced by the German company Takata Petri. To test its efficacy when combined with the raised bonnet, they cooperated into developing a prototype Fiat Stilo by engineers at the Fiat Research Centre in Turin, Italy. Then the team estimated the danger of head injuries in test collisions with a dummy pedestrian.

4 A standard Stilo test hitting a pedestrian at 40 kilometres per hour would have a score of around 1,000 on the Head Impact Criterion (HIC) scale. That is the equivalent of an 18% chance of a life-threatening injury. For pedestrians hitting Hardy's bonnet, the scores were reduced to between 234 and 682, whilst the normal windscreen airbag scores ranged between 692 and 945. [18] Hardy's team has also introduced a design in which a windscreen mounting system cushions the impact with the edge of the windscreen. [19] This consists of a flexible Z-shaped section of metal, that is a maximum of 15 millimetres wide, separating the windscreen from its frame so that it is able to flex inwards to absorb energy in a collision. [28] The team says it could decrease HIC scores by over 50%.

5 [23] Another APROSYS collaboration led by Jurgen Gugler at Graz

ACADEMIC READING

University of Technology in Austria researched how changing the shaping of the front of a truck could reduce the risk to pedestrians. Computer stimulations of 20 accident scenarios indicated that a smooth sloping surface with a central bulge decreases the likelihood of a pedestrian involved in a front-end accident being run over by 80 to 90%. Gugler says, "The pedestrian is knocked to the side, rotated and pushed towards the ground. You are out of the path of the oncoming truck."

6 Fiat researchers managed by Roberto Puppini have also had some success in early tests of an adaptive bumper system. Four gas springs kick in at high speeds to move the bumper forward so that it will absorb energy of an impact. So will manufacturers actually incorporate any of these safety innovations into their cars? [24]Over the next two years, the European car safety commission (Euro NCAP), will be phasing the results of pedestrian safety tests into its essential rating system. [25]Poor Euro NCAP test results could result in less safe car models being withdrawn from the market. This suggests that buyers and manufacturers can be persuaded to take the safety of drivers and their passengers seriously, but it remains to be seen whether the welfare of pedestrians is as persuasive a selling point.

7 For now at least, there is little else to convince car-manufacturers to install these safety devices. [20]Hardy says, "Recently, from the legislative point of view, there is not a colossal incentive for manufacturers to utilise these technologies." Perhaps ultimately the law will have to step in so that external airbags and energy-absorbing bodywork enhance pedestrian safety as dramatically as seat belts and internal airbags have enhanced driver and passenger safety.

---

enhance v. ~를 강화하다   pedestrian n. 보행자   release v. 해방하다   absorb v. ~을 흡수하다   efficacy n. 효능   dummy n. 연습용 인형   bulge a. 볼록한 부분   adaptive a. 적응성의   withdraw v. 철수하다   persuasive a. 설득력이 있는   legislative a. 입법권이 있는   colossal a. 거대한   utilise v. ~을 이용하다

Questions 14-20

Complete the summary below.

Choose **NO MORE THAN THREE WORDS** from the passage for each answer.

Write your answers in boxes **14-20** on your answer sheet.

Every month there are about 3,400 people hit by a car in the US and a similar number of casualties in **14** Europe. Actually, around 30% of them are a result of **15** (a) windscreen or its frame. To decrease road traffic accidents, a European-wide collaboration devised automatic lifting rear of 16 (the) bonnet, and a 17 (a) giant airbag ahead of the windscreen working at the same time.

Hardy's team has researched a system to cushion impacts with the outline of 18 (the) windscreen. It includes an easily bent and 19 z-shaped metal frame with the windscreen and frame separated. But he said: According to law, although having safety devices for protection against a crash, now any manufacture companies to harness these devises could not have 20 (a) colossal incentive.

14 ○ 키워드인 3,400 people을 첫 번째 단락의 세 번째 문장에서 찾는다. 미국과 유럽에서 3,400명 보행자들이 교통사고로 목숨을 잃었다고 나와 있다.

정답 Europe

15 ○ 키워드인 30%를 첫 번째 단락의 네 번째 문장에서 찾는다. 부상자의 30%가 windscreen이나 frame과 충돌에 원인이 있다고 나와 있다.
a result of = caused by

정답 (a) windscreen

16 ○ 키워드인 a European-wide collaboration을 두 번째 단락의 첫 번째 문장에서 찾을 수 있다.
automatic lifting rear of = automatically raises the rear of

정답 (the) bonnet

17 ○ 키워드 ahead of the windscreen과 working은 두 번째 단락의 마지막 문장에서 찾을 수 있다. 두 번째 단락에서 자동차 앞유리 앞의 큰 에어백을 풀어 놓는다고 했다.
ahead of the windscreen = in front of the windscreen
working = releasing

정답 (a) giant airbag

18 ○ 키워드인 Hardy's team을 네 번째 단락의 네 번째 문장에서 찾을 수 있다. 자동차 앞유리의 가장자리에 쿠션 효과를 주는 windscreen-mounting 시스템을 도안하는 것을 도와주었다고 제시했다.
the outline of = the edge of

정답 (the) windscreen

19 ○ 키워드 easily bent와 metal frame은 네 번째 단락의 다섯 번째 문장에서 찾을 수 있다. 시스템은 쉽게 구부러지는 z 모양으로 된 금속으로 이루어져 있다고 했다.
easily bent = able to flex

정답 z-shaped

20 ○ 키워드 now any manufacture companies to harness는 본문의 마지막 단락의 두 번째 문장에서 찾을 수 있다. 이러한 기술을 이용하는 제조업체들을 위한 엄청난 인센티브는 없다고 언급하고 있다.
harness these devises = utilise these technologies

정답 (a) colossal incentive

ACADEMIC READING

Questions 21-25

*Complete the each sentence with the correct ending, **A-G**, below.*

*Write the correct letter, **A-G**, in boxes **21-25** on your answer sheet.*

A	be part of schemes to decrease hazardous situations for pedestrians.
B	help judge less safe vehicle models between buyers and companies.
C	improve testing under the condition that a crash decreased.
D	make a solution within frequency of tests for safe pedestrians.
E	study how replacing a lorry's front side protects pedestrians.
F	be persuasive as a selling point.
G	improve a pedestrian's chances.

A	보행자들을 위해서 위험한 상황을 단절시키는 계획의 한 부분이다.
B	구매자들과 회사들 간의 안전성이 낮은 자동차의 모델을 평가하는 것을 돕는다.
C	충돌을 줄이는 조건하에 실험을 향상시킨다.
D	보행자들의 안전을 위한 실험의 빈도수 내에서 해결 방안을 만들어 줄 것이다.
E	대형 트럭의 앞면의 교체로 보행자들을 보호하는 방법을 연구한다.
F	판매할 때의 강조점으로 설득력이 있다.
G	보행자의 기회를 향상시킨다.

21 A European-wide collaboration [키워드]

➤ 본문에서 A European-wide collaboration은 두 번째 단락의 첫 번째 문장에서 찾을 수 있다.

정답 C

22 European Union-funded Integrated Project [키워드]

➤ 본문에서 European Union-funded Integrated Project는 세 번째 단락의 첫 번째 문장에서 찾을 수 있다.
hazardous situations for pedestrians = risk of severe injury to the pedestrian

정답 A

23 APROSYS collaboration [키워드]

➤ 본문에서 APROSYS collaboration은 다섯 번째 단락의 첫 번째 문장에서 찾을 수 있다.
how replacing a lorry's front side protects pedestrians = how changing the shaping of the front of a truck could reduce the risk to pedestrians

정답 E

24 Euro NCAP [키워드]

➤ 본문에서 Euro NCAP는 여섯 번째 단락의 네 번째 문장에서 찾을 수 있다.
make a solution within frequency of tests for safe pedestrians = be phasing the results of pedestrian safety tests

정답 D

246

25 Poor Euro NCAP [키워드]

○ 본문에서 Poor Euro NCAP는 여섯 번째 단락의 다섯 번째 문장에서 찾을 수 있다.
help judge less safe vehicle models = result in less safe car models being withdrawn from the market

정답 B

Questions 26-28

*Choose the correct letter in boxes, **A, B, C** or **D**.*

*Write the correct letter in boxes **26-28** on your answer sheet.*

26 Which one of the following is found in the passage?
  A the number of traffic accidents and rubbish on the road
  B the amount of petrol gas misused and recycled
  C the number of casualties in traffic accidents on the road in Europe
  D the cases of car insurance in a court

다음 중 이 글에서 발견되는 것은 무엇인가?
A 교통사고 수와 도로의 쓰레기
B 페트롤 가스의 악용과 재활용의 양
C 유럽의 도로에서 교통사고의 희생자 수
D 법정에서 자동차 보험의 소송 건수

○ 보기 중 본문에 언급되어 있는 것은 C뿐이다.

정답 C

27 What are the main technical devices made by Roger Hardy?
  A brake system
  B automatic both bonnet and airbag system
  C instant front door and trunk open
  D anti-slip tires whilst heavy rain and snow

Roger Hardy에 의해 만들어진 주된 기술 고안품은 무엇인가?
A 제동장치
B 자동 덮개와 에어백 시스템
C 순간 앞문 장치와 개방된 트렁크
D 폭우 및 폭설 중 미끄럼 방지 타이어

○ 질문에서 키워드 Roger Hardy를 두 번째 단락의 첫 번째 문장에서 찾을 수 있다. 두 번째 단락의 두 번째 문장에서 그가 이끄는 범유럽적 공동연구에서 자동차 덮개 뒷부분과 에어백을 고안했다는 것을 추론할 수 있다.

정답 B

28 The writer believed that the "Hardy's team" on system could
  A decrease the Head Impact Criterion(HIC) score until over half per cent.
  B be almost as safe as computer stimulation test.
  C be causing significant damage to half a per cent of the Head Impact Criterion(HIC).
  D reduce converting the windscreen airbag.

저자는 시스템에 대해서 Hardy 팀이 ~라고 믿었다.
A 50% 이상까지 HIC 스코어를 줄일 수 있다.
B 컴퓨터 시뮬레이션 테스트만큼 거의 안전하다.
C HIC의 50% 정도 주요한 손상을 야기할 수 있다.
D 앞 유리 에어백 변형을 감소시킬 수 있다.

○ 질문에서 키워드 Hardy's team을 네 번째 단락의 마지막 문장에서 찾을 수 있다.
until over half per cent = by over 50%

정답 A

ACADEMIC READING

READING PASSAGE 3

You should spend about 20 minutes on Questions 29-40 which are based on Reading Passage 3 on the following pages.

The Harmony of Food and Drink

A [35]Food is not only a necessity for life, but also our greatest sources of pleasure. The taste of things such as champagne, chocolate and chips offer your brain a big "pleasure hit" that keeps us coming back for more. [30]And the preparation of food is as important as the ingredients. Recently, food, science and technology have become more closely linked than ever. Scientifically-minded chefs like Harold McGee, Heston Blumenthal and Ferran Adria sometimes utilise science to enhance startling new dishes.

B [32]Before the Agricultural Age, humans were hunter-gatherers. [36]Sheep were probably the first animals to be farmed, followed by cattle and pigs. We are still unsure what our earliest ancestors actually ate and how much of their diet was meat. We know that Otzi the iceman had consumed ibex, deer, vegetables and possibly grains.

C [29]Controversially, it has been suggested that the invention of cooking was a main factor in human evolution (as well as our alveolar bone) – a question that partly depends on when humans discovered fire. Like us, apes also prefer cooked food to raw – possibly because cooked food offers more energy than raw food does. [37]Recently, almost all our food comes from farming for the huge increase in human population over the last 200 years. Farming has become much more intensive and dependant on technology and the so-called Green Revolution in the 20th century was a vital boost. At the same time, technologies for conserving food have come along in leaps and bounds.

D But, the grains have not been without cost. Soil quality has been damaged, and crops like bananas have become less genetically diverse, rare breeds of animals have been pushed close to extinction, and habitats have been destroyed. Also, the increasing demand for meat puts pressure on agriculture. One possible solution to food shortages is genetic modification of crops plants to enhance yield and to make them resistant to disorder. [34]But GM has proved unpopular with the public, in spite of efforts to grow environmentally friendly solutions.

Concern for environmental damage from farming led to the development of "sustainable" techniques, like organic farming which rejects the use of artificial fertilisers, pesticides and other agricultural technologies. [38]Organic farming produces lower yields, but there is evidence that it produces suitable amounts of food with less environmental damage.

E [31]The overfishing of the world's oceans has also led to serious damage, causing population crashes in many species. Recently, fish farming has become more widespread. It decreases the burden on wild fish, but has other problems such as escaping fish, excessive food consumption, infectious viruses and louse infestation. Unless the population recessions are stopped, we will have to turn to less appetizing species for our seafood like jellyfish.

F Nowadays, many people suffer from food allergies, and must avoid common foods like peanuts and wheat. A condition called food intolerance looks the same on the surface, but its effects are slower to appear and longer lasting. Charles Darwin may have been a sufferer of this condition. The allergy epidemic has been related to modern clean living.

G Today, one of the biggest health problems is obesity. [39]Through a diet rich in fats and sugars, many people in developed countries are overweight increasing the risk of cancer, diabetes and an early death. Unfortunately, mild obesity takes two to four years off the average lifespan. The risks are particularly concerning for children and being overweight as a child makes you more obese as an adult. The causes of obesity have been a source of debate. Surprisingly, a lack of exercise may not be a critical factor. [33]It is possible that it could be a genetic condition and may also be caused by eating lots of fructose. [40]Some cases have been linked to a virus that causes fat cells to increase. Also, obesity is socially contagious. A huge range of possible treatments for obesity have been developed.

---

preparation n. 준비   ingredient n. 성분   utilise v. ~을 이용하다   enhance v. ~를 강화하다   in leaps and bounds 높이 도약해서   infestation n. 내습   recession n. 후퇴   intolerance n. 완고함   obesity n. 극대비만   diabetes n. 당뇨병   critical a. 결정적인   fructose n. (화학) 과당   contagious a. 전염성의

ACADEMIC READING

Questions 29-34

Reading Passage 3 has seven paragraphs, **A-G**.

Which paragraph contains the following information?

Write the correct letter, **A-G**, in boxes **29-34** on your answer sheet.

29 cooked food relative to human evolution and structure of teeth

> 키워드 human evolution, teeth는 C단락에서 찾을 수 있다. C단락의 첫 번째 문장에서 요리의 발명은 (우리의 치조골뿐 아니라) 인간의 진화에 중요한 요소가 되어 왔다고 주장하고 있다.
> teech = alveolar bone

정답 **C**

30 a change of food taste and importance of preparation

> A단락의 세 번째와 네 번째 문장에서 '음식 준비는 재료만큼 중요하다.'와 '최근 들어, 음식, 과학 그리고 기술은 그 어느 때보다 밀접한 관련을 갖게 되었다.'에서 답을 찾는다.

정답 **A**

31 problems of population crash caused by overfishing

> 키워드 overfishing은 E단락에서 찾을 수 있다. E단락의 첫 번째 문장에서 '전 세계의 바다에서 이뤄지는 물고기의 남획 역시 심각한 피해를 주며, 많은 종자들 속에서 개체군의 파괴를 야기한다.'에서 답을 찾는다.

정답 **E**

32 the earlier hunting of human

> 키워드 the earlier hunting of human을 B단락의 첫 번째 문장에서 찾을 수 있다.(Before the Agricultural Age, humans were hunter gatherers.) 인류의 초기의 사냥에 대한 단락은 B이다.

정답 **B**

33 overweight influenced with gene and overeating

> 키워드 gene, overeating은 G단락에서 찾을 수 있다. G단락의 일곱 번째 문장에서 몇 가지 유전자들과 과당의 과잉 섭취가 비만의 원인이 될 수 있다고 언급한다.

정답 **G**

34 indifference of genetic modification crops

> 키워드 indifference, genetic modification crops는 D단락에서 찾을 수 있다. D단락의 다섯 번째 문장에서 유전자 변형은 대중적으로 인기가 없다고 밝히고 있다.

정답 **D**

Questions 35-40

Complete the sentences below.

Choose **NO MORE THAN TWO WORDS** from the passage for each answer.

Write your answers in boxes **35-40** on your answer sheet.

35 Food is one of human's essential materials of ---------------.

○ 키워드 food와 essential을 A단락의 첫 번째 문장에서 찾을 수 있다.
human's essential materials = our greatest source

음식은 유쾌함을 갖고 있는 인간의 본질적인 물질 중 하나이다.

정답 pleasure

36 --------------- might be the first creature to be tamed for farming.

○ 키워드 the first creature to be tamed을 B단락의 두 번째 문장에서 찾을 수 있다.
the first creature to be tamed = the first animal to be farmed

양이 아마도 농경을 위해 사육된 최초의 동물일 것이다.

정답 sheep

37 The population has increased over the last 200 years, accelerating with technology triggered ---------------.

○ 키워드인 last 200 years는 C단락에서 찾을 수 있다.
accelerating = intensive 형 격렬한

지난 200년 동안 사람의 수가 증가해 오고 있으며, 기술은 녹색혁명을 이끌었다.

정답 Green Revolution

38 --------------- is yielded with less environmental damage and non-fertilisers.

○ 키워드 less environmental damage는 D단락의 마지막 문장에서 찾을 수 있다.
fertilisers = pesticides

유기농업은 환경 손상을 덜 주며 비료도 없이 수확하는 농업이다.

정답 Organic farming

39 From overeating fats and sugars, modern people are suffering from ---------------.

○ 키워드 overeating fats and sugars를 G단락의 두 번째 문장에서 찾을 수 있다.
overeating fats and sugars = a diet rich in fats and sugars

지방과 설탕 과다 섭취로, 현대인들은 비만에 고통을 받고 있다.

정답 obesity (or overweight)

40 Health problem have been linked to --------------- which makes fat cells.

○ 키워드 Health problem과 fat cells를 G단락의 여덟 번째 문장에서 찾을 수 있다.

건강 문제는 지방세포를 만드는 바이러스와 밀접한 관계가 있다.

정답 (a) virus

ACADEMIC WRITING

TASK 1

You should spend about 20 minutes on this task.

> ***The bar chart below shows the number of employees from the European Union in the United States (1999).***
> 아래 막대그래프는 미국에서 근무하는 유럽 근로자의 수를 보여 주고 있다.
>
> ***Write a report for a university lecturer describing the information shown below.***
> 아래 정보를 묘사하여 대학 강의를 위한 리포트를 작성하시오.

You should write at least 150 words.

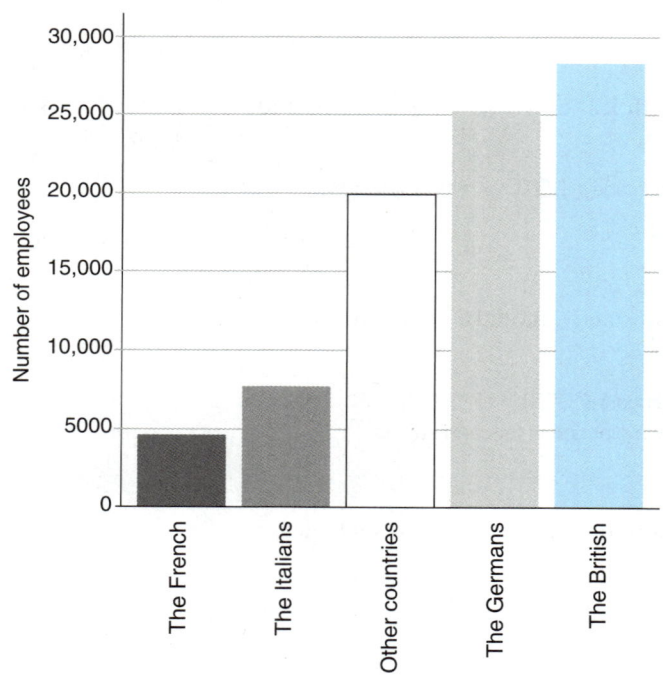

EU-Born Science & Technology Employees Working in The US in 1999

먼저 도입단락(Introduction)을 작성한다. 글의 서론부분으로 그래프의 이름을 만드는 것이다. 항상, 도입단락은 정관사 The로 시작하고 시제는 현재시제를 사용한다.

1   **The bar graph above indicates** the employment of Europeans in the field of both science and technology in the United States in 1999.
   위의 막대그래프는 1999년 미국에서 과학과 기술 분야에서 근무하는 유럽인들의 고용 현황을 보여 주고 있다.

문제와 동일하게 작성하면 감점이 되므로 문법구조를 약간 활용하여 구조는 다르지만 의미는 같게 표현하면 된다. 문제에 주어진 차트의 이름은 bar graph(bar: 막대)이며, 장소부사 below 대신 above(위에 있는)가 쓰였다. 동사는 일반동사 현재시제(indicates: ~을 가리키다), 다음은 목적대상인 the employment of Europeans(유럽인들의 고용 현황), 그 다음엔 적당한 명사와 명사를 이어 주는 전치사 in(~에서), 그 다음엔 both A and B 구문(A와 B 두 가지 모두)에서 특징적인 설명 science와 technology를 적고 다음엔 전치사 in + 명사구 in the United States를 사용했고, 마지막으로 그래프의 특정 년도 in 1999를 명시하였다.

두번째 단락으로 일반화 진술(General statement)을 작성한다. 본론에 들어가기 전에 그래프의 전반적인 상황과 분위기를 서술하는 것이다.

2   **In general,** there were five broad countries categorised, including France, Italy, Germany, Britain and other countries.
   일반적으로, 프랑스, 이탈리아, 독일, 영국, 그 밖의 나라를 포함한 5개의 주요 국가군이 있다.

처음 문장은 연결어(linking word)인 In general(일반적으로)로 시작하고 다음엔 유도부사구문으로 그래프의 시제에 맞추어 작성해 나간다. there were ~(~이 있다) 그리고 그래프의 전반적인 분위기는 5개의 막대차트로 나열된 것을 간략히 서술한다. 유도부사구문은 본 주어가 be동사 다음에 위치하므로 복수명사 five broad countries와 categorised(수동분사/서술형용사)를 언급하고 다음엔 전치사 including을 사용하고 차트에 나온 나라명을 작성한다.

세번째 단락으로 설명묘사(Descriptions)를 작성한다. 본론단락으로, 그래프를 문법과 어휘를 활용하여 자세히 객관적으로 나라 간의 특징을 비교해 가면서 서술하는 것이다. (단, 반복적인 문장은 가급적 사용하지 않는다.)

3   **With** the trend of moving engineering, both the French and Italians were at a low rate of around 4,900 and 7,500 people each, among the developed European nations.
   기술 이전의 추세와 함께, 프랑스와 이탈리아는 각각 대략 4,900명과 7,500명으로 선진 유럽국가들 중에서 낮은 비율을 보였다.

4   **In contrast,** the rate of German employees was more than five times that of the French.
   반면에, 독일은 프랑스보다 약 5배 이상 높았다.

ACADEMIC WRITING

5 **Also**, the British had the highest rate at roughly 28,000.
또한, 영국은 약 28,000명으로 다른 나라들 중에 가장 높았다.

6 It was more than twice the number of the French plus Italians.
이것은 프랑스와 이탈리아를 합산한 인원 수보다 두 배 이상 많았다.

7 **But** the total number of other European countries' workers was around 20,000 people.
그러나 다른 유럽 국가들의 노동자의 합계는 약 20,000명이었다.

8 Each country showed a few people working.
각 국가는 적은 노동 인원 수를 보여 주었다.

전치사(With)로 시작하고 다음에 명사어구(the trend of moving engineering)를 쓰고, 주어(both the French and Italians)와 be동사복수과거동사(were) 어순대로 서술해 나간다. 그래프상의 상위 집합과 하위 집합을 서술하면서 서로 간의 간격을 구체적으로 비교(In contrast) 설명한다. 또한 Other countries 영역의 특징으로 맺었다.

네 번째 단락으로 결론(Conclusion)을 작성한다. 글의 마지막 단락으로 그래프를 분석(analysis)하고 맺으면 된다.

9 **As a result**, we can see that, from this bar graph, both the Germans and British have a significant science and technology workforce in the United States.
결론적으로, 이 그래프를 통하여, 우리는 미국 내에 독일과 영국의 과학 기술 노동자들이 많다는 것을 알 수 있다.

결론부분은 연결어(Linking word)인 As a result(결론적으로)로 시작하고 다음엔 we can see that + S + V ~로 특징을 요약하고, from this chart를 두 개의 콤마를 사용하여 문장 내에 삽입해 놓고, 최종적으로 그래프를 종합 분석하여 글을 끝맺었다.

샘플 답안

The bar graph above indicates the employment of Europeans in the field of both science and technology in the United States in 1999.

In general, there were five broad countries categorised, including France, Italy, Germany, Britain and other countries.

With the trend of moving engineering, both the French and Italians were at a low rate of around 4,900 and 7,500 people each, among the developed European nations. In contrast, the rate of German employees was more than five times that of the French. Also, the British had the highest rate at roughly 28,000. It was more than twice the number of the French plus Italians. But the total number of other European countries' workers was around 20,000 people. Each country showed a few people working.

As a result, we can see that, from this bar graph, both the Germans and British have a significant science and technology workforce in the United States.

(total words: 150)

ACADEMIC WRITING

TASK 2

You should spend about 40 minutes on this task.

> *Central and local governments make a frantic attempt to promote festivals to create a lot of revenue. Some people think this money should be invested in social programmes for the poor.*
> 중앙정부와 지방정부는 막대한 예산이 드는 축제행사를 홍보하기 위해서 혈안이다. 몇몇 사람들은 이런 돈을 그 나라의 가난한 사람들을 위한 사회보장프로그램에 사용해야 한다고 생각한다.
>
> *To what extent do you agree or disagree with this statement?*
> 이 진술에 대해 당신은 어느 정도 찬성 혹은 반대하는가?
>
> *Give reasons for your answer.*
> 당신의 대답에 대한 이유를 들어라.

You should write at least 250 words.

You should use your own idea, knowledge and experience and support your arguments with examples and relevant evidence.

먼저 도입단락(Introduction)을 작성한다. 글의 서론부분으로, 주어진 문제의 내용을 활용하여 관련된 분위기를 만드는 것이다.

도입단락은 Recently, we are living within a society of ~로 작성한다. '최근에 우리는 ~한 사회에서 살고 있다' 로 부드럽게 서두를 시작한다. 문제에서 문화산업인 국가경축행사는 higher quality of life(삶의 더 높은 질)으로 함축한다.

1 **Recently, we are living within a society of** higher quality of life.
   최근에, 우리는 삶의 질이 더 높은 사회에 살고 있다.

그리고 다음 문장으로 대다수의 사람을 문장의 '주어'로 놓고 관심분야와 이에 대한 이유를 간단히 서술한다.

2 **Most people are able to** enjoy the attractions of the tourism industry.
   대부분의 사람들이 관광 산업의 매력을 즐길 수 있다.

그리고 다음 문장에서 문장의 분위기 전환으로 국가행사의 양면성을 서술한다.

3 **Of course**, government sponsored national ceremonies and other such events have a number of positive effects but there is a also a strong need to prioritise the development of community welfare services for the poor.

물론 정부가 지원하는 국가 기념행사와 다른 행사들은 여러 긍정적인 효과를 가지고 있지만, 가난한 사람들을 위한 공동체 복지 서비스를 우선적으로 해결해 달라는 강력한 요구 또한 존재한다.

◑ 찬성/반대의 문제가 아닌 경우에서는 (4)번은 생략한다.

4 **So, I do** agree **with the statement above** because I believe that things **such as** public education and health service should be prioritised.

그래서 나는 위에 언급된 진술에 당연히 찬성한다. 왜냐하면 나는 공교육과 의료 서비스와 같은 것들이 우선시되어야 한다고 생각하기 때문이다.

두 번째 단락으로 [제1단락]을 작성한다. 여기선, 서론에서 언급한 두 가지 대안 중 첫 번째인 public education(공교육)에 대한 구체적인 사례와 본인의 의견을 들어 논리성을 높여 나간다.

'질 높은 삶' 으로 시작하면서 사람들의 문화에 대한 강조점을 비교 역설한다.

5 **As a result of** higher quality living, people are no longer concerned with just their basic needs but are able to gain a lot from cultural industries.

더 질 높은 삶의 결과로, 사람들은 더 이상 기본적인 욕구에만 관심을 갖는 것이 아니라, 문화산업으로부터 더 많은 것을 얻을 수 있게 되었다.

그리고 자기계발에 대한 열정을 서술한다.

6 **They are enthusiastic** about self-development.

그들은 자기계발에 대해 열정적이다.

그리고 역접접속사를 넣어 배움에 대한 욕구를 해결할 금전적 여유가 없다고 설명한다.

7 **However**, some people don't have enough money to meet all of their desires.

그러나 몇몇 사람들은 그들의 모든 욕구를 채울 수 있는 충분한 돈을 가지고 있지 않다.

그리고 우리 사회의 능력 있는 소외계층과 그들의 안타까운 처지를 서술한다.

8 **There are a lot of poor people with good abilities in our society, but unfortunately they give up on education too soon.**

우리 사회에는 훌륭한 능력을 가진 가난한 사람들이 많다. 그러나 불행하게도 그들은 너무 일찍 배움의 길을 포기한다.

그리고 공신력 있는 언론자료를 허구적으로 인용하여, 현재 영국정부의 지나친 허례허식에 대한 비난을 이야기한다.

ACADEMIC WRITING

9 **According to the BBC (2009),** the British government has been criticised for investing a lot of money in the preparations for the 2012 London Olympic games.

2009년 BBC에 따르면, 영국정부는 2012년 런던 올림픽 준비에 막대한 금액을 투자한다고 비판받고 있다고 한다.

그리고 이에 관련 예시로 본인의 대학시절을 현실성 있게 허구로 인용한다.

10 **For example, when I was at** university, my classmate abandoned his studies in Britain.

예를 들어, 내가 대학을 다녔을 때, 나의 동급생은 영국유학을 포기했다.

그리고 그 친구의 안타까운 처지를 언급해 준다.

11 He was a very keen dancer but did not have the support of his parents.

그는 매우 열정적인 댄서였지만, 부모님의 지원을 받을 수 없었다.

그리고 지금은 평범하게 일하고 있다고 설명한다.

12 Now, he is working for a small company in their marketing department.

현재, 그는 작은 회사의 마케팅부서에서 일하고 있다.

세 번째 단락으로 [제2단락]을 작성한다. 여기선, 서론에서 언급한 두 가지 대안 중 두 번째인 welfare service (복지 서비스)에 대한 구체적인 사례와 본인의 의견을 들어 논리성을 높여 나간다.

안락한 생활은 비만 등의 문제를 유발한다고 서술한다.

13 Living a comfortable life can also cause a number of problems such as obesity.

편안한 삶을 사는 것은 비만과 같은 여러 문제들을 유발할 수도 있다.

그리고 현대인들의 운동 결핍에 대해 설명한다.

14 These days, people don't exercise regularly and often eat and drink too much whilst working or studying through the night.

최근 들어, 사람들은 규칙적으로 운동하지 않고, 밤에 일을 하거나 공부할 때 먹고 마시기를 즐긴다.

그리고 이런 현상을 정보사회의 부정적인 면이라고 서술한다.

15 This is a negative aspect of living in a society of information.

이것은 정보화 사회의 부정적인 면이다.

그리고 이에 관련된 WHO의 보고 결과를 사례로 들어 좀 더 정당성을 높여 나간다.

16 **For instance**, according to the WHO, 4% of people living in New York suffer from obesity, high blood pressure or diabetes.
예를 들어, WHO에 따르면, 뉴욕 인구의 4%가 비만, 고혈압, 혹은 당뇨로 고통받고 있다고 한다.

네번째 단락으로 결론(Conclusion)을 작성한다. 글의 마지막 단락으로 주제를 언급하고 본인의 의견으로 맺으면 된다. 결론의 맺음말로 시작하면서, 국가경축행사에 대한 양면성을 다시 역설한다.

17 **In conclusion**, although national ceremonies have some good points and positive effects, it is more important to support the poor and improve their living conditions first.
결론적으로, 국가 기념행사가 여러 장점을 가지고 있고 긍정적인 효과도 있지만, 저소득층을 지원하고 그들의 삶의 조건을 먼저 향상시키는 것이 더욱 중요하다.

그리고 이런 현상을 동전에 비유함으로써 사회현상에 대한 함축성을 보인다.

18 **This situation is like two sides of a coin.**
이런 상황들은 동전의 양면과 같다.

그리고 본인의 의견을 들어 정부에 대한 각성을 촉구한다.

19 **So, in my opinion**, it is essential that governments invest plenty of revenue in welfare services.
그래서, 개인적 의견으로는, 정부가 복지 서비스에 많은 예산을 투자하는 것이 필수적이다.

ACADEMIC WRITING

샘플 답안

Recently, we are living within a society of higher quality of life. Most people are able to enjoy the attractions of the tourism industry. Of course, government sponsored national ceremonies and other such events have a number of positive effects but there is a also a strong need to prioritise the development of community welfare services for the poor. So, I do agree with the statement above because I believe that things such as public education and health service should be prioritised.

As a result of higher quality living, people are no longer concerned with just their basic needs but are able to gain a lot from cultural industries. They are enthusiastic about self-development. However, some people don't have enough money to meet all of their desires. There are a lot of poor people with good abilities in our society, but unfortunately they give up on education too soon. According to the BBC (2009), the British government has been criticised for investing a lot of money in the preparations for the 2012 London Olympic games. For example, when I was at university, my classmate abandoned his studies in Britain. He was a very keen dancer but did not have the support of his parents. Now, he is working for a small company in their marketing department.

Living a comfortable life can also cause a number of problems such as obesity. These days, people don't exercise regularly and often eat and drink too much whilst working or studying through the night. This is a negative aspect of living in a society of information. For instance, according to the WHO, 4% of people living in New York suffer from obesity, high blood pressure or diabetes.

In conclusion, although national ceremonies have some good points and positive effects, it is more important to support the poor and improve their living conditions first. This situation is like two sides of a coin. So, in my opinion, it is essential that governments invest plenty of revenue in welfare services.

(total words: 334)

TASK 1

You should spend about 20 minutes on this task.

The chart below shows the number of hidden costs of the UK's annual food bill.
아래 차트는 영국에서 매년마다 식품 청구서의 숨겨진 손실에 대한 수치적 비율을 보여 준다.

Write a report for a university lecturer describing the information shown below.
아래 정보를 묘사하여 대학 강의를 위한 리포트를 작성하시오.

You should write at least 150 words.

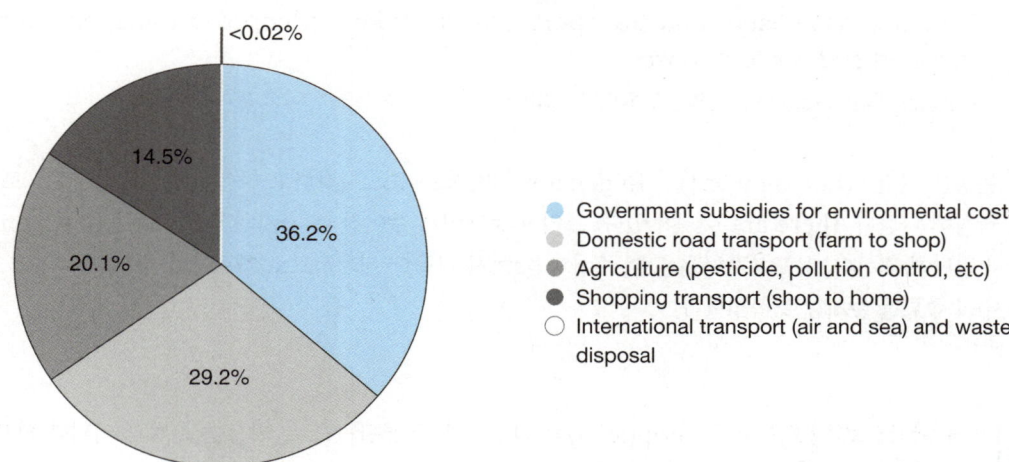

ACADEMIC WRITING

먼저 도입단락(Introduction)을 작성한다. 글의 서론부분으로 차트의 이름을 만드는 것이다. 항상, 도입단락에서는 정관사 The로 시작하고 시제는 현재시제를 사용한다.

1 **The pie chart above indicates** the recent percentages of the covered loss of Britain's annual food bill.
   위의 파이차트는 영국의 연간 식품청구서의 숨겨진 손실에 대한 최근의 비율을 보여 준다.

문제와 동일하게 작성하면 감점이 되므로 약간 다른 단어를 활용하여 의미는 같게 표현하면 된다. 문제에 주어진 차트의 종류는 pie chart(pie: 원판)이며, 장소부사 below 대신 above(위에 있는)가 쓰였다. 동사는 일반동사 현재시제 (indicates: ~을 가리키다), 다음은 목적대상인 the recent percentages of the covered loss(숨겨진 손실에 대한 최근의 비율), 그다음엔 적당한 명사와 명사를 이어 주는 전치사 of(~의), 그다음엔 Britain's annual food bill을 적는다.

두 번째 단락으로 일반화 진술(General statement)을 작성한다. 본론에 들어가기 전에 차트의 전반적인 상황과 분위기를 서술하는 것이다.

2 **In general,** there are four broad categorised environmental costs.
   일반적으로, 네 가지 항목의 환경적 손실이 있다.

3 They are "Domestic road transport," "Agriculture," "Shopping transport" and "International transport and waste disposal."
   이를테면, '국내 도로교통', '농업', '쇼핑배달' 그리고 '국제 운송과 쓰레기 처리' 등이다.

처음 문장은 연결어(linking word)인 In general(일반적으로)로 시작하고 다음엔 유도부사구문으로 차트의 시제에 맞추어 작성해 나간다. there are ~(~이 있다) 그리고 문제에서 주어진 네 가지의 환경적 비용(environmental costs)에 대해서 간단히 적는다. 유도부사구문은 본 주어가 be동사 다음에 위치하므로 차트상의 네 가지 비용을 언급한다. 다음 문장에서 그 종류를 순서대로 작성한다.

세 번째 단락으로 설명묘사(Descriptions)를 작성한다. 본론단락으로, 차트를 문법과 어휘를 활용하여 자세히 객관적으로 서로 간의 특징을 비교해 가면서 서술하는 것이다. (단, 반복적인 문장은 가급적 사용하지 않는다.)

4 **With** the government subsidies, the cost of domestic road transport was the highest among them at 29.2%.
   정부보조금과 함께, 국내 도로교통 비용이 가장 높은 29.2%를 차지했다.

5 This was more than twice the cost of shopping transport which was only 14.5%.
   이것은 14.5%인 쇼핑 배달 비용보다 두 배 이상 많은 수치이다.

6 Also, the agricultural costs made up of pesticides and pollution control was at 20.1%.
또한 살충제와 오염 방지 항목으로 이루어진 농업 관련 비용은 20.1%였다.

7 Surprisingly, that of "International transport and waste disposal" was much less at 0.02%.
놀랍게도, '국제운송과 쓰레기처리'에 대한 비용은 0.02%로 다른 것보다 훨씬 낮게 나왔다.

8 It does not affect the cost of the food bill directly.
이것은 식품 청구서의 비용에 직접적으로 영향을 주지는 않는다.

9 In order to reduce costs, the British government supports about half (36.2%) compared with the sum loss (63.8%) per year.
이런 손실을 줄이기 위해서, 영국 정부는 매년마다 총 손실(63.8%)에 비교해 반 정도(36.2%) 후원을 해 준다.

전치사(With)로 시작하고 다음에 명사어구 쓰고, 주어(the cost)와 be동사(was) 어순대로 서술해 나간다. 차트상의 네 개의 환경적 손실(Environmental costs)에서 가장 높은 것을 설명하면서 가장 낮은 것과의 차이점을 서술하고, 서로 간의 특징을 수치적으로 비교하기 쉬운 요소를 선택적으로 서술하면서, 첨가부사(Also), 놀람부사(Surprisingly) 그리고 to부정사 용법으로 본문을 맺었다.

네번째 단락으로 결론(Conclusion)을 작성한다. 글의 마지막 단락으로, 차트를 분석(analysis)하고 맺으면 된다.

10 Consequently, from this chart we can see that the cost of domestic delivery and pesticides is excessive and the British government supports much money.
결과적으로, 이 차트에서 우리는 국내 지역의 운송료와 살충제 관련 비용이 과도하게 지출되며, 영국 정부가 많은 금액을 지원하고 있음을 알 수 있다.

결론부분에선 연결어(Linking word)인 Consequently(결론적으로)로 시작하고 we can see that + S + V~로 특징을 요약한다. 국내지역의 운송료 비용과 살충제의 과다 지출과 정부의 많은 지원금을 결론으로 삼았다.

ACADEMIC WRITING

샘플 답안

The pie chart above indicates the recent percentages of the covered loss of Britain's annual food bill.

In general, there are four broad categorised environmental costs. They are "Domestic road transport," "Agriculture," "Shopping transport" and "International transport and waste disposal."

With the government subsidies, the cost of domestic road transport was the highest among them at 29.2%. This was more than twice the cost of shopping transport which was only 14.5%. Also, the agricultural costs made up of pesticides and pollution control was at 20.1%. Surprisingly, that of "International transport and waste disposal" was much less at 0.02%. It does not affect the cost of the food bill directly. In order to reduce costs, the British government supports about half (36.2%) compared with the sum loss (63.8%) per year.

Consequently, from this chart we can see that the cost of domestic delivery and pesticides is excessive and the British government supports much money.

(total words: 151)

TASK 2

You should spend about 40 minutes on this task.

> *Studying abroad can be highly motivational for students and also inspire their dreams. However, whilst studying abroad can have a number of positive effects on students, there are also many difficulties that they may meet along the way. With this in mind, it is more advantageous to study at home.*
> 유학은 학생들에게 큰 동기 부여가 될 수 있으며, 또한 그들의 꿈을 고무시킨다. 하지만 유학은 긍정적인 면이 많은 반면에, 그들이 맞닥트릴 많은 어려움도 또한 존재한다. 이런 것들을 염두에 두면 국내에서 공부하는 것이 더 이득이 많다.
>
> *To what extent do you agree or disagree with this statement?*
> 이 글에 대해서 당신은 어느 정도 찬성 혹은 반대하는가?
>
> *Give reasons for your answer.*
> 당신의 대답에 대한 이유를 들어라.

You should write at least 250 words.

You should use your own idea, knowledge and experience and support your arguments with examples and relevant evidence.

먼저 도입단락(Introduction)을 작성한다. 글의 서론부분으로, 주어진 문제의 내용을 활용하여 관련된 분위기를 만드는 것이다.

도입단락은 These days, we are living within in a ~ society로 작성한다. '오늘날 우리는 ~한 사회에서 살고 있다.'는 의미로 부드럽게 시작한다. 이 문제에서는 a globalized society(국제화 사회)로 추론 가능하다.

1. **These days**, we are living in a globalized society.
   오늘날 우리는 국제화 사회에서 살고 있다.

그리고 다음 문장에서는 대다수의 사람을 문장의 '주어'로 놓고 관심분야와 이에 대한 이유를 간단히 서술한다.

2. **Most people are interested in** higher education because it enables students to get a deep understanding of their subject area by working with specialist professors at the universities.
   대부분의 사람들은 더 높은 수준의 교육에 관심을 보인다. 왜냐하면 대학에 있는 전문 교수들과 함께 작업함으로써 학생들이 그들의 과목을 더 깊이 이해할 수 있게 해 주기 때문이다.

그리고 다음 문장에서 유학이 우리에게 주는 양면성을 서술한다.

ACADEMIC WRITING

3 **Of course**, there are some disadvantages to studying abroad but there are also many future benefits for students that study abroad.
물론 유학에는 여러 단점도 있지만 또한 유학생들이 얻을 수 있는 많은 미래의 이득도 있다.

그리고 본문단락에 들어가기 전에 찬성 혹은 반대에 대한 입장을 밝힌다.

4 **Therefore, I disagree with the statement above**.
그러므로, 나는 위 언급에 반대하는 입장이다.

두번째 단락으로 [제1단락]을 작성한다. 여기선, 서론에서 언급한 반대하는 입장에서 유학에 대해서 좋은 점으로 선진국의 질적인 교육 시스템을 나열하면서 구체적인 사례와 본인의 의견을 들어 논리성을 높여 나간다.

5 **Due to the nature of the international education market**, most people usually want to attend universities in more economically developed countries.
국제 교육 시장의 환경 때문에, 대부분의 사람들은 경제 선진국의 대학교에 입학하고자 한다.

자국에서 졸업한 아시아 학생들의 현실을 언급한다.

6 **Actually**, students who have graduated from Asian universities are aware that their educational systems can sometimes be of a lower quality.
사실상 아시아의 대학교를 졸업한 학생들은 그들의 교육 체계가 때때로 질이 더 낮을 수도 있다는 것을 인식하고 있다.

그리고 공신력 있는 BBC방송사의 보도 자료를 적당히 문장의 내용에 맞게 허구적으로 언급한다. 객관화된 보도 자료는 개인적인 논술에 논리성을 높여 나간다.

7 **According to a BBC survey in 2009**, most Asians studying in UK were satisfied with the British educational system due to its free thinking style and good teaching methods.
BBC의 2009년 조사에 따르면, 영국에서 공부하는 대부분의 아시아인들은 자유로운 사고를 추구하는 스타일과 훌륭한 교육 방법들을 가지고 있는 영국의 교육 체계에 만족한다고 한다.

그리고 사례를 들어 동화작가가 되고 싶어 하는 사람들이 해리 포터의 영향을 받아 문학의 독특성을 배우러 유학을 간다는 내용을 설명한다.

8 **For example**, aspiring fantasy authors can take a lot of inspiration from novels such as Harry Potter because of the way in which traditional British children's culture is expressed through a unique method of storytelling.
예를 들어, 판타지 소설 작가를 꿈꾸는 사람들은 해리 포터와 같은 소설에서 많은 영감을 얻을 수 있다. 전통적인 영국의 어린이 문화가 독특한 이야기 방식을 통해 잘 표현되어 있기 때문이다.

세 번째 단락으로 [제2단락]을 작성한다. 여기선, 서론에서 언급한 반대하는 입장에서 유학에 대해서 좋은 점으로 고용의 혜택을 나열하면서 구체적인 사례와 본인의 의견을 들어 논리성을 높여 나간다.

첫 문장에서는 첨가부사와 함께 지금 세계 경제가 침체되어 다국적 기업에서는 유능한 인재를 찾고 있으며, 많은 이들이 좋은 직장을 얻기 위해 유학을 결심하게 되는 것을 언급한다.

9 **Furthermore**, due to the current economic climate most international corporations need able workers from excellent schools.

게다가 현재의 경제 분위기로 인해 대부분의 다국적기업은 훌륭한 학교를 졸업한 능력 있는 직원을 필요로 한다.

10 So, many young people are studying overseas in order to gain professional language skills.

그래서 많은 젊은이들이 전문적인 언어 기술을 습득하기 위해 유학을 선택하고 있다.

11 **For instance**, the zPod player made by A company was invented by special web designers who had graduated from Art schools in advanced countries.

예를 들어, A사가 만든 zPod 플레이어는 선진국의 예술학교를 졸업한 전문적인 웹 디자이너들에 의해 발명되었다.

12 Now, the zPod player is the leading product in the personal stereo market.

현재 zPod 플레이어는 휴대용 음악 재생기 시장에서 가장 많이 팔리는 제품이다.

네 번째 단락으로 결론(Conclusion)을 작성한다. 글의 마지막 단락으로 주제를 언급하고 본인의 의견으로 맺으면 된다. 결론의 맺음말로 시작하면서, 유학이 자국에서 얻을 수 없는 교육적 경험이며 든든한 내일을 위한 멋진 투자라고 결론짓는다.

13 **To sum up**, in my opinion, although there are some difficulties for students studying abroad such as learning a new language and culture, it is certainly possible to adapt well to a new environment.

결론적으로, 유학생들이 새로운 언어나 문화와 같은 어려움을 겪을 수 있겠지만, 새로운 환경에 충분히 잘 적응할 수 있다.

14 **Furthermore**, studying abroad can open a lot of doors in terms of opportunities in the international job market.

게다가 유학은 국제 취업 시장에서 많은 기회를 얻게 해 줄 수 있다.

ACADEMIC WRITING

샘플 답안

These days, we are living in a globalized society. Most people are interested in higher education because it enables students to get a deep understanding of their subject area by working with specialist professors at the universities. Of course, there are some disadvantages to studying abroad but there are also many future benefits for students that study abroad. Therefore, I disagree with the statement above.

Due to the nature of the international education market, most people usually want to attend universities in more economically developed countries. Actually, students who have graduated from Asian universities are aware that their educational systems can sometimes be of a lower quality. According to a BBC survey in 2009, most Asians studying in UK were satisfied with the British educational system due to its free thinking style and good teaching methods. For example, aspiring fantasy authors can take a lot of inspiration from novels such as Harry Potter because of the way in which traditional British children's culture is expressed through a unique method of storytelling.

Furthermore, due to the current economic climate most international corporations need able workers from excellent schools. So, many young people are studying overseas in order to gain professional language skills. For instance, the zPod player made by A company was invented by special web designers who had graduated from Art schools in advanced countries. Now, the zPod player is the leading product in the personal stereo market.

To sum up, in my opinion, although there are some difficulties for students studying abroad such as learning a new language and culture, it is certainly possible to adapt well to a new environment. Furthermore, studying abroad can open a lot of doors in terms of opportunities in the international job market.

(total words: 289)

TEST 3

TASK 1

You should spend about 20 minutes on this task.

The graph below shows the average levels of Methane (CH_4) globally. Line A shows the trend together with seasonal variations. Line B indicates the trend that emerges when the seasonal cycle has been removed.

아래 그래프는 세계적인 평균 메탄의 양을 보여 준다. A선은 계절 변화에 따른 변화를 보여 준다. B선은 계절 변화 주기를 배제한 경향을 보여 준다.

Write a report for a university lecturer describing the information shown below.

아래 정보를 묘사하여 대학 강의를 위한 리포트를 작성하시오.

You should write at least 150 words.

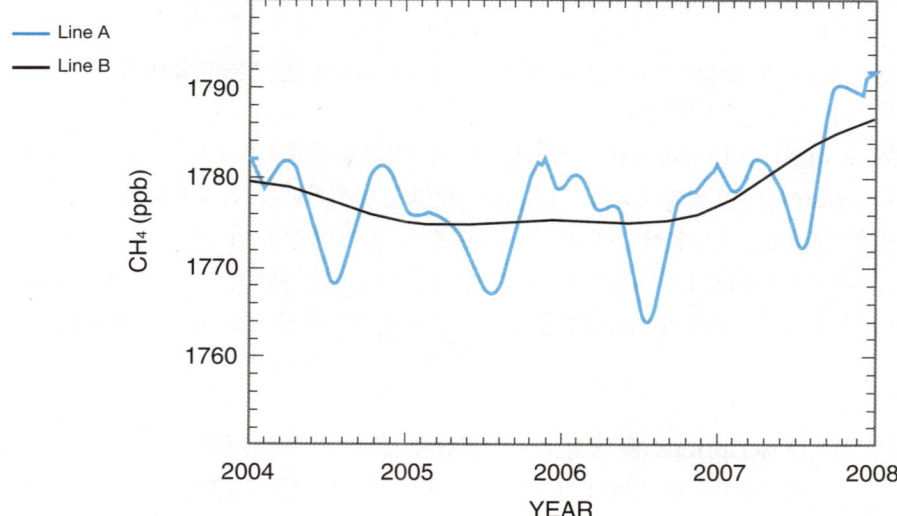

ACADEMIC WRITING

먼저 도입단락(Introduction)을 작성한다. 글의 서론부분으로, 그래프의 이름을 만드는 것이다. 항상, 도입단락은 정관사 The로 시작하고 시제는 현재시제를 사용한다.

1. **The line graph above indicates** the Methane (CH₄) levels in conditions with and without variations caused by the seasonal cycle from 2004 to 2008.
   위의 선 그래프는 2004년부터 2008년까지의 계절 주기로 인한 계절 변화가 있는 경우와 없는 경우 메탄의 정도를 보여 준다.

문제와 동일하게 작성하면 감점이 되므로 문법구조를 약간 활용하여 구조는 다르지만 의미는 같게 표현하면 된다. 문제에 주어진 차트의 이름은 line graph(line: 줄/실)이며, 장소부사 below 대신 above(위에 있는)가 쓰였다. 동사는 일반동사 현재시제(indicates: ~을 가리키다), 다음은 목적대상인 the Methane levels(메탄의 정도), 그 다음엔 in condition(~한 조건), 그 다음엔 with and without variations caused by the seasonal cycle로 condition을 설명했고, 마지막으로 그래프의 기간 from 2004 to 2008(from A to B: A에서 B까지)를 명시하였다.

두번째 단락으로 일반화 진술(General statement)을 작성한다. 본론에 들어가기 전에 그래프의 전반적인 상황과 분위기를 서술하는 것이다.

2. **In general, there were** two trends from both line A and line B.
   일반적으로, A선과 B선의 두 가지 흐름이 있다.

3. **They were not similar to each other because line A had fluctuated greatly, whilst line B hadn't so much.**
   두 개의 선들은 서로 유사한 관계성이 없다. 왜냐하면, A선은 매우 변동이 심하나, B선은 변동이 심하지 않다.

처음 문장은 연결어(linking word)인 In general(일반적으로)로 시작하고 다음엔 유도부사구문으로 그래프의 시제에 맞추어 작성해 나간다. there were ~(~이 있다) 그리고 그래프의 전반적인 분위기로 두 선의 비교되는 특징을 간략히 서술한다. 유도부사구문은 본 주어가 be동사 다음에 위치하므로 그래프상의 두 개의 선을 언급하고 다음엔 이들(They)은 서로 간의 유사점이 없다는(be not similar to) 식으로 문장을 나열하며 이를 위한 뒷받침 문장으로 because + S + V 접속사절을 놓는데 line A는 변동이 심하고(fluctuated), line B는 변동이 심하지 않음(hadn't so much)을 언급한다.

세번째 단락으로 설명묘사(Descriptions)를 작성한다. 본론단락으로, 그래프에 대해 문법과 어휘를 활용하여 자세히 객관적으로 서로 간의 특징을 비교해 가면서 서술하는 것이다. (단, 반복적인 문장은 가급적 사용하지 않는다.)

4. **With** the trend of seasonal variations, line A met four outstanding negative points from 2004 to 2008.
   계절적 변동으로 A선은 2004년부터 2008년까지 네 개의 두드러진 (–) 점을 접하고 있다.

5 In mid-2006 the Methane level hit its lowest point at around 1764 ppb.
2006년 중반 들어 메탄의 정도는 약 1764ppb로 최저점을 찍었다.

6 This line started at 1782 ppb in 2004, and finished at 1792 in 2008.
이 선은 2004년도에 1782ppb에서 시작했고, 2008년도에 1792ppb로 끝났다.

7 It had changed greatly over the 4 years.
이것은 4년에 걸쳐 매우 크게 변했다.

8 After mid-2007 the Methane level sharply increased.
2007년 중반 이후, 메탄의 정도는 가장 급격히 상승하였다.

9 In contrast, line B had few ups and downs.
비교적으로, B선은 굴곡이 작았다.

10 1780 ppb was the start and it reduced slowly and increased slightly in the second half of 2006, reaching its highest point at 1786 ppb in 2008.
1780ppb로 시작하여 서서히 감소하다가 2006년 하반기에 약간 증가하여 2008년에 최고점인 1786ppb까지 도달하였다.

전치사(With)로 시작하고 다음에 명사어구를 쓰고, 주어(line A)와 과거동사(met) 어순대로 서술해 나간다. 그래프 상의 네 개의 (-) 꼭짓점들을 서술하고, 그중에서 가장 낮은 점을 설명하면서 시작점과 끝나는 점 그리고 후반부의 급격히 상승하는 부분을 묘사한다. 다음은 비교(In contrast)되는 line B에 대해서 설명하는데, 굴곡(ups and downs)이 심하지 않다고 언급하며, 시작점을 설명하면서 그래프의 2006년 하반기의 특징과 2008년의 끝나는 점까지 설명하면 된다.

네번째 단락으로 결론(Conclusion)을 작성한다. 글의 마지막 단락으로, 그래프를 분석(analysis)하고 맺으면 된다.

11 As a result, we know that, from the graph, Methane was rising dramatically in 2007.
결론적으로, 우리는 이 그래프를 통해서 2007년에 메탄의 양이 급격하게 증가하고 있음을 알 수 있다.

12 And we can see that the burning of fossil fuels such as coal, oil and gas may affect the primary source of increasing the green house effect.
그리고 우리는 석탄, 기름, 가스와 같은 화석연료의 연소는 지구의 온난화 효과 증가의 주된 원인에 영향을 줄 수 있다는 것을 알 수 있다.

ACADEMIC WRITING

결론부분에선 연결부사(Linking word)인 As a result,(결론적으로)로 시작하고 다음엔 we know that + S + V ~로 특징을 요약하고, 분석하여 결론을 맺으면 된다. 메탄은 2007년을 기점으로 급속히 상승하며, 화석연료(fossil fuels)의 소각(the burning)이 온실효과(the green house effect)를 증가시키는 주된 원인이 되기도 한다는 것으로 정리한다.

샘플 답안

The line graph above indicates the Methane (CH$_4$) levels in conditions with and without variations caused by the seasonal cycle from 2004 to 2008.

In general, there were two trends from both line A and line B. They were not similar to each other because line A had fluctuated greatly, whilst line B hadn't so much.

With the trend of seasonal variations, line A met four outstanding negative points from 2004 to 2008. In mid-2006 the Methane level hit its lowest point at around 1764 ppb. This line started at 1782 ppb in 2004, and finished at 1792 in 2008. It had changed greatly over the 4 years. After mid-2007 the Methane level sharply increased. In contrast, line B had few ups and downs. 1780 ppb was the start and it reduced slowly and increased slightly in the second half of 2006, reaching its highest point at 1786 ppb in 2008.

As a result, we know that, from the graph, Methane was rising dramatically in 2007. And we can see that the burning of fossil fuels such as coal, oil and gas may affect the primary source of increasing the green house effect.

(total words: 193)

TASK 2

You should spend about 40 minutes on this task.

> ***Due to the increasing density of living areas in a city, most residents are suffering from physical and social dangers so that they are against it.***
> 도시의 생활공간의 밀도 증가로, 대부분의 사람들은 물리적·사회적 위험으로 고통받고 있기에 이런 현상에 저항하는 입장에 있다.
>
> ***To what extent do you agree or disagree with this statement?***
> 당신은 이 내용에 어느 정도 찬성 혹은 반대하는가?
>
> ***Give reasons for your answer.***
> 당신의 대답에 대한 몇 가지 이유를 들어라.

You should write at least 250 words.

You should use your own idea, knowledge and experience and support your arguments with examples and relevant evidence.

먼저 도입단락(Introduction)을 작성한다. 글의 서론부분으로, 주어진 문제의 내용을 활용하여 관련된 분위기를 만드는 것이다.

도입단락은 These days, we are living in ~ society로 작성한다. '오늘날 우리는 ~한 사회에 살고 있다.' 이렇게 부드럽게 서두를 시작한다. 문제의 분위기는 an urbanized society(도시화 사회)으로 추론 가능하다.

1   **These days**, we are living in an urbanized society.
    오늘날, 우리는 도시화 사회에 살고 있다.

그리고 다음 문장에서 대다수의 사람을 문장의 '주어'로 놓고 관심분야와 이에 대한 이유를 간단히 서술한다.

2   **Most people are attracted to** the convenience of living in an urban area because of the amenities and employment opportunities.
    대부분의 사람들은 편의시설과 취업 기회 때문에 도시의 편안함에 매력을 느낀다.

그리고 다음 문장에서 도시화가 우리에게 주는 양면성을 서술한다.

ACADEMIC WRITING

3 **Of course**, there are a number of advantages to living in a city but there are also some negative aspects such as social problems and pollution.
물론, 도시 생활에는 여러 장점이 있지만, 또한 사회적 문제나 오염과 같은 몇몇 부정적인 면도 존재한다.

그리고 본문단락에 들어가기 전에 찬성 혹은 반대 입장을 언급한다.

4 **I therefore agree with the statement above.**
그러므로 나는 위의 진술에 동의한다.

두 번째 단락으로 [제1단락]을 작성한다. 여기선, 도시화를 반대하는 입장에서 서론에서 언급한 찬성하는 첫 번째 이유로 도시부동산 가격상승에 대한 구체적인 사례와 본인의 의견을 들어 논리성을 높여 나간다.

사회적인 분위기를 담은 문장으로 본론을 시작한다.

5 **As a result of** global industrialization, these days most people tend to move to urban areas where life is more comfortable.
세계적인 산업화의 결과로, 오늘날 많은 사람들은 더욱 편안한 삶을 살 수 있는 도시 지역으로 이주하는 경향이 있다.

사회적 서비스가 결핍된 시골의 현실을 언급한다.

6 **Actually**, people find it difficult to enjoy a high quality of life in rural areas because there are not enough social services such as good educational facilities.
사실상, 사람들은 시골에서 높은 삶의 질을 즐기기가 어렵다는 것을 알게 된다. 왜냐하면 교육 시설과 같은 사회적 서비스가 충분하지 않기 때문이다.

그리고 공신력 있는 BBC방송사의 보도 자료를 적당히 문장의 내용에 맞게 허구적으로 언급한다. 객관화된 보도 자료는 개인적인 논술에 논리성을 높여 준다.

7 **According to the BBC**, most real estate prices have skyrocketed ten-fold recently, especially in the east of London due to the 2012 Olympic games.
BBC에 따르면, 최근 2012년 올림픽 때문에 특히 동런던 지역의 대부분의 부동산 가격이 10배 이상 폭등했다.

그리고 이에 관련하여 도시화의 밀집현상으로 삶의 공간이 없어져 가는 답답한 현실을 서술한다.

8 **However**, unfortunately, increasing the population density of a city is causing recreational facilities such as parks to become sparse and further limits car parking space.
그러나, 불행하게도 도시의 인구밀도 증가는 공원과 같은 여가시설을 줄어들게 만들고 주차공간도 제한시킨다.

세 번째 단락으로 [제2단락]을 작성한다. 여기선, 도시화를 반대하는 입장에서 서론에서 언급한 찬성하는 두 번째 이유로 매연으로 인한 도시 내 공기오염에 대한 구체적인 사례와 본인의 의견을 들어 논리성을 높여 나간다.

첨가부사와 함께 도시 안의 자동차 매연으로 인한 호흡질환과 국제기구의 객관적인 통계자료를 바탕으로 신생아들의 질병과 오염으로 인한 현대인들의 고통을 이야기한다.

9 **Furthermore**, due to the air pollution caused by traffic and construction, the number of people in big cities with respiratory diseases is increasing, meaning that residents often feel uncomfortable.
게다가, 교통과 건축에 의해 발생하는 대기오염으로 인해 호흡기질환을 앓는 도시인들이 증가했다. 거주자들이 종종 불편함을 느낀다는 의미다.

10 **According to the WHO (World Health Organization)**, around 40% of newborn babies have asthma and atopic dermatitis.
WHO에 따르면, 신생아의 40%가량이 천식과 아토피 피부염을 앓고 있다.

11 **As a result of** this kind of statistic, people are now taking more precautions.
이러한 수치의 결과로, 사람들은 더 많은 주의를 기울이고 있다.

12 **For example**, on the way to and from work many people wear masks to protect themselves from car exhaust fumes.
예를 들어, 출퇴근길에 많은 사람들이 자동차 배기가스로부터 자신을 보호하기 위해 마스크를 착용한다.

네 번째 단락으로 결론(Conclusion)을 작성한다. 글의 마지막 단락으로, 주제를 언급하고 본인의 의견으로 맺으면 된다. 결론의 맺음말로 시작하면서, 도시화의 양면성을 다시 역설하고, 부작용에 대한 보완작업으로 정부의 역할을 강조한다.

13 **In conclusion**, although most people are able to live a higher quality of life as a result of urbanization, there are negative points, such as housing price inflation and air pollution.
결론적으로, 대부분의 사람들이 도시화의 결과로 더 질 높은 삶을 살 수 있음에도 불구하고, 주택 가격의 인플레이션이나 대기오염과 같은 여러 부정적인 면이 존재한다.

그리고 이런 현상을 동전에 비유함으로써 사회현상에 대한 함축성을 보인다.

14 **This situation is like two sides of a coin**.
이런 상황은 동전의 앞면과 뒷면의 속성과 같다.

ACADEMIC WRITING

15 **So, in my opinion**, governments should invest revenue in public health services and make severe regulations against properties and business's that cause pollution.

그러므로, 개인적인 의견으로는, 정부는 국민보건서비스에 자금을 투자하고, 오염을 유발하는 부동산과 기업에 대해 엄격하게 규제해야 한다.

샘플 답안

These days, we are living in an urbanized society. Most people are attracted to the convenience of living in an urban area because of the amenities and employment opportunities. Of course, there are a number of advantages to living in a city but there are also some negative aspects such as social problems and pollution. I therefore agree with the statement above.

As a result of global industrialization, these days most people tend to move to urban areas where life is more comfortable. Actually, people find it difficult to enjoy a high quality of life in rural areas because there are not enough social services such as good educational facilities. According to the BBC, most real estate prices have skyrocketed ten-fold recently, especially in the east of London due to the 2012 Olympic games. However, unfortunately, increasing the population density of a city is causing recreational facilities such as parks to become sparse and further limits car parking space.

Furthermore, due to the air pollution caused by traffic and construction, the number of people in big cities with respiratory diseases is increasing, meaning that residents often feel uncomfortable. According to the WHO (World Health Organization), around 40% of newborn babies have asthma and atopic dermatitis. As a result of this kind of statistic, people are now taking more precautions. For example, on the way to and from work many people wear masks to protect themselves from car exhaust fumes.

In conclusion, although most people are able to live a higher quality of life as a result of urbanization, there are negative points, such as housing price inflation and air pollution. This situation is like two sides of a coin. So, in my opinion, governments should invest revenue in public health services and make severe regulations against properties and business's that cause pollution.

(total words: 301)

TEST 4

TASK 1

You should spend about 20 minutes on this task.

The table below shows the percentage of electronic products used in UK homes in 2005 and 2008.
아래 도표는 2005년과 2008년 영국의 가정에서 사용된 전자 제품의 양을 보여 준다.

Summarise the information by selecting and reporting the main features, and make comparisons where relevant.
주요 특징을 선택하고 서술하면서 정보를 요약하고, 관련 사항을 비교하시오.

You should write at least 150 words.

Percentage of electronic categories in UK Homes both in 2005 and 2008

	2005	2008
TV	93	94
computer	50	72
microwave oven	80	85
washing machine	95	95
video recorder	82	65
digital camera	15	90
Humidifier	20	62

ACADEMIC WRITING

먼저 도입단락(Introduction)을 작성한다. 글의 서론부분으로, 표의 이름을 만드는 것이다. 항상, 도입단락은 정관사 The로 시작하고 시제는 현재시제를 사용한다.

1   The table above indicates the amount of electronic products in UK households both in 2005 and 2008.
    위의 도표는 2005년과 2008년의 영국 가정에서 사용하는 전자제품의 양을 보여 준다.

문제와 동일하게 작성하면 감점이 되므로 문법구조를 활용하여 구조는 다르지만 의미는 같게 표현하면 된다. 문제에 주어진 표의 이름은 table이며, 장소부사 below 대신 above(위에 있는)가 쓰였다. 동사는 일반동사 현재시제 indicates: ~을 가리키다), 다음은 목적대상인 the amount(양), 다음엔 적당한 명사와 명사를 이어 주는 전치사 of(~의), 다음엔 명사구 electronic products를 사용했다.

두 번째 단락으로 일반화 진술(General statement)을 작성한다. 본론에 들어가기 전에 표의 전반적인 상황과 분위기를 서술하는 것이다.

2   In general, the outstanding rate of differences between 2005 and 2008, can be found in the increased use of both digital cameras and humidifiers.
    전반적으로, 디지털 카메라와 가습기의 증가분에서 2005년과 2008년의 두드러지는 비율의 차이를 알 수 있다.

3   We can see a 6 fold increase in the use of digital cameras whilst the use of humidifiers tripled.
    우리는 디지털 카메라의 사용량이 6배, 가습기의 사용량이 3배 증가하였음을 알 수 있다.

처음 문장은 연결어(linking word)인 In general(전반적으로)로 시작하고 표의 시제에 맞추어 작성해 나간다. 그리고 표의 전반적인 분위기는 표의 움직임과 진행과정에 대해 간략히 서술한다. 문제의 표에서 보는 바와 같이 전자제품 항목 중에 디지털 카메라와 가습기의 증가분이 눈에 띄게 많다는 것을 설명한다.

세 번째 단락으로 설명묘사(Descriptions)를 작성한다. 본론단락으로, 문법과 어휘를 활용하여 자세히 객관적으로 모든 표의 진행과정을 서술하는 것이다. (단, 반복적인 문장은 가급적 사용하지 않는다.)

4   Surprisingly, the product that had the lowest rate of usage in 2005 was the digital camera at 15%.
    놀랍게도, 2005년에 사용 비율이 가장 낮았던 제품은 디지털 카메라로, 15%였다.

5   However, three years later this increased to 90%.
    그러나 3년 후 90%로 증가하였다.

6 **Of course**, both TVs and washing machines were over 90%, but there was hardly any difference between the two years.
물론, 칼라TV와 세탁기의 사용률은 90%가 넘었지만 2년 사이에 차이가 거의 없었다.

7 **In contrast**, video recorders decreased at a rate of 17% between 2005 and 2008, compared to the other categorises which increased.
대조적으로, 다른 항목들이 증가한 것에 비교해 비디오 레코더는 2005년과 2008년 사이에 17% 줄어들었다.

표를 요약할 때, 디지털 카메라의 사용률이 3년 사이 큰 폭으로 증가했음을 언급한다. 또한, 꾸준히 상위그룹에 있는 세탁기와 칼라TV를 언급하고, 7가지 항목 중에서 사용률이 떨어진 비디오 레코더를 설명하면서 요약정리를 하면 좋다.

네번째 단락으로 결론(conclusion)을 작성한다. 글의 마지막 단락으로, 표를 분석(analysis)하고 맺으면 된다.

8 **As a result** of studying this table, we know that the most used electronic products in British homes are TVs and washing machines.
이 도표를 살펴보면, 우리는 영국의 가정에서 가장 많이 사용된 전자제품이 TV와 세탁기임을 알 수 있다.

9 It is also clear that the use of the video recorder went down significantly because of the arrival of more practical goods like the digital camera.
또한 디지털 카메라와 같은 더욱 실용적인 상품의 출현으로 인해 비디오 레코더의 사용률이 현저하게 줄어들었음이 분명히 나타난다.

결론부분은 연결어(Linking word)인 As a result of(~의 결과로)로 시작하고 다음엔 we know that + S + V ~로 분석하고, 디지털 카메라의 활용으로 같은 기능을 갖고 있는 비디오 레코더의 이용률이 감소한 것으로 정리한다.

ACADEMIC WRITING

샘플 답안

The table above indicates the amount of electronic products in UK households both in 2005 and 2008.

In general, the outstanding rate of differences between 2005 and 2008, can be found in the increased use of both digital cameras and humidifiers. We can see a 6 fold increase in the use of digital cameras whilst the use of humidifiers tripled.

Surprisingly, the product that had the lowest rate of usage in 2005 was the digital camera at 15%. However, three years later this increased to 90%. Of course, both TVs and washing machines were over 90%, but there was hardly any difference between the two years. In contrast, video recorders decreased at a rate of 17% between 2005 and 2008, compared to the other categorises which increased.

As a result of studying this table, we know that the most used electronic products in British homes are TVs and washing machines. It is also clear that the use of the video recorder went down significantly because of the arrival of more practical goods like the digital camera.

(total words: 176)

TASK 2

You should spend about 40 minutes on this task.

Modern society is becoming more concerned with the increase in juvenile crime.
현대 사회는 청소년 범죄의 증가에 더욱 관심을 기울이고 있다.

What do you think is the cause of the increase in juvenile crime?
청소년 범죄 증가의 원인은 무엇이라고 생각하는가?

What solutions can you suggest?
제안할 수 있는 해결점은 무엇인가?

You should write at least 250 words.

You should use your own idea, knowledge and experience and support your arguments with examples and relevant evidence.

먼저 도입단락(Introduction)을 작성한다. 글의 서론부분으로, 주어진 문제의 내용을 활용하여 관련된 분위기를 만드는 것이다.

도입단락에서는 우리가 살고 있는 사회의 현실에 대해 언급한다. 이 문제에서는 juvenile crimes(청소년 범죄)에 대해 언급하면서 글을 시작한다.

1   **In our modern society**, juvenile crime is on the rise.
현대 사회에서, 청소년 범죄는 계속 증가하고 있다.

그리고 다음 문장에서 대다수의 사람을 문장의 '주어'로 놓고 관심분야와 이에 대한 이유를 간단히 서술한다.

2   **Many people have an appreciation** for young people because they are able to consider social issues with an open mind and creative approach.
많은 사람들이 젊은이들에게 감탄한다. 왜냐하면 그들은 사회적 이슈에 대해 열린 마음과 창의적인 접근방식을 가지고 생각할 수 있기 때문이다.

그리고 다음 문장에서 청소년들의 성향의 양면성을 서술한다.

ACADEMIC WRITING

3 The thoughts and ideas of teenagers can contribute to society in a positive way but sometimes a lack of judgement can cause teenagers to act in a thoughtless way too.
청소년들의 사고는 긍정적인 방식으로 사회에 기여할 수도 있지만, 때로는 판단력의 결핍이 청소년들을 경솔하게 행동하도록 만들 수도 있다.

그리고 본문에 들어갈 원인 두 가지를 간접적으로 언급한다.

4 I would therefore like to talk about the main causes of juvenile crime.
그러므로 나는 청소년 범죄의 주요 원인들에 대해 이야기하고자 한다.

두 번째 단락으로 [제1단락]을 작성한다. 여기선, 서론에서 간접적으로 언급한 청소년 범죄의 원인 중 첫 번째인 부모와의 대화 단절(the lack of communication)에 대한 구체적인 사례와 본인의 의견을 들어 논리성을 높여 나간다.

문제의 분위기에 맞게 '자본주의'로 시작하면서 돈에 대한 욕망이 불러오는 대화의 단절을 이야기한다.

5 In a society of capitalism and consumerism, the desire to earn money can sometimes lead to a lack of family cohesion.
자본주의와 소비지상주의의 사회에서 돈을 벌고자 하는 욕망은 때때로 가족 구성원 간의 화합을 막는 결과를 가져오기도 한다.

6 Consequently, there is breakdown in communication between parents and their children.
결과적으로 부모 자식 간의 소통이 단절되었다.

그리고 공신력 있는 언론자료를 현실성 있는 허구로 인용하여, 최근 결손가정의 비행청소년의 증가를 이야기한다.

7 According to the BBC (2009), the number of students from broken homes is increasing every year.
2009년 BBC에 따르면, 결손가정에서 자라는 학생들의 수가 매년 증가하고 있다.

그리고 이에 관련된 현실성 있는 예시로 본인의 고교시절을 허구로 인용한다.

8 For example, when I was at secondary school, my classmate had poor conduct at school and abandoned his studies.
예를 들면, 내가 고등학교에 다닐 때, 나의 반 친구는 행실이 좋지 않아 학업을 그만두었다.

그리고 그 친구의 안타까운 처지를 언급해 준다.

9 It was a sad situation because his parents were unconcerned by his deviation from school.
친구의 부모님이 그의 일탈에 무관심했기 때문에 슬픈 상황이었다.

세 번째 단락으로 [제2단락]을 작성한다. 여기선, 서론에서 간접적으로 언급한 청소년 범죄의 원인 중 두 번째인 과보호(over protectiveness)에 대한 구체적인 사례와 본인의 의견을 들어 논리성을 높여 나간다.

핵가족의 가정형태로 아이를 하나만 낳아 정성 들여 키우는 현실에 대해서 작성한다.

10 These days, there are many one-child families.
오늘날 많은 가정들이 아이를 한 명만 낳는다.

그리고 이런 현상이 이런 문제를 낳았다고 정의한다.

11 The children of these families usually receive a lot of attention from their parents which can make them child become selfish and have a lack of empathy.
이러한 가정의 아이는 일반적으로 부모에게 많은 관심을 받는데 이것이 아이를 이기적이고 타인에 공감하지 못하게 만들 수 있다.

그리고 이에 관련된 현실성 있는 예시로 시사적 허구를 인용한다.

12 For instance, according to a newspaper report, a child from a wealthy home was arrested on a theft charge in a department store last week.
예를 들어, 신문기사에 따르면 부유한 가정에서 자란 한 아이가 지난주 백화점에서 절도죄로 체포되었다.

그리고 아이를 망치는 부모의 잘못된 행동에 대해서 설명한다.

13 However, instead of being scolded, the child was comforted by his parents.
그러나 그 아이는 부모에게 혼나는 대신 위로받았다.

네 번째 단락으로 결론(Conclusion)을 작성한다. 글의 마지막 단락으로 주제를 언급하고 본인의 의견으로 해결방안을 제시하고 맺으면 된다.

결론의 맺음말로 시작하면서, 청소년에 대한 양면성을 다시 역설한다.

14 In conclusion, teenagers can contribute positively to society with their creativity but they need to be nurtured by their parents.
결론적으로, 청소년들은 그들의 창의성으로 사회에 긍정적으로 기여할 수 있지만, 부모에게 양육되어야 하는 존재이다.

ACADEMIC WRITING

15 It is a two-sided situation.
이것은 양면적인 상황이다.

16 So, in my opinion, one solution to this problem could be a combination of school education and government sponsored family programmes.
그래서 개인적인 의견으로는, 이러한 문제의 해결책이 학교 교육과 정부 지원 가족 프로그램의 결합일 것이라 생각한다.

샘플 답안

In our modern society, juvenile crime is on the rise. Many people have an appreciation for young people because they are able to consider social issues with an open mind and creative approach. The thoughts and ideas of teenagers can contribute to society in a positive way but sometimes a lack of judgement can cause teenagers to act in a thoughtless way too. I would therefore like to talk about the main causes of juvenile crime.

In a society of capitalism and consumerism, the desire to earn money can sometimes lead to a lack of family cohesion. Consequently, there is breakdown in communication between parents and their children. According to the BBC (2009), the number of students from broken homes is increasing every year. For example, when I was at secondary school, my classmate had poor conduct at school and abandoned his studies. It was a sad situation because his parents were unconcerned by his deviation from school.

These days, there are many one-child families. The children of these families usually receive a lot of attention from their parents which can make them child become selfish and have a lack of empathy. For instance, according to a newspaper report, a child from a wealthy home was arrested on a theft charge in a department store last week. However, instead of being scolded, the child was comforted by his parents.

In conclusion, teenagers can contribute positively to society with their creativity but they need to be nurtured by their parents. It is a two-sided situation. So, in my opinion, one solution to this problem could be a combination of school education and government sponsored family programmes.

(total words: 275)

TASK 1

You should spend about 20 minutes on this task.

> *The table below shows the reasons why people in Australia use on-line services according to the ages.*
> 아래 도표는 호주 사람들의 나이에 따른 인터넷 사용 목적을 보여 준다.
>
> *Summarise the information by selecting and reporting the main features, and make comparisons where relevant.*
> 주요 특징을 선택하고 서술하면서 정보를 요약하고, 관련 사항을 비교하시오.

You should write at least 150 words.

**Percentage of using on-line services
in Australia according to the ages and the purpose of use**

	11~19	20~29	30~39	40 and over
Academic study	36	31	27	18
E-Banking	2	5	11	20
E-mail	40	41	41	38
Online shopping	5	8	15	20
Online Chatting	15	12	5	3
Others	2	3	1	1

ACADEMIC WRITING

먼저 도입단락(Introduction)을 작성한다. 글의 서론부분으로 도표의 이름을 만드는 것이다. 항상, 도입단락은 정관사 The로 시작하고 시제는 현재시제를 사용한다.

1   **The table above indicates** the reasons for using the Internet services based on age in Australia.
    위의 도표는 호주에서의 나이에 따른 인터넷 사용 목적을 보여 준다.

문제와 동일하게 작성하면 감점이 되므로 문법구조를 활용하여 구조는 다르지만 의미는 같게 표현하면 된다. 문제에 주어진 도표의 이름은 table이며, 장소부사 below 대신 above(위에 있는)가 쓰였다. 동사는 일반동사 현재시제(indicates: ~을 가리키다), 다음은 목적대상인 the reasons(이유), 그다음엔 명사와 명사를 이어 주는 전치사 for(~의), 그다음엔 동명사 using을 적고 다음엔 명사어구 the Internet services를 사용했다.

두번째 단락으로 일반화 진술(General statement)을 작성한다. 본론에 들어가기 전에 도표의 전반적인 상황과 분위기를 서술하는 것이다.

2   **In general**, the rate of use for e-mail is very high compared to the other categories in all age groups.
    일반적으로, 모든 연령층에서 이메일 사용률이 다른 항목들보다 훨씬 높았다.

처음 문장은 연결어(linking word)인 In general(일반적으로)로 시작한다. 그리고 표의 움직임과 진행과정에 대해 간략히 서술한다. 문제의 표에서 보는 바와 같이 나이에 따른 인터넷 사용목적에서 전자메일이 가장 많은 비중을 차지했다.

세번째 단락으로 설명묘사(Descriptions)를 작성한다. 본론단락으로, 도표에 대해 문법과 어휘를 활용하여 자세히 객관적으로 모든 진행과정을 서술하는 것이다. (단, 반복적인 문장은 가급적 사용하지 않는다.)

3   From the different services, users that prefer to use the Internet for e-mail and education account for more than half of the people questioned.
    인터넷을 이메일이나 교육의 용도로 사용하기를 선호하는 사용자가 설문에 대답한 사람들 중 절반을 넘었다.

4   **Also**, not including e-mail, 36 per cent of the 11-19 age group like to use Internet services for education, whereas 20% per cent of the over 40 age group like to use online shopping services.
    또한 이메일을 제외하고, 11-19세 층의 36퍼센트가 인터넷 서비스를 교육의 용도로 사용하며, 40세 이상 층의 20퍼센트가 온라인 쇼핑 서비스를 사용하고 있다.

5   **Surprisingly**, they do not care about on-line chatting compared with the 11 to 19 age group.
    놀랍게도, 그들은 11-19세 층과 비교했을 때 온라인 채팅에는 관심이 없다.

6 However, only 2 per cent of the younger users use on-line banking services.
그러나 젊은 사용자층의 겨우 2퍼센트만이 온라인 뱅킹 서비스를 사용한다.

도표를 요약할 때, 먼저 인터넷 서비스의 주된 이용에 대해서 언급하면서, 젊은 층과 40세 이상 층의 인터넷 서비스 이용 세부 항목에 대해서 서로 비교와 대조를 하면서 요약정리를 하면 좋다.

네번째 단락으로 결론(Conclusion)을 작성한다. 글의 마지막 단락으로, 도표를 분석(analysis)하고 맺으면 된다.

7 From studying this table, we can see that most of the users are using Internet services for convenience by using them to save time and money.
이 도표에서, 우리는 대다수 사용자들이 시간과 비용을 절약하여 편리함을 얻기 위해 인터넷 서비스를 사용한다는 것을 알 수 있다.

결론부분에선 인터넷 서비스 이용의 목적으로 편리함을 간접적으로 역설하면서 다음 아래와 같이 내용을 다시 요약 정리한다.

8 Of course the difference between the age groups is interesting.
물론 연령층에 따라 나타나는 차이점은 흥미롭다.

9 It seems the young use the Internet for education and people over 40 use the Internet for practical things.
젊은이들은 인터넷을 교육의 용도로 사용하고 40세 이상의 사용자는 실용적인 용도로 사용하는 것으로 보인다.

10 Although all of them are accustomed to connecting with other people by using e-mail.
하지만 모든 연령대의 사용자들은 이메일을 통해 타인과 연락하는 것에 익숙하다.

ACADEMIC WRITING

샘플 답안

The table above indicates the reasons for using the Internet services based on age in Australia.

In general, the rate of use for e-mail is very high compared to the other categories in all age groups.

From the different services, users that prefer to use the Internet for e-mail and education account for more than half of the people questioned. Also, not including e-mail, 36 per cent of the 11-19 age group like to use Internet services for education, whereas 20% per cent of the over 40 age group like to use online shopping services. Surprisingly, they do not care about on-line chatting compared with the 11 to 19 age group. However, only 2 per cent of the younger users use on-line banking services.

From studying this table, we can see that most of the users are using Internet services for convenience by using them to save time and money. Of course the difference between the age groups is interesting. It seems the young use the Internet for education and people over 40 use the Internet for practical things. Although all of them are accustomed to connecting with other people by using e-mail.

(total words: 190)

TASK 2

You should spend about 40 minutes on this task.

> ***Whilst informational systems are now being utilised to aid the old, some people are worrying about the possible negative outcomes.***
> 정보화 시스템이 현재 노인을 돕기 위해 이용되고 있지만, 몇몇 사람들은 생길지 모르는 부정적인 결과를 걱정하기도 한다.
>
> ***To what extent do you agree with this statement?***
> 이 진술에 대해 당신은 어느 정도 찬성하는가?
>
> ***Give reasons for your answer.***
> 당신의 대답에 대한 이유를 제시하라.

You should write at least 250 words.

You should use your own idea, knowledge and experience and support your arguments with examples and relevant evidence.

먼저 도입단락(Introduction)을 작성한다. 글의 서론부분으로, 주어진 문제의 내용을 활용하여 관련된 분위기를 만드는 것이다.

도입단락은 These days, we live in a world ~로 작성한다. '오늘날 우리는 ~한 사회에 살고 있다.' 이렇게 부드럽게 서두를 시작한다.

1 **These days**, we live in a world full of information.
   오늘날 우리는 정보로 가득 찬 세계에 살고 있다.

그리고 다음 문장에서는 대다수의 사람을 문장의 '주어' 로 놓고 관심분야와 이에 대한 이유를 간단히 서술한다.

2 **Most people have interest in** online services and are able to get updated information quickly.
   대부분의 사람들은 온라인 서비스에 관심이 있으며 업데이트되는 정보를 빠르게 얻을 수 있다.

그리고 다음 문장에서 문장의 분위기 전환으로 인터넷 서비스가 고령자에게 주는 양면성을 서술한다.

3 There are of course, a number of benefits of Internet use for the elderly but also some problems caused by incorrect use.
   물론 고령자들이 인터넷 사용으로 얻을 수 있는 이득들이 있지만, 잘못된 사용으로 생길 수 있는 문제들도 있다.

ACADEMIC WRITING

그리고 본문에 들어갈 주제를 직접/간접적으로 언급한다.

4 I would like to talk about these problems.
   나는 이러한 문제들에 대해 이야기하고자 한다.

두 번째 단락으로 [제1단락]을 작성한다. 여기선, 서론에서 간접적으로 언급한 역부작용 중 첫 번째인 인터넷활용의 미숙(poor ability with the service)에 대한 구체적인 사례와 본인의 의견을 들어 논리성을 높여 나간다.

문제의 분위기에 맞게 '인터넷 서비스' 로 시작하면서 요즘 노인들의 온라인 의료서비스의 혜택을 설명한다.

5 Most elderly people are able to see an online doctor whenever they need by using Internet services.
   대부분의 고령자들은 인터넷 서비스를 사용함으로써 필요할 때 언제든지 온라인 병원 진료를 받을 수 있다.

그리고 노인들의 인터넷 학습에 대한 열정을 보여 준다.

6 They are also enthusiastic about learning how to use the Internet.
   그들은 또한 인터넷 사용법을 배우는 데에도 열정적이다.

그리고 자판 사용법에 익숙지 않은 점을 설명한다.

7 However, unfortunately some elderly people have difficulties controlling online systems and using the keyboard correctly without a guide.
   하지만, 불행하게도 일부 노인들은 안내 없이 온라인 시스템을 다루고 키보드를 올바르게 사용하는 데 어려움을 겪는다.

그리고 공신력 있는 언론자료를 현실성 있는 허구로 인용하여, 최근 온라인 의료 서비스를 노인이 취급하기에 어렵다는 점을 역설한다.

8 The BBC criticised online health services in 2009 as they were difficult for elderly people to use without assistance.
   BBC는 2009년에 온라인 의료 서비스에 대해 도움 없이 고령자가 사용하기에는 어렵다며 비판했다.

그리고 이에 관련된 예시로 본인의 대학시절을 허구로 인용한다.

9 When I was at university I worked as a volunteer assisting elderly people that lived alone.
   내가 대학교에 다닐 때 독거노인을 돕는 자원봉사를 했었다.

그리고 노인들의 인터넷 활용 미숙에 대한 안타까운 처지를 언급해 준다.

10 They often had to wait a long time for council staff because of problems with the online service.
그들은 온라인 서비스를 이용하면서 생기는 문제들 때문에 종종 시청 공무원을 오래 기다려야 했다.

그리고 이와 관련된 인터넷 범죄 사건을 언급해 준다.

11 I also heard of an old man that lost a lot of money because of an online banking scam.
나는 또한 온라인 뱅킹에서 거금을 사기당한 노인의 이야기를 들었다.

세 번째 단락으로 [제2단락]을 작성한다. 여기선, 서론에서 간접적으로 언급한 부작용 중 두 번째인 노인병(disease of old age)에 대한 구체적인 사례와 본인의 의견을 들어 논리성을 높여 나간다.

첫 문장에서는 편리한 온라인 문화로 노인들의 운동 부족에 대한 현실에 대해서 서술한다.

12 There is also a chance that becoming to comfortable with online culture could result in the elderly starting to exercise less.
또한 온라인 문화로 더욱 편리한 생활을 영위할 수 있는 기회는 고령자들에게 운동 부족의 결과를 가져오기도 한다.

13 Compared with the agricultural societies of old, these days more and more people are suffering from conditions such as diabetes and high blood pressure.
예전의 농업사회와 비교해 보면, 오늘날 더욱더 많은 사람들이 당뇨나 고혈압과 같은 질병으로 고통받고 있다.

그리고 이에 관련된 현실성 있는 예시로 시사적 허구를 인용한다.

14 For instance, according to a recent newspaper report, old age obesity is increasing.
예를 들어, 최근의 신문 기사에 따르면 노인층의 비만이 증가하고 있다.

그리고 나이가 들수록 건강을 관리하지 않는 노인들의 성향을 설명한다.

15 As people get older they are less inclined to look after themselves well.
나이를 먹을수록, 사람들은 자기 자신을 덜 돌보는 경향이 있다.

네 번째 단락으로 결론(Conclusion)을 작성한다. 글의 마지막 단락으로 주제를 언급하고 본인의 의견으로 맺으면 된다. 결론의 맺음말로 시작하면서, 정보사회에 대한 양면성을 다시 역설한다.

16 In conclusion, although there are some advantages to the elderly using modern technology, there are also problems caused by their inability to use it effectively.
결론적으로, 고령자들이 현대의 기술을 이용하는 것은 많은 도움이 되지만 또한 효율적으로 이용하지 못하는 미숙함으로 인해 생기는 문제들도 존재한다.

ACADEMIC WRITING

17 This is a difficult situation.
이것은 매우 어려운 상황이다.

그리고 본인의 의견으로 정부가 노인층을 도울 수 있는 온라인 서비스 사회프로그램에 투자할 것을 촉구한다.

18 In my opinion, governments should begin investing in support programmes in order to help the elderly use online services.
나는 고령자들이 온라인 서비스를 이용하는 것을 돕기 위한 지원 프로그램에 정부가 투자해야 한다고 생각한다.

샘플 답안

These days, we live in a world full of information. Most people have interest in online services and are able to get updated information quickly. There are of course, a number of benefits of Internet use for the elderly but also some problems caused by incorrect use. I would like to talk about these problems.

Most elderly people are able to see an online doctor whenever they need by using Internet services. They are also enthusiastic about learning how to use the Internet. However, unfortunately some elderly people have difficulties controlling online systems and using the keyboard correctly without a guide. The BBC criticised online health services in 2009 as they were difficult for elderly people to use without assistance. When I was at university I worked as a volunteer assisting elderly people that lived alone. They often had to wait a long time for council staff because of problems with the online service. I also heard of an old man that lost a lot of money because of an online banking scam.

There is also a chance that becoming to comfortable with online culture could result in the elderly starting to exercise less. Compared with the agricultural societies of old, these days more and more people are suffering from conditions such as diabetes and high blood pressure. For instance, according to a recent newspaper report, old age obesity is increasing. As people get older they are less inclined to look after themselves well.

In conclusion, although there are some advantages to the elderly using modern technology, there are also problems caused by their inability to use it effectively. This is a difficult situation. In my opinion, governments should begin investing in support programmes in order to help the elderly use online services.

(total words: 293)

TEST 6

TASK 1

You should spend about 20 minutes on this task.

> *The pie chart below shows the causes of worldwide global warming and the table shows the percentage of CO_2 by causes in three continents.*
> 아래 파이 차트는 지구 온난화의 원인을 보여 주고, 도표는 세 대륙의 원인별 이산화탄소의 수치를 보여 준다.
>
> *Write a report for a university lecturer describing the information shown below.*
> 아래 정보를 묘사하여 대학 강의를 위한 리포트를 작성하시오.

You should write at least 150 words.

Causes of worldwide global warming

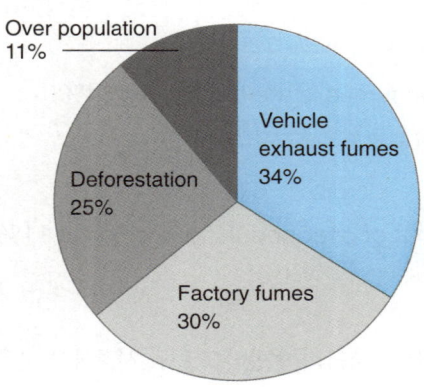

Percentage of CO_2 by causes in three continents

	Percentage of CO_2				Total percentage of CO_2
	Vehicle	Factory	Deforestation	Population	
Europe	35	33	15	17	100
America	33	19	31	17	100
Asia	33	27	9	31	100

ACADEMIC WRITING

먼저 도입단락(Introduction)을 작성한다. 글의 서론부분으로, 차트의 이름을 만드는 것이다. 항상 도입단락은 정관사 The로 시작하고 시제는 현재시제를 사용한다.

1 **The pie chart and the table above indicate** the reasons for the amount of CO_2 emission that cause world global warming among three continents.
   위의 파이차트와 도표는 세 대륙의 지구온난화를 유발하는 이산화탄소 방출량의 원인에 대해서 언급하고 있다.

문제와 동일하게 작성하면 감점이 되므로 문법구조를 활용하여 구조는 다르지만 의미는 같게 표현하면 된다. 문제에 주어진 두 개의 도표의 이름은 pie chart와 table이며, 장소부사인 below 대신 above(위에 있는)가 쓰였다. 동사는 일반동사 현재시제(indicate: ~을 가리키다), 다음은 목적대상인 reasons and the amount of CO_2 emission causing(원인 제공이 되는 이산화탄소의 방출량과 이유), 다음엔 마지막으로 world global warming among three continents를 명시하였다.

두 번째 단락으로 일반화 진술(General statement)을 작성한다. 본론에 들어가기 전에 차트의 전반적인 상황과 분위기를 서술하는 것이다.

2 **In general**, there are four main causes of global warming: vehicle exhaust fumes, factory fumes, deforestation and over population.
   일반적으로 지구온난화에는 네 가지 주요 원인이 있다. 자동차 배기가스, 공장 매연, 삼림벌목과 과잉인구이다.

3 Among them, vehicle exhaust fumes is the highest, at 34%.
   이 중 자동차 배기가스가 34%로 가장 높은 비중을 차지한다.

4 It is more than three times that of over population, which is 11%.
   이는 과잉인구가 차지하는 11%보다 세 배 이상 많다.

처음 문장은 연결어(linking word)인 In general(일반적으로)로 시작하고 다음엔 유도부사구문으로 차트의 시제에 맞추어 작성해 나간다. there are ~(~이 있다. 주어진 차트에서 시간적 개념이 명시되어 있지 않으면, 현재시제를 사용한다.) 그리고 파이 차트의 지구온난화의 발생 원인 4가지의 수치에 대해 간략하게 서술한다.

세 번째 단락으로 설명묘사(Descriptions)를 작성한다. 본론단락으로, 두 번째 도표를 문법과 어휘를 활용하여 자세히 객관적으로 서로 간의 특징을 비교해 가면서 서술하는 것이다. (단, 반복적인 문장은 가급적 사용하지 않는다.)

5 CO_2 emissions in Europe are mainly caused by both vehicle exhaust fumes and factory fumes, with these things accounting for more than 60%.
   유럽의 이산화탄소 배출의 주원인은 자동차 배기가스와 공장 매연으로, 이 두 개가 60% 이상을 차지한다.

6   Both vehicle exhaust fumes and deforestation are severe in America, at over 60%.
    자동차 배기가스와 벌목은 아메리카대륙에서 60% 이상으로 아주 치명적이다.

7   Finally, a combination of exhaust fumes, factory fumes and over population accounts for 90% of Asia's CO_2 emissions.
    마지막으로, 자동차 배기가스, 공장 매연, 과잉인구의 합이 차지하는 비중은 아시아의 이산화탄소 배출량의 90% 정도이다.

8   Surprisingly, both vehicle exhaust fumes and factory fumes cause more than 50% of all emissions.
    놀랍게도, 자동차 배기가스와 공장 매연의 합은 모든 국가에서 50% 이상의 비중을 차지한다.

주어(CO_2 emissions)와 be동사(are) 어순대로 서술해 나간다. 두 번째 도표상의 4종류의 CO_2의 생성원인을 비교 설명하면서 놀람부사(Surprisingly)를 넣어 두드러진 특성이 자동차 배기가스와 공장 매연이라는 것을 강조 설명한다.

네번째 단락으로 결론(Conclusion)을 작성한다. 글의 마지막 단락으로 도표들을 분석(analysis)하고 맺으면 된다.

9   These charts therefore show that 30% of CO_2 emissions are caused by vehicle exhaust fumes, which means it is the main problem in terms of global warming.
    이 차트는 이산화탄소 배출량의 30%가량이 자동차 배기가스로 인해 발생하며, 이는 지구온난화의 주요 문제임을 의미한다.

CO_2 배출량에서 가장 큰 비중을 차지하는 것은 자동차 배기가스라는 결론으로 글을 끝맺는다.

ACADEMIC WRITING

샘플 답안

The pie chart and the table above indicate the reasons for the amount of CO_2 emissions that cause world global warming among three continents.

In general, there are four main causes of global warming: vehicle exhaust fumes, factory fumes, deforestation and over population. Among them, vehicle exhaust fumes is the highest, at 34%. It is more than three times that of over population, which is 11%.

CO_2 emissions in Europe are mainly caused by both vehicle exhaust fumes and factory fumes, with these things accounting for more than 60%. Both vehicle exhaust fumes and deforestation are severe in America, at over 60%. Finally, a combination of exhaust fumes, factory fumes and over population accounts for 90% of Asia's CO_2 emissions. Surprisingly, both vehicle exhaust fumes and factory fumes cause more than 50% of all emissions.

These charts therefore show that 30% of CO_2 emissions are caused by vehicle exhaust fumes, which means it is the main problem in terms of global warming.

(total words: 162)

TASK 2

You should spend about 40 minutes on this task.

> ***With the increase in global tourism, it has become obvious that there are many advantages and disadvantages that can be found from the effects of tourism.***
> 세계적인 관광업의 증가로 관광의 영향력에 많은 장단점이 있다는 사실을 알 수 있다.
>
> ***Do you believe that the advantages outweigh the disadvantages?***
> 당신은 장점이 단점을 능가한다고 생각하는가?
>
> ***Give reasons for your answer.***
> 당신의 대답에 대한 몇 가지 이유를 들어라.

You should write at least 250 words.

You should use your own idea, knowledge and experience and support your arguments with examples and relevant evidence.

먼저 도입단락(Introduction)을 작성한다. 글의 서론부분으로 주어진 문제의 내용을 활용하여 관련된 분위기를 만드는 것이다.

도입단락은 These days, we live ~ 으로 작성한다. '오늘날 우리는 ~한 사회에 살고 있다.' 이렇게 부드럽게 서두를 시작한다.

1. **These days** we live in a world of convenient travel.
   오늘날 우리는 편하게 여행할 수 있는 세상에서 살고 있다.

그리고 다음 문장에서는 대다수의 사람을 문장의 '주어' 로 놓고 관심분야와 이에 대한 이유를 간단히 서술한다.

2. **Most people** have an interest in travelling, whether it be domestically or abroad.
   대부분의 사람들은 국내여행이든 해외여행이든 여행에 흥미를 가지고 있다.

3. There are many attractions to see all over the world as well as a number of great places to rest and recuperate.
   세계적으로 휴양지뿐 아니라 관광할 수 있는 많은 명소들이 있다.

그리고 다음 문장에서 관광여행이 우리에게 주는 양면성을 서술한다.

ACADEMIC WRITING

4   **Of course**, tourists may be faced with problems such as traffic, theft and over charging whilst they are travelling.
    물론 관광객들은 여행하는 도중에 교통, 절도, 바가지요금과 같은 문제에 부딪치기도 한다.

5   **However**, there are many positive things too.
    그러나 여행에는 긍정적인 면 또한 많다.

두번째 단락으로 [제1단락]을 작성한다. 여기선, 서론에서 언급한 여행의 이로운 점들 중 흥미를 위한 여행에 대해서 구체적인 사례와 본인의 의견을 들어 논리성을 높여 나간다.

6   For cultural and historic spots many tourists visit Europe, Africa or Asia because there are many things to see and cheap flight tickets available.
    문화적, 역사적 명소들을 보기 위해 많은 관광객들이 유럽, 아프리카, 아시아 등을 방문한다. 왜냐하면 볼거리가 풍부하고 비행기값이 저렴하기 때문이다.

여흥을 찾는 현대인들에 대해서 언급한다.

7   They may want to visit an area of natural beauty or perhaps some places of historical interest.
    그들은 자연적인 아름다움을 지닌 장소 혹은 역사적으로 흥미로운 장소를 방문하고 싶어 할 수도 있다.

그리고 문제의 분위기에 맞게 영국 문화재관리청(the National Heritage)을 언급해 준다. 본문단락에서 국가 혹은 세계 기구를 언급해 주면 개인적인 의견에 대한 객관적인 타당성을 높일 수 있다. 관광문화에 대한 문제가 출제되면 the National Heritage를 꼭 이용하자. 여기에서는 사례로 영국의 Bath city에 대해 이야기한다.

8   **For example**, according to the National Heritage in UK, most people that visit Bath are interested in seeing the old Roman sites.
    예를 들어, 영국 문화재 관리청에 따르면 Bath를 방문하는 많은 사람들은 예전의 로마 유적지를 보는 것을 흥미로워한다.

9   They have the opportunity to enter a luxury Roman bathhouse and enjoy a modern style spa treatment.
    그들은 고급 로마 목욕탕에 입장할 기회를 얻으며, 현대식 온천도 즐길 수 있다.

세번째 단락으로 [제2단락]을 작성한다. 여기선, 서론에서 언급한 여행의 이로운 점들 중에서 여행객들이 교육적인 견문을 넓힐 수 있다는 점에 대해서 구체적인 사례와 본인의 의견을 들어 논리성을 높여 나간다.

10 Some tourists travel not only for entertainment but also for educational reasons.
몇몇 관광객들은 즐기기 위해서뿐만 아니라 교육적인 이유로 여행을 하기도 한다.

11 They may have a strong desire to visit wonderful attractions like temple or national parks that they have previously learnt about.
그들은 이전에 배웠던 절이나 국립공원과 같은 훌륭한 유적지를 방문하고자 하는 바람을 강하게 가지고 있다.

12 These attractions show the importance of cultural values.
이러한 명소들은 문화적 가치의 중요성을 보여 준다.

13 For example, a visit to Stonehenge enables tourists to learn about prehistoric customs and consider how they relate to the modern day.
예를 들어, 스톤헨지를 방문하는 것은 관광객들에게 선사시대의 관습을 배우고 그것들이 현재와 어떻게 관련이 있는지를 생각해 볼 수 있게 해 준다.

네번째 단락으로 결론(Conclusion)을 작성한다. 글의 마지막 단락으로 주제를 언급하고 본인의 의견으로 맺으면 된다. 결론의 맺음말로 시작하면서, 사람들은 여행을 통해 좋지 않은 일을 겪기도 하지만, 휴식과 배움을 제공받는다고 서술한다.

14 In conclusion, despite a few potential problems, tourists appreciate the beauty of travel, cultural enjoyment and relaxation.
결론적으로, 몇몇 잠재적인 문제들에도 불구하고, 관광객들은 여행의 아름다움과 문화적 즐거움, 휴식을 즐긴다.

15 In my opinion, travel offers a refreshing escape from the stress of the real world and motivates us to learn.
나는 여행이 현실 세계의 스트레스로부터 신선한 탈출구를 제공해 주고 배움에 대한 동기를 부여해 준다고 생각한다.

ACADEMIC WRITING

샘플 답안

These days we live in a world of convenient travel. Most people have an interest in travelling, whether it be domestically or abroad. There are many attractions to see all over the world as well as a number of great places to rest and recuperate. Of course, tourists may be faced with problems such as traffic, theft and over charging whilst they are travelling. However, there are many positive things too.

For cultural and historic spots many tourists visit Europe, Africa or Asia because there are many things to see and cheap flight tickets available. They may want to visit an area of natural beauty or perhaps some places of historical interest. For example, according to the National Heritage in UK, most people that visit Bath are interested in seeing the old Roman sites. They have the opportunity to enter a luxury Roman bathhouse and enjoy a modern style spa treatment.

Some tourists travel not only for entertainment but also for educational reasons. They may have a strong desire to visit wonderful attractions like temple or national parks that they have previously learnt about. These attractions show the importance of cultural values. For example, a visit to Stonehenge enables tourists to learn about prehistoric customs and consider how they relate to the modern day.

In conclusion, despite a few potential problems, tourists appreciate the beauty of travel, cultural enjoyment and relaxation. In my opinion, travel offers a refreshing escape from the stress of the real world and motivates us to learn.

(total words: 251)

TEST 7

TASK 1

You should spend about 20 minutes on this task.

The diagram below shows the visual apparent motion.
아래 도형은 시각적 외견상 움직임을 보여 주고 있다.

Write a report for a university lecturer describing the information shown below.
아래 정보를 묘사하여 대학 강의를 위한 리포트를 작성하시오.

You should write at least 150 words.

Visual apparent motion
시각적 외견상의 움직임

When displayed on a screen, this creates an impression of motion that doesn't exist.
스크린에 비칠 때, 이것은 존재하지 않는 동작의 인상을 만들어 낸다.

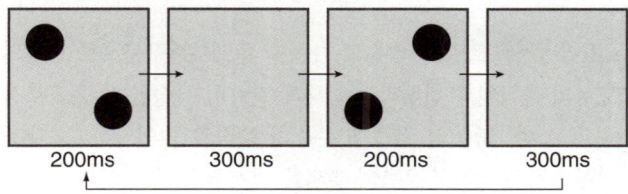

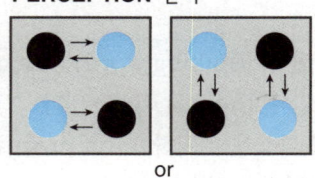

ACADEMIC WRITING

먼저 도입단락(Introduction)을 작성한다. 글의 서론부분으로 도형의 이름을 만드는 것이다. 항상, 도입단락은 정관사 The로 시작하고 시제는 현재시제를 사용한다.

1   The diagram above indicates the visual impression of intangible motion.
    위의 도형은 무형의 움직임의 시각적인 인지를 보여 주고 있다.

문제와 동일하게 작성하면 감점이 되므로 약간 문법구조를 활용하여 구조는 다르지만 의미는 같게 표현하면 된다. 문제에 주어진 도형의 이름은 diagram이며, 장소부사 below 대신 above(위에 있는)가 쓰였다. 동사는 일반동사 현재시제 (indicates: ~을 가리키다), 다음은 목적대상인 the visual impression(시각적 인지), 그 다음엔 적당한 명사와 명사를 이어주는 전치사 of(~의), 그 다음엔 서술형용사 intangible을 적고 다음엔 motion을 사용했다. 여기서 intangible(무형의)을 사용한 것은 문제의 that doesn't exist의 동의어로 표기한 것이다.

두 번째 단락으로 일반화 진술(General statement)을 작성한다. 본론에 들어가기 전에 도형의 전반적인 상황과 분위기를 서술하는 것이다.

2   In general, there is a processing from the left side to the right side.
    일반적으로, 왼쪽 면에서 오른쪽 면으로 진행하는 과정이 있다.

3   As the stimulus loop is repeating by a continuous tester, the result of experience meets the perception.
    stimulus loop는 실험자에 의해 반복되면서, 그 실험의 결과는 인식과정을 만나게 된다.

처음 문장은 연결어(linking word)인 In general(일반적으로)로 시작하고 다음엔 유도부사구문으로 도형의 시제에 맞추어 작성해 나간다. there is ~(~이 있다) 그리고 도형의 움직임과 진행과정에 대해 간략히 서술한다. 유도부사구문은 본 주어가 be동사 다음에 위치하므로 a processing라고 쓰며, 도형의 좌측과 우측의 움직임을 언급하고, 다음엔 stimulus loop에 대한 문장을 서술한다. 실험자의 반복된 실험으로 좌측에서 우측의 결과를 얻게 되었다는 식으로 서술하면 된다.

세 번째 단락으로 설명묘사(Descriptions)를 작성한다. 본론단락으로, 도형에 대해 문법과 어휘를 활용하여 자세히 객관적으로 모든 진행과정을 서술하는 것이다. (단, 반복적인 문장은 가급적 사용하지 않는다.)

4   With the stimulus loop, the first box is two dots on the left corner of ups and the right corner of downs, moving to the second box which is empty.
    stimulus loop로 첫 번째 상자는 좌측 상단 그리고 우측 하단에 점이 위치해 있으며, 이것은 두 번째 비어 있는 상자로 옮겨 간다.

5   The third one was located on the opposite side to the first one, transferring to the forth one which is vacant.
    세 번째 상자는 첫 번째 상자와 반대 방향으로 위치해 있으며, 이것은 네 번째 비어 있는 상자로 옮겨진다.

6   These processes are re-operating with intervals of 200ms or 300ms respectively.
    이런 과정들은 시간의 간격, 즉 각각 200ms와 300ms의 반복된 작업으로 진행된다.

7   Both the second and the forth clear are a space of moving.
    비어 있는 두 번째와 네 번째 상자는 움직임 간의 간격을 말한다.

8   So, the speed of motion is based on the length of a time.
    그래서, 움직임의 속도는 시간의 길이에 비례한다.

9   Therefore, the dots will appear to jump vertically or horizontally, and then after some time, they will switch directions spontaneously.
    그러므로, 점들은 수직과 수평으로 점프하면서 나타나고 그리고 나서 얼마 후에 점들은 자연스럽게 위치를 바꾼다.

전치사(With)로 시작하고 다음에 명사어구를 쓰고, 주어(the first box)와 현재동사(is) 어순대로 서술해 나간다. 도형의 진행과정을 묘사하기 전에 먼저 도형의 모양과 구조에 대해서 서술하고, 진행과정을 순서적으로 표현하면 된다. 도형의 진행과정은 적당한 시간의 간격, 200ms 혹은 300ms를 각각(respectively) 두고 반복적으로 진행한다. 두 번째와 네 번째 비어 있는 공간을 만나게 되는데, 이것은 움직임의 폭(a space of moving)을 뜻하며, 점들의 움직이는 속도는 주어진 시간의 간격에 비례한다. 그러므로 점들은 수직적(vertically) 혹은 수평적(horizontally)으로 점프동작(jump)이 자연스럽게 위치를 바꾸어 가며 움직이는 것이다.

네 번째 단락으로 결론(Conclusion)을 작성한다. 글의 마지막 단락으로 도형을 분석(analysis)하고 맺으면 된다.

10 This experiment enables us to see how a direct tactile sensation can perceptually grouped in different ways from those of the regular cycles.
    이 실험은 직접적인 촉감이 규칙적인 반복과는 다른 방법으로 인식적으로 형성됨을 알려 준다.

ACADEMIC WRITING

샘플 답안

The diagram above indicates the visual impression of intangible motion.

In general, there is a processing from the left side to the right side. As the stimulus loop is repeating by a continuous tester, the result of the experience meets the perception.

With the stimulus loop, the first box is two dots on the left corner of ups and the right corner of downs, moving to the second box which is empty. The third one was located on the opposite side to the first one, transferring to the forth one which is vacant. These processes are re-operating with intervals of 200ms or 300ms respectively. Both the second and the forth clear are a space of moving. So, the speed of motion is based on the length of a time. Therefore, the dots will appear to jump vertically or horizontally, and then after some time, they will switch directions spontaneously.

This experiment enables us to see how a direct tactile sensation can perceptually grouped in different ways from those of the regular cycles.

(total words: 172)

TASK 2

You should spend about 40 minutes on this task.

> ***Due to the increase of technology, people today have greater amounts of free time.***
> 기술의 발달로 오늘날 사람들은 여가 시간이 더욱 많아졌다.
>
> ***What are the advantages and disadvantages of the conveniences created by modern technology?***
> 현대문명이 만들어 낸 편리함의 장점과 단점은 무엇인가?

You should write at least 250 words.

You should use your own idea, knowledge and experience and support your arguments with examples and relevant evidence.

먼저 도입단락(Introduction)을 작성한다. 글의 서론부분으로 주어진 문제의 내용을 활용하여 관련된 분위기를 만드는 것이다.

도입단락에서는 These days, we live in ~으로 작성한다. '오늘날 우리는 ~한 사회에 살고 있다.' 이렇게 부드럽게 서두를 시작한다. 문제의 분위기는 mechanic world(기계문명의 사회)로 추론 가능하다.

1   **These days**, we live in a mechanical world, and we enjoy very convenient life.
  오늘날 우리는 기계문명의 세계에 살고 있으며, 매우 편리한 삶을 영위하고 있다.

그리고 다음 문장에서 대다수의 사람을 문장의 '주어' 로 놓고 관심분야와 이에 대한 이유를 간단히 서술한다.

2   **Most people** take a great deal of enjoyment from their leisure time.
  대부분의 사람들은 여가시간에서 많은 즐거움을 얻는다.

그리고 다음 문장에서 기계문명이 우리에게 주는 양면성을 서술한다.

3   Machines help us complete tasks at home or at work, but we also are facing some problems due to our lifestyles being perhaps too comfortable.
  기계는 가정에서나 직장에서나 일을 완수할 수 있도록 도와주지만, 또한 우리는 너무 편리한 생활방식으로 인해 여러 문제에 직면하게 된다.

그리고 본문단락에 들어가기 전에 기계문명의 장점과 단점을 언급한다.

ACADEMIC WRITING

4 I would therefore like to discuss the advantages and disadvantages of automatic tools.
나는 자동화 도구의 장점과 단점에 대해 논의하고자 한다.

두 번째 단락으로 [제1단락]을 작성한다. 여기선, 서론에서 언급한 장점과 단점 중 첫 번째인 기계문명으로 인한 시간과 비용의 절약에 대해 구체적인 사례와 본인의 의견을 들어 논리성을 높여 나간다.

5 Many people are given a sense of convenience by automatic systems as they help us save time and money.
많은 사람들은 시간과 비용을 절약해 주는 자동화 시스템으로 인해 편리함을 얻는다.

그리고 문제의 분위기에 맞게 제레미 리프킨(Jeremy Rifkin)의 '접속의 시대(The Age of Access)'를 인용하면서 사회 분위기를 설명한다. 본문단락에서 저명한 사람의 일화 혹은 저서를 언급해 주면 개인적인 의견에 대한 객관적인 타당성을 높일 수 있다. 정보사회에 대한 문제가 출제되면, 제레미 리프킨(Jeremy Rifkin)을 꼭 이용하자.

6 According to "The Age of Access" by Jeremy Rifkin, who is a famous scholar in the United States, the culture of mechanism is a distinctive feature of our society.
미국의 저명한 학자 제레미 리프킨의 '접속의 시대'에 따르면 기계문명 문화는 우리 사회의 독특한 특징이다.

다음 문장에서는 정보화 사회를 통한 생활의 편리성을 설명한다.

7 We can easily buy things on the Internet without spending our time going to markets or department stores.
우리는 가게나 백화점에 가서 시간을 보내지 않아도 인터넷을 통해 물건을 쉽게 구입할 수 있다.

8 Also, house chores can be arranged by online systems.
집안일도 온라인으로 처리할 수 있다.

세 번째 단락으로 [제2단락]을 작성한다. 여기선, 기계문명의 편리성으로 얻게 된 부작용을 서술하면서, 구체적인 사례와 개인적인 의견을 들어 논리성을 높여 나간다.

편리한 첨단생활로 얻게 되는 문제점에 대해서 세계보건기구(WHO)의 객관화된 자료와 현대인들의 비만의 통계학적 수치를 언급한다.

9 Unfortunately, there is also a downside, the world is now seeing an increase in obesity because there are too many convenient facilities in our lives.
안타깝게도, 좋지 않은 면도 존재한다. 편리한 시설들이 너무 많아 오늘날 비만 인구가 증가하고 있다.

10 The WHO (World Health Organization) reported that many people seem not only to be not exercising, but also to be eating fast, high calorie food with zero nutrients which causes disease.

WHO는 많은 사람들이 운동하지 않을 뿐 아니라 영양가 없고 질병을 유발시키는 고칼로리 패스트푸드를 즐겨 먹는 것으로 보인다고 보고하였다.

11 For example, around 4% of the American population are suffering from obesity according to the AMA (American Medical Association).

예를 들어, AMA에 따르면 미국 인구의 4%가량이 비만으로 고통받고 있다.

네 번째 단락으로 결론(Conclusion)을 작성한다. 글의 마지막 단락으로, 주제를 언급하고 본인의 의견으로 맺으면 된다. 결론의 맺음말로 시작하면서, 기계화 사회에 대한 양면성을 다시 역설한다.

12 In conclusion, although the culture of mechanism has its advantages, there are also some negative effects.

결과적으로 기계문화는 나름의 장점을 가지고 있음에도 불구하고, 부정적인 효과 또한 존재한다.

그리고 본인의 의견으로 정부가 부작용을 교정하기 위해서 사회 건강 관리 체계에 자금을 투자할 것을 촉구한다.

13 Therefore, in my opinion, governments should make a solution by investing in social health care systems to counter these drawbacks.

따라서 나는 이러한 문제점을 해결하기 위해 정부가 사회 건강 관리 체계에 투자함으로써 해결책을 만들어야 한다고 생각한다.

ACADEMIC WRITING

샘플 답안

These days, we live in a mechanical world, and we enjoy very convenient life. Most people take a great deal of enjoyment from their leisure time. Machines help us complete tasks at home or at work, but we also are facing some problems due to our lifestyles being perhaps too comfortable. I would therefore like to discuss the advantages and disadvantages of automatic tools.

Many people are given a sense of convenience by automatic systems as they help us save time and money. According to "The Age of Access" by Jeremy Rifkin, who is a famous scholar in the United States, the culture of mechanism is a distinctive feature of our society. We can easily buy things on the Internet without spending our time going to markets or department stores. Also, house chores can be arranged by online systems.

Unfortunately, there is also a downside, the world is now seeing an increase in obesity because there are too many convenient facilities in our lives. The WHO (World Health Organization) reported that many people seem not only to be not exercising, but also to be eating fast, high calorie food with zero nutrients which causes disease. For example, around 4% of the American population are suffering from obesity according to the AMA (American Medical Association).

In conclusion, although the culture of mechanism has its advantages, there are also some negative effects. Therefore, in my opinion, governments should make a solution by investing in social health care systems to counter these drawbacks.

(total words: 250)

IELTS READING (Academic Module) ANSWER SHEET

Are You: Female? ▭   Male? ▭

Your first language code: ▶ 0 1 2 3 4 5 6 7 8 9
                            ▶ 0 1 2 3 4 5 6 7 8 9
                            ▶ 0 1 2 3 4 5 6 7 8 9

IELTS Reading Answer Sheet

Module taken (shade one box):   Academic ▭   General Training ▭

#	Answer	✓ / ✗	#	Answer	✓ / ✗
1			21		
2			22		
3			23		
4			24		
5			25		
6			26		
7			27		
8			28		
9			29		
10			30		
11			31		
12			32		
13			33		
14			34		
15			35		
16			36		
17			37		
18			38		
19			39		
20			40		

Checker's Initials ▭   Marker's Initials ▭   Band Score ▭   Reading Total ▭

IELTS READING (Academic Module) ANSWER SHEET

Are You: Female? ☐   Male? ☐

Your first language code: 0 1 2 3 4 5 6 7 8 9

IELTS Reading Answer Sheet

Module taken (shade one box):   Academic ☐   General Training ☐

#	Answer	✓ / ✗	#	Answer	✓ / ✗
1			21		
2			22		
3			23		
4			24		
5			25		
6			26		
7			27		
8			28		
9			29		
10			30		
11			31		
12			32		
13			33		
14			34		
15			35		
16			36		
17			37		
18			38		
19			39		
20			40		

Checker's Initials: _____   Marker's Initials: _____   Band Score: _____   Reading Total: _____

IELTS READING (Academic Module) ANSWER SHEET

Are You: Female? ▭   Male? ▭

Your first language code: ▸ 0 1 2 3 4 5 6 7 8 9
                            ▸ 0 1 2 3 4 5 6 7 8 9
                            ▸ 0 1 2 3 4 5 6 7 8 9

IELTS Reading Answer Sheet

Module taken (shade one box):   Academic ▭   General Training ▭

#	Answer	✓ / ✗	#	Answer	✓ / ✗
1		✓ 1 ✗	21		✓ 21 ✗
2		2	22		22
3		3	23		23
4		4	24		24
5		5	25		25
6		6	26		26
7		7	27		27
8		8	28		28
9		9	29		29
10		10	30		30
11		11	31		31
12		12	32		32
13		13	33		33
14		14	34		34
15		15	35		35
16		16	36		36
17		17	37		37
18		18	38		38
19		19	39		39
20		20	40		40

Checker's Initials ▭   Marker's Initials ▭   Band Score ▭   Reading Total ▭

IELTS READING (Academic Module) ANSWER SHEET

Are You: Female? ☐ Male? ☐

Your first language code: 0 1 2 3 4 5 6 7 8 9

IELTS Reading Answer Sheet

Module taken (shade one box): Academic ☐ General Training ☐

#	Answer	✓ ✗	#	Answer	✓ ✗
1			21		
2			22		
3			23		
4			24		
5			25		
6			26		
7			27		
8			28		
9			29		
10			30		
11			31		
12			32		
13			33		
14			34		
15			35		
16			36		
17			37		
18			38		
19			39		
20			40		

Checker's Initials Marker's Initials Band Score Reading Total

IELTS READING (Academic Module) ANSWER SHEET

Are You: Female? ☐ Male? ☐

Your first language code: 0 1 2 3 4 5 6 7 8 9

IELTS Reading Answer Sheet

Module taken (shade one box): Academic ☐   General Training ☐

#		#	
1	✓ 1 ✗	21	✓ 21 ✗
2	2	22	22
3	3	23	23
4	4	24	24
5	5	25	25
6	6	26	26
7	7	27	27
8	8	28	28
9	9	29	29
10	10	30	30
11	11	31	31
12	12	32	32
13	13	33	33
14	14	34	34
15	15	35	35
16	16	36	36
17	17	37	37
18	18	38	38
19	19	39	39
20	20	40	40

Checker's Initials   Marker's Initials   Band Score   Reading Total

IELTS READING (Academic Module) ANSWER SHEET

Are You: Female? ☐   Male? ☐

Your first language code: 0 1 2 3 4 5 6 7 8 9
　　　　　　　　　　　　　　0 1 2 3 4 5 6 7 8 9
　　　　　　　　　　　　　　0 1 2 3 4 5 6 7 8 9

IELTS Reading Answer Sheet

Module taken (shade one box):   Academic ☐   General Training ☐

#	Answer	✓ / ✗	#	Answer	✓ / ✗
1		✓ 1 ✗	21		✓ 21 ✗
2		2	22		22
3		3	23		23
4		4	24		24
5		5	25		25
6		6	26		26
7		7	27		27
8		8	28		28
9		9	29		29
10		10	30		30
11		11	31		31
12		12	32		32
13		13	33		33
14		14	34		34
15		15	35		35
16		16	36		36
17		17	37		37
18		18	38		38
19		19	39		39
20		20	40		40

Checker's Initials ☐   Marker's Initials ☐   Band Score ☐   Reading Total ☐

IELTS READING (Academic Module) ANSWER SHEET

Are You: Female? ▭   Male? ▭

Your first language code: 0 1 2 3 4 5 6 7 8 9
                             0 1 2 3 4 5 6 7 8 9
                             0 1 2 3 4 5 6 7 8 9

IELTS Reading Answer Sheet

Module taken (shade one box):   Academic ▭   General Training ▭

#	Answer	✓ ✗	#	Answer	✓ ✗
1		1	21		21
2		2	22		22
3		3	23		23
4		4	24		24
5		5	25		25
6		6	26		26
7		7	27		27
8		8	28		28
9		9	29		29
10		10	30		30
11		11	31		31
12		12	32		32
13		13	33		33
14		14	34		34
15		15	35		35
16		16	36		36
17		17	37		37
18		18	38		38
19		19	39		39
20		20	40		40

Checker's Initials   Marker's Initials   Band Score   Reading Total